QUITTERS
NEVER
WIN

MICHAEL BISPING
WITH ANTHONY EVANS

EBURY
PRESS

1 3 5 7 9 10 8 6 4 2

Ebury Press, an imprint of Ebury Publishing
20 Vauxhall Bridge Road
London SW1V 2SA

Ebury Press is part of the Penguin Random House group of companies whose
addresses can be found at global.penguinrandomhouse.com

Penguin
Random House
UK

First published by Ebury Press in 2019
This edition published in 2020

www.penguin.co.uk

A CIP catalogue record for this book is available from the British Library

ISBN 9781529104455

Typeset in 9.42 pt/15.45 pt ITC Galliard Std
by Integra Software Services Pvt. Ltd, Pondicherry

Printed and bound in Great Britain by Clays Ltd, Elcograf S.p.A.

For Rebecca. Without her,
the following wouldn't have
happened...

QUITTERS
NEVER
WIN

CHAPTER ONE
THE COUNT

Bisping couldn't sleep the night before the big battle.

He knew nothing about the adversary he'd be fighting the next day. He felt unprepared. As the other fighters conserved their energy and took their minds off fighting with idle chatter, Bisping left the camp. He was going to spy on the enemy.

He travelled on foot into the dusk and continued until the sky was pitch-black. He walked slowly, crawling at times to avoid the attention of wolves which, he knew, could weigh over 10 stone. Finally, he reached the foot of the mountain that had been on the horizon. There was no moon but the stars, unusually bright, gave light enough for Bisping to pick his way up the slopes and through the vineyards that clung to its moist soil.

From the summit, Bisping found what he was looking for: the enemy encampment. It was too dark to see the individual soldiers, but every campfire was clearly visible in the night, and these allowed him to make an accurate estimate of the enemy's number. And Bisping – or *Bischoping* as he would have spelled it – returned to his own camp armed with that vital piece of information.

With full knowledge of the forces opposing them, the army of the Prince-Bishop, sovereign ruler of the state of Münster, attacked immediately. The rout of these invaders earned Bischoping (Germanic for 'Bishop's Man') land and the hereditary title of

Count. The family coat of arms was created – it depicts a bright star over a grapevine.

That coat of arms was worn centuries later by Thomas Bischoping when he served in the army of King Stefan Batory of Poland. Thomas had been born around 1560 in Münster but left home to seek greater fame and fortune in the war against Ivan the Terrible's Russian army. Like his ancestor, Thomas's courage and fighting ability were rewarded by the grant of lands – this time on the provision that Thomas and his descendants would defend it against invasions from the north.

Two decades later, on 4 January 1609, Thomas's younger son, Johann Bischoping, rode his horse through the gates of Hradcany Castle in Prague. He demanded an audience with King Rudolph II, the Holy Roman Emperor.

As the younger son in an age when only the eldest inherited lands and titles, Johann had left his ancestral home to seek his own fortune and glory as a commander in the army of Lithuania. But, initially, the Lithuanian military questioned whether the man who showed up was truly one of the famous Bischoping fighting noblemen.

Johann vowed to return with proof of his birthright – a letter signed by the King.

The Imperial Chancellery's endorsement of Johann's nobility, dated 5 January 1609, is still in the Vienna State Archives. Written in Latin, the document describes in minute detail the Bischoping coat of arms and warns any royal house of Europe refusing to recognise Johann Bischoping's status will be fined 50 gold marks (half of which would be paid to Johann, and half to the treasury).

Now convinced the knight was the man he claimed to be, the Lithuanian army dispatched Bischoping and a garrison of men to defend a stretch of the northern border. Johann defended it so well that he was granted ownership of much of the land. Now a nobleman in his own right, Johann had founded another Bisping dynasty.

On 12 September 1683, Teofil Bisping served gallantly in the liberation of Vienna from the Ottoman Empire forces who'd laid siege to the city since July. The Bisping banner is displayed to this day in a Viennese chapel commemorating 'the rescue'.

A century later, when Poland ceased to be recognised by the Russian, Austrian and Prussian aggressors as an independent state, Jan Bisping was among the nobles who refused to surrender. In 1812, that Bisping founded a military unit and joined forces with Napoleon to fight against their common enemies.

One hundred and thirty years later, at the onset of the Second World War, another Jan Bisping was the latest Bisping to be called upon to defend his ancestral home. This time the invading Russians wore the uniforms of the USSR's Red Army. They came with machine guns and tanks and the orders to kill every Polish noble.

Jan Bisping had no choice but to flee west into what was now German-occupied Poland. He and his wife Maria loaded their 11 children on a cart drawn by draught horses. Communist sympathisers arrived and blocked their escape. Jan handed rifles to his three eldest sons, including 15-year-old Andrzej, and charged. The communists scattered as the young Bispings fired and the cart got through.

The Germans allowed the Bispings to pass into the territory they occupied, and the family were given shelter in a farmhouse. They probably rested easy for the first time in days, but they were not out of the reach of the Red Army yet.

It was September 1939 and the Molotov–Ribbentrop Pact between Russia and Germany came into effect. The Bispings had gone to sleep in the relative safety of German-occupied Poland; when they woke the border had been moved miles to the west, and they were again deep into Russian territory. A desperate flight to the new border ensued but the Russians were determined to capture the nobleman. As they closed in on him, Jan Bisping gave himself up so his family could escape.

He was never heard from again.

Maria made it to Western Europe. Some of her children were taken in by relations in powerful families in Italy and France but she continued until reaching England. Andrzej, now a man, accompanied her. With his mother safe, Andrzej ('Andrew') joined the Free Polish unit of the British military.

His son, the latest Jan Bisping, was born in London after the war. Proud of the country of his birth, Jan served in the British Army until the 1980s.

I am Jan's son. My name is Michael Bisping. I am a fighter from a very long line of fighters.

I was born Michael Galen-Bisping on 28 February 1979. My mother, Kathleen, was taken to the Princess Mary's Hospital at the small Akrotiri British military base near Limassol, in the south of Cyprus. Like with international embassies, military bases are sovereign territory. I'd have to explain that I was actually born on British soil to UFC producers, who thought they needed to show the twin olive branch flag of Cyprus when I was introduced in the Octagon.

My parents met during my dad's previous stationing to Ballykinler Barracks in County Down, Northern Ireland. My mother was one of 12 children and contracted polio as a child; she's extremely tough and mentally strong. A British officer getting involved with an Irish civilian was not the done thing during the mid-1970s but, at 6ft 6in tall, my dad had long since gotten used to a) attracting sideways glances and b) not really giving a fuck.

They married and had a big family. I came after my big brothers Stephen and Konrad, and twins Maxine and Adam followed and then finally my little sister Shireen completed the Bisping family.

My dad left the army in 1983 after serving our country for 17 years. The Cyprian heat had somewhat alleviated the after-effects of an IRA nail bomb but as he started to get older those injuries began to prevent Dad from doing the job he loved, which he found frustrating.

Now I'm the same age he was then, I can relate.

After his honourable discharge, Dad moved the whole family to Clitheroe, Lancashire, where his mother had grown up. My nan had died in a car crash years before, but we still had family in the area and Dad felt he could better support us in the North rather than in London where he'd been raised.

Worthy of a picture postcard, Clitheroe, population 15,517, is up a bit and a little to the left of Manchester. It has very narrow streets, old stonework buildings that blend in to the countryside and even has an eleventh-century castle. At the American producers' insistence, the Norman keep has lurked in the background of many a *UFC Countdown* show. They love a castle, the Yanks.

Despite the castle, the surrounding countryside and an olde tea room that does a good trade in Cornettos during those few days a year when it's warm, Clitheroe is a working-class town. Monday to Friday, its factories and industrial estates are full of hard-grinding people and – as I'd come to know in my teens – on the weekend Clitheroe's pubs and bars are ram-packed with people celebrating the end of another week of hard work.

More of that later.

If we were underprivileged, the only reason I knew that was because bullies at St Michael and St John's school made sure of it. Wearing the same school shirt days in a row, having a mediocre brand of trainers on my feet (which may or may not have been waiting in a cupboard since they got too small for my older brothers) – these were the main avenues of attack.

I'm not going to bullshit you. I could say that, like Georges St-Pierre or Daniel Cormier, the reason I began in martial arts was with the honourable intention of learning how to defend myself. But the reason I started training was because I liked being a fighter. I followed my brother Konrad to a class one night and found that this was more than something I was good at – this was who I was.

The martial art I studied was a version of Japanese jujitsu called Yawara Ryu. It was a full-system style martial art with throws, grappling on the ground, submissions and striking with fists, feet, knees and elbows. If that sounds familiar, it should; years before the advent of the UFC or Pancrase in Japan, here was a proto-mixed martial art in the UK.

I remember the excitement of my first day of training. I didn't know what the hell I was doing, so copied everybody else. When everyone stood in a line with their left fist and left foot forward, so did I. By the time anyone explained to me that, being left-handed, I was supposed to lead with my right it was too late. Without intending it, I was now a converted southpaw and my jab would be thrown using my power hand for the rest of my martial arts career.

Yawara Ryu, as the schools which followed its curriculum called it, was developed by a visionary martial artist and sports scientist named Paul Davies.

Coming from a military background, my dad understood the life lessons I could gain from training. He was incredibly supportive of my new obsession. If I needed a new *gi* (white uniform) or gloves, I got them. He drove me all over the country as I entered not only jiu-jitsu but full-contact karate and kickboxing tournaments. My dad was my driver, advocate and cheerleader – he also enjoyed giving me grief on the occasions I didn't win.

By the middle of high school I'd usually enter and win the Under-15 category, then win the Under-18 and, if they'd let me, usually reach the final if not win the adult competition.

Paul Davies took notice. When the local Yawara Ryu club in Clitheroe shut down, Davies spoke to my dad about me training in Nottingham. Twice a week my dad would do the four-hour round trip so I could continue training.

It was a funny excuse for not doing homework:

'I couldn't do it,' I'd tell my teachers, honestly enough. 'I went to Nottingham again last night and didn't get home till 1am.'

'Michael,' they'd say, 'there's no way anyone is driving you to Nottingham – a four-hour round trip – twice a week to do martial arts.'

'My dad is.'

My favourite type of competition, by far, was Knockdown Sport Budo. Just as he'd developed his own fighting system with Yawara Ryu, Paul Davies also created his own expression of combat sports with KSBO.

If you think of modern MMA and subtract wrestling takedowns and Brazilian jiu-jitsu (BJJ) guard work and add a five-second count-out, that's essentially what a KSBO fight looked like. There were over 30 UK clubs affiliated with KSBO – including several like London Shootfighters which would, in time, become full-blown MMA gyms and produce UFC fighters of their own – and many more in Sweden, France and elsewhere in Europe.

Four times a year, these clubs would send their best fighters to compete against each other in KSBO tournaments. I won titles in 1995, 1996, 1997 and 1998. Davies would telephone me incessantly, holding me hostage on the handset plugged in near the bottom of the stairs as he waxed lyrical about how KSBO would eventually become this massive mainstream sport.

When I was 16, Davies presented me with the chance to travel to New Zealand to compete in the jiu-jitsu world championships. I'd be fighting grown men with years of experience at this level.

My family and friends helped me get just about enough money to go. Blackburn Rugby Union Football Club, where I played as a flanker, went above and beyond and threw a fundraising dinner for me. What an adventure for a 16-year-old, amazing, I couldn't wait!

I travelled with an older fighter, a 6ft 5in monster called Richard who was competing for the heavyweight title in New Zealand and then remaining in the country indefinitely. He was twice my age and, supposedly, would be looking after me on my first trip to the other side of the world. We'd be staying with a friend of his when we landed in New Zealand.

Richard was waiting for me at Heathrow airport. Right away he goes, 'Here, I got too many bags – carry this for me,' and handed me his rucksack.

Things started going wrong on the first leg of the flight. Our connection in Bali was delayed until the following afternoon. No worries, the competition wasn't until the weekend, and a day stretching our legs sounded good to me. But, unlike New Zealand, Bali requires visitors to have six months – minimum – left on their passport. Mine only had five.

'You stay here in the airport – see you tomorrow.' And with that Richard left me – and his carry-on bag – and disappeared through customs. Then the airport security threatened to put me on a plane back to England before, at 3am and after hours of me arguing with them, deciding instead I needed to leave the airport immediately.

'Come back, get on plane. No wait for plane here. Go!'

So there's me, 16 years old, with my own suitcase, Richard's suitcase and, of course, Richard's fucking rucksack. I'm basically a teenaged packhorse. I'm wearing a tracksuit and trainers which are already squelching with foot sweat in the humidity of Bali.

Dog-tired and desperate to get some sleep, I flagged a cab outside the airport and asked to be taken to a decently priced hotel. He drove by several reasonably priced hotels until I realised he was either running up his tab or taking me somewhere I really didn't want to go.

'Stop! Stop!' I get out the cab, with my luggage, next to open sewers on both sides of the road and straw-hat-wearing old men straight out of every martial arts movie. I drag those suitcases for over an hour – in a giant fucking circle. I'd been awake for 26 hours. I just needed somewhere to lie down – so I headed in the direction of the beach.

'Hey – young man! Young man! Come have a beer!' shouts a German accent from a beach dive bar made out of driftwood and bamboo.

Just to sit down and peel those suitcases out of my palms felt amazing – so you can imagine how the beer made me feel. I began to tell bar patrons – three impossibly drunk fat German businessmen and a local transvestite – my troubles.

'So … nowhere to stay tonight?' the transvestite repeated back to me. 'Yes, you do. You come stay with me.'

Now, I didn't want to be impolite, but I was happy when the Germans said I could come back to their posh hotel instead. A monkey woke me up. Jet-lagged and drunk off bottled beers, I'd passed out on the German guys' balcony. Now I was getting woken up by a monkey – a wild animal who apparently lived nearby – laughing at me. Of course he was – I'd pissed my tracksuit in my sleep.

The Germans rolled through the door, back from what I imagined was a breakfast of piled sausages. I didn't want them to see that I'd pissed myself, so I thanked them for their hospitality and got outta there.

Time to get back to the airport – only, I had no clue where the airport was. I dragged those bloody suitcases around in the heat and sweat of the city all morning. By 10am I was croaking like a frog: '… water … please … water'.

Everywhere I turned, I was mobbed by street merchants. On every corner, I was literally surrounded me by people of all ages selling watches, T-shirts, necklaces and even electrical goods. 'Good deal for you! Good quality!' they'd holler as they stalked after me into the next crowded street – where I'd immediately find myself in another fence's patch and then I'd be harassed all over again. There were these two girls – about my age, 16, 17 years old – who were the most aggressive of the lot. They pulled and tugged at me as I walked, begging me to buy a leather bracelet.

'Okay, you have for free!' they said and tied a bracelet on each of my wrists as I hauled my suitcases behind me.

'No, get those off me,' I said. 'No thanks.'

As I stopped to untie the bracelets, I spotted a KFC. Like an oasis in the desert! I pushed my way by the street sellers and swung open the door into the beautifully air-conditioned fast-food restaurant. I ordered a giant Sprite and sucked it down like it was life-force itself! I went to pay and ... those fucking girls had pickpocketed me. They'd stolen everything.

There are probably legends in Bali to this day of a crazed teenager trucking two lumpy suitcases through the streets and over the sewers – but the two girls were long gone.

And I was even more lost. I almost passed out from thirst getting to the airport but I made it back in time for my flight on to New Zealand. My bad luck followed me. The trip from hell continued with me contracting a crazy foot disease. My left foot was bleeding and reeked like a zombie's fart.

When I landed in New Zealand, Richard was waiting for me

'Where the fuck have you been?' he demanded.

'Where the fuck have *you* been!' I answered.

'Have you got my bag? Where's my bag?'

'Here's your fucking bag!'

Richard tore the zipper down – and pulled out over $20,000 in cash. He was planning to stay in NZ – and didn't want to pay tax on the money he was bringing in.

Whatever, I just needed to get medical attention for my foot. The doctor I saw had no idea what I'd caught in Bali. He prescribed me antibiotic tablets the size of Big Macs.

Richard's friend we were supposed to be staying with? Turned out not to be much of a friend at all, so we stayed in a hostel that a serial killer would be ashamed to visit. Capping off a grand experience, Richard – 30-something and huge – also beat the shit out of 16-year-old me every day in sparring.

In the end, though, he was knocked out in the opening round. I took home the silver medal in the light heavyweight division and a series of anecdotes I've been telling ever since.

It wasn't as much that I was losing interest in martial arts (I continued to kickbox) as much as I became more interested in DJing.

One night when I was 16 and walking home from work, I popped in to see a mate and he had a set of decks. I thought it was the coolest thing I'd ever seen. He let me have a go and I was hooked. Like with martial arts, I drove myself into an obsession DJing. I got my own decks and practised relentlessly. I secured a paid gig at a club and improved to where I was one of the more popular and respected DJs in the northwest of England.

I played a lot of the major clubs of that time including having the 2am and 6am slots at the infamous Monroe's nightclub in Great Harwood. The best DJs in the country worked Monroe's.

Monroe's was a crazy place. During one set during my first few nights there, I saw a pushing and shoving match on the dance floor escalate to where one guy bit the nose off another. I'd learn that was a slow night; several months later during one of my breaks, a man stormed passed me wearing a red balaclava and wielding a Samurai sword. He was making his exit after chopping someone up on the dance floor. Then there was the time when my records got stolen between sets. I went outside to the car park and forced two dodgy-looking guys to show me whatever it was they were obviously hiding in their boot ('Open your fucking boot now,' I said. 'No problem – but when you see what is in there, walk away'). Instead of my records, it was some poor guy gagged and wrapped in duct tape.

The place was finally closed down in 2004 after 200 police descended and arrested everyone in sight. Along with a mountain range of ecstasy tablets, the cops found CS-gas sprays and various weapons including, you guessed it, samurai swords.

I was around those sorts of people here and there but while I was no angel – and no stranger to street fights – I was never interested in being part of that kind of lifestyle in the slightest. All I cared about was having a good night out with my mates. But, even though I didn't go looking for trouble, one night trouble came looking for me.

On a summer's night in 1996, a man came to my apartment to kill me.

I'd moved out of the family home in April. I was 17, earning some money and after growing up in a noisy house of eight, I couldn't wait to have a place all to myself. I'd found a fully furnished apartment for 67 quid a week. It was fully furnished with funky plastic furniture from the 1980s but, hey, 67 quid a week.

The five rooms I was renting had been requisitioned from the homes on either side of it. It was basically a bedsit space zig-zagging through the larger building. While everyone else who lived in Bawdlands (no 'Street', no 'Lane', just 'Bawdlands') entered their home via the main street, the only way in – or out – of my apartment was via a back alley behind a greengrocer's.

The back/front door opened into a vestibule. To the right was a slender, rectangular kitchen area which was separated from the living room by a very 80s-style door – clear glass held in a wooden frame. From the living room you could take the Mount Everest of steep staircases to the upstairs bathroom and bedroom.

Like any 17-year-old kid would, I thought the place was fantastic. I didn't consider that entering via a dark alleyway could be in any way unsafe. I didn't care how dark the yard outside my door was. I didn't think about how low to the ground the bedroom window stood. Why would it occur to me that having only one way in – one way out – could be so dangerous?

The unthinkable happened at 11:45pm on a Saturday night in mid-July. I'd arrived home about 20 minutes before. I was a little drunk from that evening as well as hung over from the night before. Thank God I didn't let the lads talk me into another late one. I collapsed on the old-fashioned PVC sofa and finished off the last few sips of a can of Foster's I found in the fridge. I was knackered from the two-day bender with my mates. I kicked off my shoes, socks and jeans, lay on the couch and began to watch a late-night Channel 4 movie.

I'll have a doze here, I thought. *Maybe when I wake up I'll have the energy for the hike upstairs to bed.*

I don't think I fell asleep, but, if I did, it was for a minute tops.

My eyes flickered open. I'd heard a noise. A faint tapping. I sat up and listened. I couldn't hear anything. I started watching the movie again when …

Knock-knock, knock-knock-knock …

I definitely heard that! I was a little spooked. I was 17, living on my own for the first time. I got up and turned the TV down a bit. I waited a few minutes, listening. Then I heard it again.

Knock-knock, knock-knock-knock …

It was faint, it was intermittent, but there was definitely a knocking. It was creepy; loud enough for me to hear but only just about. Something wasn't right.

It came again:

14

Knock-knock, knock-knock-knock …

Fuck. *Fuck!*

It was coming from the kitchen. I skulked to the glass door to the kitchen and opened it, placing one hand on the pane to stop it from rattling in its frame. Something wasn't right. I left the kitchen lights off. Instead I crept on my hands towards the door. It was pitch-black outside. Blacker than when I'd arrived home 25 minutes before.

I waited, crouched there in the dark. I calmed down a little and almost felt silly when …

Knock-knock, knock-knock-knock …

I freaked the fuck out. I could hear my heartbeat. No doubt about it now – someone was outside my door. Someone was in the dark knocking on my door, remaining silent for long minutes and knocking again.

'Who is it?' The words shot out of my mouth.

They were met with a stretch of silence. Then a muffled voice replied: 'It's Jon …'

Ron? Jon? I didn't make it out. 'Who?'

'Jon.'

I didn't know a Jon. 'Jon who?'

More silence. I stood up and switched the kitchen light on. The light made everything look normal.

'Who is it?' I asked.

'It's me! It's Jon!' This time the voice was assertive. Annoyed, almost. I unlocked the door and pulled it open, expecting to see the familiar face of a friend of a friend who I knew only by a nickname.

There was no face. Only the glimpse of a large outline in the dark – and a *hisssss.*

'AGGHHH!!!'

15

I'd been sprayed in the face. My eyes were welded tight shut. I couldn't open them. I stumbled into the kitchen. Snot exploded from my nose and my throat burned. I wrenched and coughed. I'd been CS-gassed in the face. What the fuck was happening? I had to get my eyes open! What was all that *splashing*? I tore my left eyelid open. I couldn't believe what I saw. An intruder was standing inside the kitchen. He was over 6ft 3in, decked in black. Black boots, black combats, black bomber jacket and what I can best describe as a black KKK hood. There were two holes for his eyes and one for his mouth. The intruder was swinging a can of petrol everywhere. It was slapping against the walls and the kitchen counters. And all over the floor.

He saw my eye was open and threw petrol on me. It splashed my clothes. I was beyond scared. I screamed words but I can't remember what.

Terrified, I realised this intruder was here to hurt me. Maybe more.

'AGGGH! STOP! STOP! WHO ARE YOU?' I screamed. The intruder said nothing. He shook the last drops of petrol on the floor and placed the can by his feet. Looking directly at me, he took out a box of Swan matches. He struck one against the box. Too hard, it snapped. He struck another; it snapped. As he went for a third I scrambled – half-blind – deeper into the house. I flipped another light on and reached the landline phone just inside the living room. I dialled 999 without taking my eyes off the doorway to the kitchen.

'Emergency Services—'

'Help! Please send police! There's someone in my house trying to kill me.'

The voice on the line told me to calm down. The voice asked if I required police, ambulance or fire brigade.

'Please send someone!'

'Sir, I understand you are—'

I'd stopped listening. The intruder was stood near the doorway, looking right at me. He was huge. The look in his eyes …

'He's here right now!'

A coat-hanger smile stretched behind the intruder's hood. He was six paces from me. He still hadn't uttered a word. He was absolutely motionless. He was just watching, watching me on the phone.

'Sir, it is important that you—'

I slammed my finger down to hang up on the emergency operator.

The smile tightened beneath the mouth hole. I could see teeth.

I hit speed-dial.

It rang twice and then: 'Hello?'

'Mate – it's Mike! Call nine-nine-nine! Someone's in my house! He's trying to kill me! Please! Seriously! There's a man here right now! Nine-nine-nine wouldn't believe me! Call the police! Please!'

The intruder jerked his head to one side. Something had surprised him. His thin lips crushed the smile gone. Slowly and deliberately he reached into his black jacket. He pulled out a lump hammer.

I leapt to the door and slammed it shut. I jammed my bare foot against the doorframe and pressed my entire weight against it. I dug in, pushing with all my strength. The masked intruder pressed his forehead against the glass. Our faces were less than a foot apart.

A smile stretched across the mouth hole again. Without moving his head off the glass, the intruder lifted the hammer up.

Clink, clink, clink …

He gently rapped the hammer on the glass.

Clink, clink, clink ...

'Who the fuck are you?! What do you want?!'

More smiling.

Clink, clink, clink ...

There was nowhere to run. There were no doors to lock behind me. What could I do? Who the fuck *was* this? In a split-second my mind raced over anyone – everyone – it could possibly be. It returned one name. The name of a thirty-something lout who I'd had several run-ins with. A bully who, finally, I'd snapped on and decked with a punch earlier that month.

'Bruno?'

His face startled back from the glass. The smile was gone.

'Bruno – is that you?'

He took a step back.

It was fucking Bruno!

'YOU FUAGH—' I couldn't shout. My throat was a cube and my lips had curled back.

White-hot anger flushed out the panic and terror in an instant. This was no practised killer, no horror-movie madman. He was just a bloke. Just a bloke named 'Bruno' who'd picked – and lost – a fight with me outside a pub a few weekends before.

I swung the door open ready for the fight of my life. The hammer arced just inches away from my head. I felt the draught on my neck hair. He turned and ran out outside. Barefoot, wearing only boxers and a T-shirt doused in petrol, I chased. I was across the backyard, down the alley, I hurtled around the corner into the street. Black boots thumped down on the pavement down Bawdlands. He skittled a family saying goodbye to visitors about to get into a car. It's crazy, but I apologised for my would-be immolator's poor manners ('Sorry! Sorry! Excuse us!').

I couldn't keep up with him. My adrenaline was burned to fumes and the soles of my feet were already red raw. The man in the black hood was now at the end of the road. Without glancing back, he turned the corner and disappeared.

My mate arrived first. The cold and the adrenaline dump had me shivering but I didn't want to go back inside my apartment. We went back to his place and called the police again from his phone.

'It was Bruno!' I told the police as two cars of them pulled up. 'It was (I gave his real name)! Lives on (I gave the street he lived on)! Calls himself Bruno! I said his name and he stopped. As soon as I said, "Bruno!" he ran off. It was him!'

They radioed that information to their colleagues and continued to take my statement in between me washing my eyes out with cold water. They stung but I didn't need to go to the hospital.

The police told me that crime-scene experts had looked over my apartment. They confirmed petrol had been thrown everywhere – and found something chilling. My attacker had been inside my home earlier in the day.

'There's evidence of forced entry through the bedroom window,' the officer said. 'And your doorbell wire was cut.'

'My doorbell?'

'It appears the assailant thought he was cutting your phone wire.'

I swallowed hard. That explained him standing there smirking when I was on the phone – he thought the line was dead and was getting off on me trying to use a phone he'd taken out of commission. That puzzled look, the tilt of the head, when I phoned my mate – that's when he realised he'd messed up and the phone was working. Even the quiet knocking at the door – he'd probably tried the doorbell as soon as I got home.

He'd been waiting for me. Planned it so I was blinded in a house set on fire and unable to call for help.

But it wasn't Bruno. The police were at his house – miles across town – within minutes of me giving them his name. They found Bruno asleep in bed; his flatmate said they'd been in all evening.

'There's no way he could have gotten from Bawdlands to his house in such a small window of time,' the cops pointed out.

'So why'd he run, then?' I gasped. 'Why'd he run when I said the name "Bruno"?'

The coppers didn't know, but put forward a theory.

'Things were going wrong for him,' one of them pointed out. 'The doorbell was cut, so he'd spent a long time trying to get you to answer the door. Every time he knocked he risked being spotted by a neighbour or setting a dog off. Then the matches didn't light. He'd gone to a lot of trouble to cut the phone line while you were out, but he'd messed that up and you'd alerted Emergency Services and your friend. He knew assistance was on the way. His plan was falling apart – you mis-identifying him offered him a way out – someone else would get the blame – and he took it.'

I never stepped foot in that apartment again by myself. My mates came with me the next day to collect my stuff.

You'd think a masked man trying to murder a 17-year-old by burning him alive would be worth a follow-up, but the police didn't contact me about the incident again.

I still get chills when talking about what happened – what could have happened – that night. But I never had nightmares or anything like that. I moved back in with my mum (my parents had now divorced) for a while, but moved back out as soon as I found another place I could afford.

I'm not a psychologist, but if I were to guess why something like that didn't affect me more I'd say it was because I got some measure of closure.

A month after the knocks on the door, I got word who the masked man was. It was credible. The guy in question – we'll call him Ronnie – was a well-known psychopath around town who believed he had a reason to dislike me. Ronnie wasn't just a local hardman, he was a violent criminal.

Literally the night I was given Ronnie's name, I spotted him in a pub. He was the right height and bulk. I walked towards him.

'Alright, Jon?'

He turned around. He recognised me.

'I said, are you alright, Jon?'

'My name's Ronnie.' He kept his teeth behind his lips. But I was almost positive, just from the eyes.

'I know your name is Ronnie. But you say it's Jon some nights, don't you, Jon?'

We looked at each other.

'You're nuts,' he said. He turned around but as I walked away his eyes kept darting back towards me.

That was 24 years ago. I've thought about that night a lot. I'm not 100 per cent sure that Ronnie was the man who broke into my house looking to do me harm. Maybe 85 per cent.

The other reason I don't think the incident affected me that much is that I chased him away. He came to my home in the middle of the night with a plan, CS gas, a can of petrol, matches and a lump hammer. But it was him who ran away – not me.

Now you understand why I rolled my eyes whenever internet MMA fans accused me of being 'afraid' of any fighter in the UFC. I haven't been afraid of any man since I was 17 years old.

CHAPTER TWO

LAST CALL

I returned to doing martial arts in the late 1990s. I wanted something a little different, so began to do kickboxing with Allan Clarkin's Black Knights in Burnley. Over the course of two stints there, I won several national and international titles.

Then I moved on from martial arts entirely. I felt like I needed to focus on 'real life'. I was enjoying my DJing but, while the money was good, working weekend nights wasn't going to be a living any time soon. And I now had responsibilities.

I'd first noticed Rebecca when she worked in the office of a factory I was slaving at. She was blonde and Australian and when I spotted her on a night out with her friends I used my best cheesy chat-up lines. She remembers I was very sure of myself and funny. Let's go with that. Two years later we'd bought a house on Nelson Street and were expecting our first child.

My personal life had never been better, but I felt professionally I could be doing so much more than lurching from one dead-end job to the next. I felt like life hadn't yet left the station for me – then, on the night of 12 January 2002, it jumped the tracks.

The evening began like any other Saturday night. I was running late to meet my mates in town, my mobile phone was vibrating with 'WHRE R U?' messages. Rebecca – who is now my wife – was calling upstairs to see if I needed help.

'Nah, you rest,' I shouted down the stairs. 'I can iron my shirt, babe.'

The shirt was quickly thrown around my back and buttoned up as I thumped down the stairs. The stairwell was narrow and steep, as stairwells tend to be in two-up, two-down terraced houses up North.

Rebecca was flicking through Saturday night TV, waiting for a friend to come over. I kissed her goodnight, told her not to wait up, and then hurried on foot into town to join my mates. It was absolutely freezing out; too cold to turn the drizzle to snow. The newspapers that weekend had stories about sheep freezing to death in farmers' fields and Manchester airport runways turning into black-ice slides. But Arctic enough to kill farm animals or not – I wasn't going to commit social suicide and actually wear a coat in public.

We don't wear coats in the North of England.

Blenky, Benty, Burge, Robbie and Aspy were already two and a half pints into a good time when I arrived, damp and ready for a session, at the Castle pub at about 7:30pm. This was my stress release from the soul-decaying boredom of my Monday to Friday, nine to five life. I was working as a door-to-door double-glazing salesman at the time so, needless to say, I was well up for a pint and overtook my mates' lager consumption easily enough over the next four hours.

We sloshed our way through beer and rainy streets along our usual Saturday night circuit of Clitheroe's public houses. A few in the Castle, one or two in the Starkies, then we hit the Swan, the White Lion and the Pit before picking up speed in the Social and the Dog until, at about 11:30pm, we dived out of the heavier rain into the Key Street.

From the outside the Key Street still looked like the stonework cottage it was decades before, but this was no quiet country pub, my friend. It was the closest thing Clitheroe had to a nightclub – drink was served until 1am, there was a dance floor and DJ and, best of all, you didn't need to spend thirty quid on a cab into Blackburn or Manchester.

Stepping past the bouncers and through the double front door, we found ourselves in the middle of our natural habitat. The ceiling was low and the air wet with sweat. It was sweaty in the Key Street no matter the weather outside because it was always ram-packed with drinkers. To the right was the ever-busy bar. It was six deep with customers on the near side that night and on the other side of the draught handles and overflowing beer trays a small army of bartenders were grabbing twenties and handing over pints, wine and shots.

To the side of the bar was an archway into a dance-floor area. It wasn't much of a space, maybe 12 metres or so surrounded by high chairs and a few tables ordered from Argos. That's where the DJ was set up and to the side of him – for use during warmer weather – there was a door to a decent outside courtyard with wooden tables. Completing our tour of this fine establishment, I'll tell you that to the far left of the front door was a short series of narrow hallways which led to the toilets.

We managed to get served in record time and took up one of our usual positions around a high table near the archway.

'I'M GOING TO TAKE A PISS,' Benty proudly announced after a couple of pints. The music and noise of the place made every conversation a shouting match. 'YOUR ROUND, MIKE. GET ME A VODKA AND COKE!'

With that, Benty crabbed his way sideways and disappeared in the direction of the toilets. After getting in the round (vodkas plus a pint for all of us … we got there late, remember?) I also needed a piss. I turned and began picking my way through the crowd, retracing Benty's route through a haze of aftershave, perfume and wine breath.

This is where it stopped being like any other boozy Saturday night.

Having reached the end of the first corridor, I pushed open the door on the left, which stood under a big sign that read 'MEN'. The sounds of the bar and dance floor were muffled to almost nothing as the door shut behind me. I made my way down the short corridor towards a second door. That door opened into the bogs.

There were two guys between me and that second door. They looked about late twenties and were dressed in shirts and smart jeans. The bigger of the two spoke: 'You can't go in there.'

'I need a piss, mate,' I said. Although I'd seen their faces before I didn't really know these two. Why couldn't I go in? Was there broken glass, puke – maybe both – on the other side of that door?

Now the other one pushed his palms against my shoulders and said, 'You're not fucking going in!'

The way he said it, I just knew. *Shit! Where's Benty?*

'Out of my fucking way!' I said, shoving the pair of them aside and pushing through the door.

Shit!

My mate Benty was on the floor near the urine trough. Two lads were kicking the crap out of him. Benty had crawled under the twin sinks to get some protection for his head and was lying on his side, covering his balls and guts with his knees. His face was bloody. He was clearly done in – and they were still kicking him.

I jumped in between them – arms extended – to get them to stop. I began dragging Benty to his feet ...

BANG!

The top of the back of my head exploded in pain and a ringing started in my left ear. The two dickheads who had tried to stop me from discovering what was going on had followed me in. Obviously.

Now it was on. I punched one of them, then another. Benty was swinging, too, and then I was grabbed from behind and we fell into a mess of flailing arms and ripping shirts. Our two-on-four brawl in the bogs was cut short, though, as a platoon of bouncers appeared out of nowhere. The scrap was broken up before it could begin. It wasn't the first time these bouncers had earned their money in that place, and we were quickly escorted outside. I was the last one to be pushed out into the night air. Even though it was still cold and drizzling, there were 25 or 30 people milling about waiting for taxis just across the narrow street by the big car park.

Benty was sat down on the wall across the road. He was alone; our mates were still inside, wondering where we'd got to. I went over to Benty to see how bad his cuts were. He looked alright. He was telling me what happened when I laid eyes on one of the two guys who'd been sticking the boots to him.

Clitheroe is a small place, so I knew the guy's name. He was an ex-military type who fancied himself as the 'ardest man in our little town. It is a slightly embarrassing thing to brag about, being the toughest guy out of such a small population. (It must have been what Brian Stann felt like when he was the WEC 'world' light heavyweight champion!)

Every town in Britain has a self-appointed 'Ardest Man. This was Clitheroe's. He saw me, too, and we moved towards each other, near the middle of the road.

(Note to reader: I'm not going to name him or anyone else involved here. I'm telling this story to show how a series of stupid mistakes I made when I was 22 followed me around for years and, several times, almost wrecked the life I wanted to give my family. It would be hypocritical of me to bring any embarrassment to the other lads all these years later. For all I know – and I really do hope it's the case – everyone involved in this petty brawl has long since grown the hell up.)

But back to the brawl outside the pub: 'Ardest Man started yelling insults. I was drunk. My mate had been bashed up. My ear was swollen fat from a sneak-attack punch. He didn't need to goad me – I'd already made the decision he was gonna pay for what he'd done to my mate.

He sensed that was the case and grabbed a young girl – 19, tops – in a full-nelson hold and literally hid behind her. He'd taken a hostage! She was yelling and trying to get away as he kept on talking shit to me. 'I just kicked the shit outta your mate – I'm about to do the same to you.' That sort of stuff.

Then, out the corner of my eye, I noticed his mate. It was the other one who'd been kicking Benty. He was keeping to my left and behind me, edging closer and closer to me. He was wearing his right fist on the side of his face.

Got it, I thought, *the idea is to hit me from behind again and, no doubt, 'Ardest will then throw the girl aside and join his sneaky mate in their second double-team of the night.*

Well, no. No, you fucking won't!

If this prick takes one step closer to me I'll …

WHAM!

My left shin baseball-batted off the guy's head. Regrettably, after years of martial arts, a head kick was what my mind selected to defend myself with. It was a total overreaction. I knew that and I regretted it. I wasn't fending off knife-wielding muggers here, this was a continuation of a stupid scrap that had begun in a toilet.

The sight of Sneaky getting dropped like a stone was enough for the 'Ardest Man. He threw his captive towards me and took off in the other direction. I remember how funny he looked, legging it down the road in tight trousers and sliding here and there in dress shoes. Then I noticed Sneaky was slowly getting to his feet, at least, and that was when the whole street blazed up blue.

VOOP! VOOP! VOOP!

A vanful of coppers had responded to a call from the Key Street. The side doors whipped open and four policemen wearing padded coats and waterproof hats rushed towards me. They had handcuffs and pepper sprays clipped onto big black belts.

I fucking legged it.

I didn't think – I set off sprinting towards the stone steps on the far side of the cark park. The steps would take me into the darker back alleys, where I thought I'd be able to put in enough distance for the police to lose interest. I was positive they had seen who the real aggressor was and would be more interested in having a word with 'Ardest Man.

A large shape jumped out of a parked car and blocked my way to the steps. Then another flipped out the other side. 'Don't bother running,' the first one shouted towards me. 'We know where you live, Michael!'

Michael?

Now this side of the car park lit up with that same swirling blue. Blue/white/blue/white was reflecting off the wet houses and tarmacked puddles. The vehicle I'd been sprinting towards was an unmarked police car. I stopped – and within seconds I was surrounded. My head got shoved across the bonnet of the police car. The front of my recently ironed shirt and one side of my face soaked up the rainwater while two bobbies snapped handcuffs around my wrists.

'You are under arrest,' I was told, but I'd already figured that part out.

I was thrown in the back of the van. One officer got in with me, the door slammed and the van began driving to Blackburn police station.

As you would when you'd gone about the last few years believing a bit of a scrap didn't *necessarily* have to ruin a great night out, I didn't understand *why* I was under arrest. There were scuffs and scraps every Friday and Saturday night. No big deal. The police usually dealt with it with the obligatory indifference of a supply teacher. ('Break it up, lads. You walk that way – and you go that way. I'd better not see either of you two again the rest of the night!')

I'd been arrested for scrapping before – and all it'd cost me was a bit of embarrassment and a taxi fare home. I'm offering an explanation rather than any excuse here. To be blunt, what had happened outside the Key Street was nothing compared to some of the incidents I had managed to get myself involved in previously. When my brother Konrad and me were cornered in Blackpool by a whole gang armed with broken bottles and baseball bats wrapped in barbed wire (years before *The Walking Dead* made it cool) – well, *that* was a big deal. That was worth calling the police for.

Sparking out some arsehole who was trying to sneak-attack me? And so obviously in self-defence? I couldn't understand why the cops had even wasted the petrol to drive me to the station.

Naturally, I told them as much in the interview room. I wasted no time in laying out what I thought was a pretty devastating case for my immediate release and – quite probably – a cup of tea and a lift home:

It was just a bit of a ruck ... That guy was going to blindside me ... they started it ... he grabbed a girl in a full-nelson – you must have seen that, surely? ... Well, I had to protect myself, didn't I? There was two more inside the pub, as well. They kicked fuck out of my mate. Those guys are well known for causing fights, ask anyone. No, really, you should ask anyone ...

It was still raining when I started the walk to Blackburn bus station at eight o'clock the next morning. Becky was having toast in the kitchen when I got home. I was ashamed to I tell her I'd got arrested, again.

I hired a solicitor from Clitheroe town centre when I got word I might actually face charges. In early March I was on the phone with him for an update. The good news, he began, was the guy I'd kicked was declining to press charges, but ...

But?

'But the local authorities are on a "zero tolerance of antisocial behaviour" drive. And they have filed charges.'

I couldn't believe it, 'Pressing charges? It's going to court?'

'Yes, Mr Bisping.'

I managed to keep listening as my lawyer laid out why the Crown Prosecution Service (CPS) was so sure of a conviction. Essentially, it boiled down to: 'Six police officers saw you commit an assault – and then you resisted arrest by attempting to flee the scene.'

Given these facts, my solicitor convinced me it was in my best interest to plead guilty to a lesser 'public order' charge and avoid antagonising the authorities into considering more serious charges.

'Plead guilty to the Public Order charge,' my legal rep recommended. 'Give the CPS an easy win and the local authority something to add to their statistics showing they are doing something about the binge-drinking culture.'

Pleading guilty was a hard thing to agree to, even as a strategy to eliminate any possibility of going to prison, which was a crazy thought to consider. Why did I need a strategy to not go to prison?

'This is stupid,' I said. 'I didn't even do anything. The other guys did way worse – and they weren't even brought in for questioning?'

'You don't have to think it is fair,' answered my solicitor. 'But you do have to think about the expense and likely return on taking this to trial, especially given the testimonial evidence the CPS will be able to bring to the court.'

Crap.

'Alright, then, let's plead guilty.'

I'd like to tell you that the night before the court date was some long, lonely night of my soul. That I lay there in bed and reflected on my behaviour, contrasting it with my ambitions to be a good father to my soon-to-arrive son.

But I'm not going to bullshit you – I was way more focused on the promotion I'd be getting as a double-glazing salesman; that was scheduled four hours after what I assumed would be a ten-minute appearance before the magistrate.

Me and Rebecca arrived at Blackburn Magistrates' Court at 9am. I was dressed as a double-glazing salesman which – luckily enough – meant black shoes, black trousers and a white shirt. I signed the paperwork at the front desk, got padded down by the surprisingly small security guard and walked through the X-ray machine. Being pregnant, Rebecca didn't have to go through the machine.

My solicitor showed up about the same time. In the end, we had 40 minutes to kill in the waiting room before my name was called. I can't remember feeling worried for one second of those 40 minutes.

We filed into the courtroom. It was an old-school-looking court exactly like you've seen on TV: lots of wood, lots of gold paint and a coat of arms hanging above the raised bench where the magistrate was sitting. There was a clerk hurrying about with files but there was no one else in the courtroom except the five of us.

I didn't blame Rebecca for taking a seat near the back of the court. I took my place next to my solicitor and the proceedings began. After hearing my plea and apology, the magistrate said a few words before standing up and leaving through the door behind his bench.

That was kinda odd. The magistrate didn't leave the court the last time I was here. Then the clerk exited the court through the door to my left. It shut behind him and the courtroom was silent. I was about to ask my lawyer if I was supposed to go back into the waiting area when he dropped an atom bomb on my world.

'Michael,' my solicitor began, 'I have to inform you that when a defendant is about to be taken into custody, security guards from Group 4 arrive. And they have just entered this courtroom.'

My head shot to the right. There they were, four of them, in their dark-blue jumpers. It took me a second to catch on.

'Hold on a minute!' I said. 'You mean there's a chance *I'm* going to *prison*? Today? Now?'

'There was always that chance, Michael,' came the patronising answer. 'And that appears what is about to happen.'

This new reality – *I was going to prison right now* – was like an out-of-body experience. Without even looking at the idiot who'd talked me into pleading guilty, I hurried to the back of the court to speak to Rebecca.

'They are sending me to prison!' I said.

She rolled her eyes and smiled. The day before, I'd told her that I'd taken so long in the shower because I'd been 'practising not dropping the soap'. I'd been making silly little jokes like that for weeks.

'Rebecca! Seriously! These guards are going to take me to prison. My solicitor just told me that's what is happening!'

Shock, disbelief, fear ... I can't even describe the look on Rebecca's face. As she began to process what I was telling her, I glanced down at her belly. I don't want to describe how dejected I felt. She began to say something when I heard someone shout, 'Mr Galen-Bisping!' from the bench. My solicitor was gesturing urgently for me to retake my place next to him.

Just then the magistrate re-entered the chamber. I swear, his lips curled when he saw I'd left my seat and gone to the back of the court.

Y'know, I hold the UFC record for getting knocked down but getting back up to win (seven!). I go back and forth on whether that's a good record to hold or not, but it does show I can get about on wobbly legs. My knees could barely keep me upright as I stood there, waiting for my sentence.

'I'm disappointed to see you in this court once again,' the magistrate began. '*Clearly*, the fine you left here with last time was not a sufficient deterrent. *Clearly*, you have not learned your lesson. *Clearly*, you are not getting the message.'

Only at the end of his lecture did he say: 'I hereby sentence you to serve 28 days in prison. Take – him – down.'

My head spun around. Rebecca was already crying.

The handcuffs pinched my wrists as I was led away, taken downstairs through a back entrance and helped up into a waiting security van. The veins in my neck were throbbing an inch thick. I had no idea what would come next and I was going quietly mental inside my head.

I was driven the nine miles to Preston Prison, an over-crowded, high-security facility for 'those whose escape would be highly dangerous to the public or national security'.

Every second of the way I couldn't believe what was happening to me. I shouldn't have kicked that guy. I knew that the second he hit the tarmac. Prison, though? I wasn't the type of guy, the type of man, who needs to be sent to prison. I didn't belong here! How could I be here?

More than anything, I thought about my girlfriend. My pregnant girlfriend. The woman who I was going to marry when I could give her the wedding I wanted to give her. I had driven our Volkswagen Polo to the court with her, and she was driving it back alone.

Like you've seen in the movies, I was told to strip and hand over my clothes and belongings. Then I was showered and given a crappy prison tracksuit, tatty slippers and told to step into a holding cell. Putting the prison-issue underwear on was soul-destroying.

There were seven or eight prisoners in the holding cell. They were all skinny, scrawny dregs of society. Two of them were engrossed in the football highlights on the TV mounted on the far wall. The rest were greeting each other like old mates, swapping stories of what they were in for. I was in that room for an hour and blanked the lot of them whenever they tried to talk to me.

Why? I kept thinking. *Why am I here with these people in this room? Is this really happening to me? I shouldn't have kicked the guy, yeah, but was the choice really let him punch me from behind again or prison? What should I have done instead?*

In twos and threes the dregs were taken out of the holding pen to whatever prison cell was now expecting them. Then it was my turn to be led away by men in uniform who referred to me by a number. The metal stairs, the industrial-estate décor, the cells and the thin cot beds – it all looked just like what I'd seen on TV or in films. Maybe because the first prisoners I saw were cigarette-stained older men, I don't know, but I wasn't scared. I was sad, sick and dejected.

My cell was also just like on TV. My cellmate was an arsonist. He told me that within minutes of me sitting down on my cot, on the left of the grey room that had been his home for a long time. He was a little guy, nine stone maybe. He was definitely weird and off-putting but I didn't get a 'dangerous' vibe off him.

Preston Prison had a 24-hour lock-up. At 7am each morning, prisoners – like me – got woken up and marched downstairs to get breakfast. We'd splat our food on a plastic tray and get marched right back to the cells, where we'd eat it with the doors already locked again behind us. A while later the trays would be collected through a slit in the door. At noon, we'd be marched downstairs to get dinner (lunch) and marched back to the cells to eat it. The tray would be collected through the slit in the door. Then a long crawl to 5pm. There'd be another march downstairs, another plastic tray would be carried upstairs and the same door would be locked. Repeat the next day, and the day after and so on. Once a week there was an hour of walking in a circle outside in a dusty yard.

Just one month to do, I kept saying to myself. Just one month in this place. I could do that. I've no idea how anyone copes any longer.

On the fifth day two guards came into the cell to do a routine search. One of them was a stocky guy, with longer hair than I thought was sensible for his line of work. Anyway, somehow he knew that I'd been a martial artist once. He'd seen me compete somewhere. I can't quite remember the details, but we had a conversation about a karate fighter from Liverpool we both knew a little.

Then the guard asked me what I was in for and I told him all about it.

'What was the charge?' he asked.

'Public order. I pleaded guilty because I was told I'd avoid coming here.'

'You sound like a prospect to be transferred. You should be in a lower-security prison,' he said.

He shut the door behind him. When it opened again the next morning, I was informed I'd been transferred.

Her Majesty's Prison Kirkham was like a Pontins but you weren't supposed to leave. It had once been an RAF base and the 'billets' – basically, villas with six bedrooms – did have a real Second World War BBC period drama feel to them. It was a palace compared to Preston! We all had our own rooms which we could lock with our own key. We had our own bathrooms; there was a communal kitchen, a living room – and even a games room.

Three hours after waking up next to a creepy fire-starter and surrounded by murderers and rapists, I was playing Space Invaders with tax evaders.

Then I caught another break. I was scheduled to be released on 1 April but that was Easter Monday and, luckily for me, the staff who process releases didn't work bank holidays. They didn't work Sundays either. Nor Saturdays. And, of course, the Friday before Easter Monday is Good Friday, another bank holiday. So, I was released from prison at 9:05am on Thursday, 28 March.

The elderly guy who signed me out gave me my double-glazing salesman white shirt, black trousers and black shoes along with an envelope with a train ticket and 50 quid. 'That's ta get home with, my mate,' he said. 'Bus station is o'wer d'are. Don't get a return ticket, eh? Ha-ha-ha!'

As the small, single-deck bus rattled along the A583 I let myself turn around for a second. *I'm never going back there*, I knew.

Easy for me to say now, but that magistrate did me a big favour. He sent me a message; a message I'd received before but had just laughed off with the arrogance of someone who'd gotten away with too much shit for too long.

What was the message?

It was pretty simple, really: *Stop getting into scraps – and stop getting arrested.*

Real life isn't like one of those pre-fight vignettes designed to encapsulate a fighter's life in a few minutes. I didn't get to skip the boring parts like you can when bingeing on Netflix Originals. There wasn't an inspirational music track to let me know better times were coming.

Even though I swore to myself, Rebecca and everyone who cared about me that I'd never, ever put myself in a situation to be arrested again, I still didn't have a direction in life. Vowing to do better than getting locked up for scrapping outside pubs is a pretty low bar as far as life ambitions go, y'know?

Rebecca and I were sitting down for a meal with her parents when the call came. It was the evening of Tuesday, 14 January 2003, and we were all excited that Rebecca and I were about to become parents to a baby girl.

My phone rang. I answered to hear my mum – who's about as tough as they come – wailing in agony. She was frantic, panic-stricken and incoherent. Something awful had happened, that was clear, but she was so heartbroken and hysterical she wasn't making any sense.

'Mum, calm down,' I said. 'Take a deep breath. Tell me what's happened. Mum ... mum!'

'Konrad,' I heard. Then, '... With an axe.'

Konrad was serving as a lance corporal in the Queen's Lancashire Regiment. He was due to be shipped out to Iraq in a few months' time, but was still in England.

What could have happened to him to upset my mum like this?

'You've got to take a breath, mum. Calm down!'

Rebecca and her parents looked on with increasing concern on their faces. Then my phone beeped with another call. It was a landline number I didn't recognise. I declined it and continued to try to get my mum to calm down a little. The landline number called again – and somehow I knew whoever it was had information about Konrad.

It was a Families Officer from the British Army. Konrad had been attacked by a private from his own platoon during a training exercise on Salisbury Plain. He'd been airlifted to Southampton General Hospital.

'Is he alive?' I heard myself ask of my brother.

'He is right now. He's undergoing surgery to try to get the brain swelling under control.'

The entire family – my parents and siblings – flew down the motorway to Konrad's bedside. He'd always been my hero; I'd looked up to Konrad since I was a toddler. I'd started martial arts because Konrad did it. I'd played rugby because Konrad did. He was now 6ft 6in tall and always the toughest, strongest – and funniest – guy in the room.

He was out of surgery when we reached the hospital. I stared down at the man in the bed with wires and tubes leeching blood out of his bandaged skull. His neck and cheeks were swollen around a breathing mask that held the tube that was helping him cling to life in his mouth. He was surrounded by white plastic machines that were keeping him alive.

His wife said a priest had been to perform last rites.

Later, I met a colleague of Konrad's who witnessed the attack. What he said – and what was said at the trial – has never left me or my family.

My brother was leading his platoon through a war game in preparation for the deployment to Iraq. A little shit named Grant Kenyon couldn't handle the pace. This coward waited for Konrad to take off his helmet and sit down during a break. Then he crept up on Konrad and swung a 3ft-long army issue pickaxe with a 1ft-wide blade head into my brother's skull.

'Your brother died,' the solider told me. 'He dropped to the ground with the axe sticking out his head. He turned blue. We checked his vitals. He was dead, gone! Then – I still can't believe it – he jumped up gasping for breath! He tried to pull the axe out before falling on the ground again. It was the craziest thing I've ever seen.'

We all stayed in the hospital for days waiting for signs of improvement. The staff – who were great – found a bed for my mum and sister to sleep in and I slept on a couch. On the fourth day, with Konrad still in a coma, I had to go back north to be with Rebecca who was due to give birth and looking after Callum on her own.

I'd been home for a couple of days when my mum called with the news. Konrad was awake! I'm not religious, but I struggle to find a better word for it than 'miracle'.

But the life Konrad had made for himself was over. He received compensation from the army but his career, his sight, his health – even his ability to take care of himself – they'd been taken away from him.

But he's a Bisping. He battled back. He's a father and husband. He still loves to compete – and came close to reaching the Paralympics in 2012. I'm so incredibly proud of him.

(Kenyon was released after serving only two years in prison. It wasn't long before he committed another cowardly and sickeningly violent act.)

On 5 February, I held my newborn daughter in my hands. After trying out several different names, Rebecca and me named her Ellie. I remember driving my young family home from the hospital, knowing Konrad had a long stay in series of hospitals in front of him.

What had happened to Konrad made me realise I needed to make the most of life – for myself and my family – while I could. I could do better than bounce around minimum wage factory jobs during the prime of my life. I had to do something different!

After bouncing around a few jobs here and there, including time as a postman and slaughterhouse worker, I'd settled into a role at an upholstery business on the edge of Clitheroe. It was boring work but I really liked my direct supervisor, a guy 35 years or so older than me named Mick. To me, Mick had life all figured out. He was a decent man earning an honest living for his family. I looked up to him and he was a mentor at a time when I really needed one. We worked side by side for over a year – which was the longest I'd ever held down a job. I was determined to keep regular money coming in for Callum's and Ellie's sake.

On tea-breaks during the warm months Mick and I would go outside, lean against the wall and pass the ten minutes talking. One day he asked me what I wanted to do with my life.

'Mick, that's what I've been trying to figure out for ages. I dunno.'

'You're a smart lad,' Mick said. 'You should really try to figure it out sooner rather than later – or do you want to be working here in ten years' time?'

'Sorry ...' I hesitated before continuing my thought. 'Please don't take this the wrong way but, if I'm honest, I don't want to be here in one month's time.'

Mick knew I wasn't insulting him or denigrating what he did for a living. He liked his job and had been encouraging me to find one that, at the very least, I didn't hate.

'Don't spend your life watching the clock until it's time to go home,' he said. 'Everybody is good at something; you owe it to yourself to work out what that is. You are young enough to do it. If you are unhappy at work, you can't help but take that home with you eventually. So really think about it – what are you good at? And then think about how you can go about doing that for a living.'

Over the weekend, with my babies cooing on my lap, I did think about it. I picked up the conversation with Mick on

Monday over the steam of a cooling chicken and mushroom pot-noodle lunch.

'So, Mick,' I began. 'I've thought about it. I *am* good at something – very good at something!'

'Let's have it then – what?'

'From the age of six to about seventeen I was a really good, world champion level, martial artist. So – I'm going to become ... a professional boxer.'

Mick looked at me as if he was embarrassed to have called me a 'smart lad' the week before.

'Oh, a boxer,' he said.

In the summer of 2003, I'd never heard of the UFC, PRIDE FC, Cage Warriors, Cage Rage or anything remotely to do with mixed martial arts. I'd seen a few minutes of an early UFC – maybe *UFC 1* – while in New Zealand when I was 16 but I hadn't been entirely sure it wasn't pro-wrestling (which I loathe). As far as I knew back then, getting paid as a professional fighter meant one thing: boxing.

'That's what I'm going to do, Dad,' I told the old man when he came round my house one evening.

My dad was 100 per cent on board with it. He'd always been so supportive of my KSBO fighting and I think he missed the road trips we'd taken around the country. He was more than encouraging about me becoming a boxer – he actually came up with a great plan of action.

'Join the army and, from there, join the army boxing team,' he said. 'I know how good you are at this – and the army love athletes. After basic training, you'll never have to deploy or do much of anything other than train boxing. It'll be fantastic for you. You'll get paid a decent wage to train and compete as a boxer for the army.

Then after a few years you come out, turn professional, and you'll have all that experience under your belt. Basically, the British Army will pay you to train and box for them.'

Of course, this wasn't the first time Dad had suggested the armed forces. He was a military man and had passed on his patriotic pride to all us kids. Not only Konrad but also my younger brother Adam had joined up when they'd got old enough and I'd given it thought here and there too. But I'd always considered the services as a back-up, a Plan B.

This suggestion, though – this was genius. My dad, brothers and I had been big fans of two-division boxing world champion Nigel Benn, a massive star on ITV in the early 1990s. Benn had learned to box while serving in the Royal Regiment of Fusiliers.

'That's the blueprint,' I told Rebecca when she got in from work. She got it immediately and was on board, even if it meant moving our family to live on a base somewhere in the world. Her father was an ex-serviceman, and he'd left the Australian Air Force with a degree, a pilot's licence and a secure future.

'Let's go for it,' she said. 'I'm with you.'

Literally the next day, I was stood in the British Army Recruitment Services office in Blackburn, filling in paperwork to join up.

There are a lot of empty words thrown around – particularly in America – about 'supporting the troops' but, having signed my name on those papers, I got a new appreciation for the men and women who volunteer. When I handed my signature over, neither me nor Rebecca had any idea what the next few years would look like – we'd waived all say in where we'd live and how much time we'd be able to spend together.

What our servicemen do is essentially hand our country a blank cheque, to be cashed in at any time, anywhere in the world, for a sum up to and including their lives. It is an incredibly generous thing to do, I realised in that moment, which is why whenever I've been asked to visit soldiers the answer has always been 'yes'.

I was proud of myself. I felt the pride of my family, my dad, my brothers and Rebecca. I had a mission, a purpose, and I began attacking it with a determination I hadn't felt in a long time. And while I was waiting for the paperwork to come through I pushed myself in weight-lifting, running, and also started training at an amateur boxing club.

Assessing my fitness levels from an athlete's perspective, the four years away from competition had left me out of shape. I'd made some efforts to trim the beer belly around my waist but, stood next to guys who trained even four times a week, I looked a little soft.

Still, after my first night of sparring, three things were obvious to me:

First, I was still fast. (Faster than these boxers, anyway.)

Second, I was still good. (Good enough for a beginner, anyway.)

And, finally, I had badly, badly missed competition fighting.

This was my direction – the one I was always heading in but didn't realise it.

I was at the upholstery place, helping Mick and another lad carry a sofa from one side of the workshop to another. Work now had a last-week-of-school feel to it. From my brothers, I knew it would be a matter of days until I was interviewed by the army and then it would be a two-day stay at an assessment centre and, maybe three weeks after that, I'd be ordered to report for basic training.

The army had assigned me a CSM – a Candidate Support Manager – who was my point of contact during the wider enrolment process.

He had my mobile, home and work numbers. He called me at work.

'Mikey – phone!' said Mick. I walked over to the phone that was mounted on the wall next to the ladies' bathroom. There were people using hammers all around me so I pressed the handset hard against my ear and turned my back to the noise. The CSM got right to the point.

'I regret it is my duty to inform you, you are not a candidate for recruitment into the British Army at this time.'

Wha?

'Background check ...'

Wha— No!

'... this type of conviction ...'

Fuck, no, no, no.

'... encouraged to reapply in five years.'

No. Please, just ... no.

At some point the CSM was gone and I was still pressing the phone against my ear with my back turned to everyone. There were tears in my eyes and I didn't want anyone to see. I was at rock bottom. I had no options in life. Not even the Army. I was going nowhere. I stood facing the wall and pressing the phone against my ear for over ten minutes. I pretended to talk until the tears were gone.

'I don't know what to do next,' I said to Rebecca at home. 'The army was Plan B – and they don't want me. My entire family is in the forces, but they don't want me. I've fucked everything up.'

This was a real low point for me. I felt very sorry for myself and angry against myself. The two emotions would roll together like in a barrel, one was on top, then the other, then the first one would be back and then they'd mix together and I'd feel just … I dunno, despair maybe. I was stuck, trapped. Every negative thought I'd ever had was churned up. *Rebecca is too good for me. I don't deserve to be happy. I didn't deserve to go to prison. I did it, though. I fucked up and went to prison. I did all this – it is my fault. There's nothing in front of me but 50 years of dead ends.*

Whenever I was at my lowest, Rebecca was at her best. She was amazing; solid as a rock and twice as tough. Let's go one step at a time, together, she said. As bad as one aspect of my life was, she quickly reminded me that we were lucky in others. We were very happy together in our terraced house in Nelson Street. We had a home, we had each other and we had Callum.

Those doubts and negative thoughts sunk beneath the surface again, and I starting gathering myself to search for something else to do. One night I was on the computer in the kitchen and, as a last resort, I googled Paul Davies's name. I found he was still lecturing sports science at Nottingham University. There was an email listed and I clicked on it. I poured my heart out a little to my childhood guru.

A week later, Rebecca told me someone was on the phone for me. It was Paul, and it was the most important phone call of my life. We caught up, and he raved about how sad he'd been when I drifted away from competing.

'You're still the best fighter I've every trained,' he said. 'You made a mistake quitting, but it's not too late. In fact, there's never been a better time to come back because big things are happening.'

Paul had always said that martial arts would become like boxing – big business and sold-out arenas and TV-rights fees. Kickboxing promoters had been saying that, too, for decades. It never happened. The only 'fights' anyone bought a ticket or turned on a TV to see was boxing.

'Things have changed since you've been away from martial arts,' Paul insisted. 'It is already happening – just like I said. Have you seen what's been happening with the UFC in America?'

I hadn't a clue. Unless the term had been used in the two minutes of that early event I saw, this conversation could literally have been the first time I'd heard the words 'Ultimate', 'Fighting' and 'Championship' strung together in a sentence.

Paul went on for hours, describing this whole other world. The UFC was taking over America, he said, doing pay-per-view events and creating champion millionaires who guest-starred in movies and drove sports cars. It was owned by two of the richest men in the US; a pair of Las Vegas casino owners. It was run by a friend of theirs. And in Japan, the sport of mixed martial arts was even bigger – crowds of 40,000 people and half the country watching on TV.

'Mixed martial arts is a sport that combines striking and grappling,' Paul said. Then he paused, dramatically, before adding, 'I prepared you for a sport which combines striking and grappling since you were six years old! You can kickbox. You know submissions and how to defend submissions. You know elbow strikes. Knees. You have a head-start on most fighters in the UK.'

My head started buzzing with where this was obviously going.

Paul informed me, 'I'm putting a squad of the best fighters in the country together. I want you on it ... if you can still fight?'

'I can still fight,' shot out of my mouth.

Paul didn't take my word for it. He arranged for me to attend a training camp in Wales. I went about my business that weekend like a man possessed. I wasn't in shape, but I squeezed every drop of

48

effort out of my body. My skills were dull from lack of use, but they were exactly where I'd left them. Paul liked what he saw.

The deal I worked out with Paul was that he'd provide me with food, accommodation and 25 quid towards my petrol money while training me four days a week in Nottingham. I would have to quit my job at the upholstery place, of course, but if I could make it to the top five MMA fighters in the UK, he would pay me a weekly wage.

'It will take four to six months to get you ready for your first MMA fight,' he said. 'I'll take a percentage of your earnings from fights, but don't worry, I won't put you in a pro-fight unless a) you are ready and b) it is for life-changing money!'

It wasn't boxing but, with respect to Nigel Benn and Frank Bruno, it was better than boxing. I didn't have to learn a new style of fighting; I'd take the style that I'd used to great success for over a decade and build on its foundation.

Again, the support from my partner was absolute. Rebecca and I sat down with a notepad and figured out a budget. It cut to the bone but it was manageable if I continued to get 200 quid or so cash every weekend. So that was the plan – I'd drive to Nottingham early Monday and train during the week. Then I'd drive home Fridays to be with my family and on Saturday I'd DJ for money.

Rebecca bought me a UFC DVD, *Ultimate Submissions*. We couldn't believe the size of the spectacle, the celebrities in the front row. It was all rock music and lights and money. It was a million miles away, in Las Vegas and exotic places with open-top cars and palm trees. It was something I knew I could do.

'You are going to be great at this,' Rebecca said. 'This is what you were supposed to be doing all along. This is the beginning of something big for you.'

I shook my head. 'For us. I'm doing this for us.'

CHAPTER THREE
THE BEGINNING

Just after teatime on Sunday, 4 January 2004, I threw two bags of clothes, a small mattress and a sleeping bag into my dad's Peugeot 306 estate. It was bitter cold and dark, and I appreciated him driving me to Nottingham to begin training. 'It's been a while since we did this,' he said.

It had been years.

It was pitch-black down the M1 and there was little traffic all the way to Junction 25. We were on the road to Nottingham, but my real destination was Las Vegas.

Paul Davies was very connected not only in martial arts but with gyms, sports halls and venues. He knew the right people to get a good rate on hiring a sports hall on Nottingham University campus and taught Yawara Ryu jiu-jitsu there on weeknights. I recognised the others there from the training camp I'd attended in Wales. Like me, they stood out in a room full of martial arts hobbyists.

This smaller group also trained together during the day at Sherwood Community Centre, where Davies was well known, and also in a makeshift MMA gym, which was little more than a room with a punching bag and mats set up in an unused space in an industrial unit owned by, you guessed it, someone Paul knew.

My new colleagues included a Thai boxer called Mark Ferron and a hairy-backed heavyweight named Andy Harby, who was at least ten years older than the rest of us but had developed scary physical strength working on the farm he owned. Then there was Freddy, who claimed to be an Olympic wrestler originally from Iran (he was from Iran), a hard-hitting kickboxer, Paul Daley, and finally a prickly 21-year-old local lad named Dan Hardy.

At first glance, I figured Dan was pursuing fighting as just another part of his counter-culture experimentation, like with his tattoos, Eastern philosophy books and punk rock music. In fact, despite having a university place waiting for him, Dan was just as determined to fight as I was. He was also the most talented guy in our team of rivals (except for me, of course, ha!) and was a great partner during those early months of my MMA training.

Davies was a taskmaster as a trainer. I knew that already, but from my first day in Nottingham he worked me like I was a professional athlete and with the expectation I would knuckle down like a pro-athlete. And that's what I did. Every week was a blur of classes with Paul and our elite group: weight-lifting sessions, submission lessons, cardio training. Afterwards, Paul would take me and occasionally Dan to the specialist stores to get whey protein, creatine, fish oils and other nutrients vital for building the body of a professional fighter. He was light years ahead of the game in terms of nutrition and strength and conditioning.

'You can't out-exercise a poor diet,' he'd say over and over.

We did pad work together but much of my striking practice was done at a boxing gym twice a week and a Thai boxing club, both in Nottingham and on the schedule Paul had packed back-to-back for me. It was a crash course; I was getting information dumped into me like a first-year law student. This sport wasn't fully formed. We were all pioneers, making shit up as we went along, cobbling together drills from trial and error and copying techniques we'd seen on UFC tapes or instructional videos mail-ordered from America.

And I absolutely *loved it*. I was happier than I'd ever been in any job I'd had. I felt fulfilled. MMA was strategic, athletic and it required strength, speed, stamina and – most of all – imagination. There were infinite ways to combine the martial arts forms – grappling, striking and wrestling – and the most unexpected amalgamations, the fastest transitions from one to the other, were what separated tough-guy 'cage fighters' from a true mixed martial artist.

Spending so much time away from my family was very tough, though. Paul set me up with a job as a lifeguard at a local swimming baths but I quit after a day of learning CPR. I made better money DJing and if I wasn't training, I wanted to be with my family.

Paul would use his contacts to either bring in or have us travel to train with combat sports specialists. When he did, he'd always seek to test my progress with these little challenges: like, one day, he offered me an extra 50 quid if I could last ten minutes grappling with four-time BJJ world champion Braulio Estima (he got me just after nine minutes, dammit).

As much as I loved the training in the days, I sort of dreaded the evenings. My accommodation from Monday nights to Friday mornings was a sleeping bag laid out in the living room of, all together now, some bloke Paul knew. Where Paul had met this guy … I couldn't begin to guess. It wasn't from martial arts or fitness training, that's for sure.

My host was about 32, nerdy and dressed as though his mum still had the final say on what clothes he bought. He was monosyllabic and made zero effort to make me feel welcome. Any attempt by me to make conversation was met with an exasperated gesture towards the always-on TV and two words: 'Watching telly!'

That fucking TV was on until at least midnight – every single night – and I was supposed to sleep in that very same room. My sleeping bag was rolled out in a crawl space behind a wooden cabinet. Getting any rest was impossible.

Proving the theory that there's someone out there for everyone, my host had a girlfriend. On the nights she visited I had two of them telling me 'Shhh! Watching telly!' if I made a sound from my cubby-hole. I felt like a red-headed step-child.

These were the strangest humans I'd ever come across. The only thing worse than getting shushed by them ('Shhhh! Telly!') was getting falsely accused of the most mental of transgressions.

A lot of the time, I had my evening meals at Paul's house. It was awkward, gate-crashing his family's evenings together. Whenever I had some spare money from DJing at the weekends, I'd treat myself to a room in a twenty-quid-a-night B&B. I also started sleeping in my car – a banged up Volvo that Paul loaned me – outside the Sherwood Leisure Centre; anything but stay in that room with that TV.

There was a snowstorm one of those nights. The swirling flakes were orange in the street lamppost's light, and when they began sticking to the windscreen the temperature in the car plummeted.

I reclined the seat as far as it would go and climbed into my sleeping bag (I may have left my trainers on, it was that bloody cold). The palm trees and flashing lights of a big fight day in Las Vegas felt a like a long way away at that moment, but I had no doubt this was the path I was supposed to be on.

That's when Rebecca called. Another bill had come in. We'd already borrowed money from our parents.

54

'We will be okay,' I said. 'I'm going to book a fight. I'm going to tell Paul tomorrow that – fuck more training – I'm ready to fight. Time to earn some money from the sport.'

I got paid literally nothing for my first professional fight.

No, that's not quite right. When I fought Steve Mathews on 10 April 2004, I actually paid the promoter 25 quid because – despite me bringing over 40 family and friends up to Newcastle-upon-Tyne, the promoter wouldn't comp me a single ticket for Rebecca.

The cheap so-and-so in question was a promoter/fighter/ referee/MC named Ian Freeman. Freeman, I'd learned by now, was British MMA royalty.

Known as 'The Machine', the sawn-off Sunderland heavyweight had turned professional before there really was a profession. In the 1990s Ian had gotten hold of early UFC and PRIDE FC videotapes and, God knows what possessed him, off he flew to cramped dojos in Tokyo and sweatboxes in the United States to learn ground-fighting. In March 2000 Freeman became the first Brit to compete in the UFC – but his legacy is more than just the answer to a trivia question.

When the UFC first brought the Octagon to the UK in the summer of 2002, Freeman stood in front of the Fleet Street press as a passionate advocate for the sport. Then, in the most publicised fight on the 13 July *UFC 38* event at London's Royal Albert Hall, Freeman wrecked the undefeated reputation of heavyweight-champ-in-waiting Frank Mir.

It was the first major British success in the UFC. What's so heart-breaking about it is when Ian got back to the dressing room; he was informed his father had passed away two days before. As a former boxer himself, his dad's dying wish was that no one say a word to Ian, so he could fight his best.

Like all British fighters who followed him should, I tip my hat to the Machine ... even though he paid me fuck-all for my first fight. Ha!

A few days before my pro-debut in Newcastle, Davies informed me that there wouldn't actually be any pay.

'That is ... *not* life-changing money,' I said.

'Let's just get the ball rolling,' Davies answered. 'Freeman's well known and a lot of the bigger promoters attend his shows. This is a chance to get your name out into the British MMA community.'

Maybe I could have been pissed off about the pay, particularly because over 40 of my family and friends all bought tickets, so it wasn't like I didn't earn my place on the card in terms of putting arses on seats. But, spending months orienting my life around fighting without actually fighting was driving me nuts. I've never been afraid of a fight in my life and I didn't see any reason not to supercharge my training with actual fights.

The event, *Pride and Glory 2: Battle of the Ages*, took place in a leisure centre in Eldon Square. A boxing ring set up in a gym hall with netball court lines painted on the floor was a long way from Las Vegas's MGM Grand, but it was a start.

Every fighter on the card – including my opponent and everyone else's opponent – got changed in the same poky storage backroom. There were 24 of us rubbing against each other's shoulders and nerves.

My anxiety was throbbing out of my eyeballs. It wasn't fear. Fear I knew what to do with. I was literally shaking under the pressure to win this thing. If I couldn't beat someone named Steve Mathews, on a card held in a Tyneside netball court, in a fight so insignificant the promoter saw no need to pay for it ... well, this whole thing was over, wasn't it?

There wasn't any reason to worry. I took Mathews – who apparently had some sort of hard-man rep – apart in a blaze of strikes. (Somehow, the fight was recorded as a submission win via armbar, and for the rest of my career I was credited with one extra sub and one less TKO.)

'The ball's rolling now, Paul,' I said afterwards.

Even as I hit the bar with Rebecca and my friends, I kept turning back to the action in the ring. The nervous energy I'd felt was something else. It was a hundred times more pressure than in my competitions as a kid but I knew I could control it better in my second fight and, in time, learn to use it as a positive force. I couldn't wait to get back in there.

My second pro-fight came just 50 days later. It was on a Sunday afternoon card at the Circus Tavern, the venue of choice for Essex wedding receptions and bar mitzvahs. The event was billed as *UK MMA 7: Rage and Fury!* which sounded like a charming evening's entertainment. My opponent, John Weir, was 3–1 with three KOs.

The way the 600 or so fans pressed up against the boxing ring was a fire hazard, but it made for a great atmosphere. The fight was raw. Weir had skills – he landed several knees before I overwhelmed him with strikes against the ropes and he planted face-first into the canvas.

After two fights, I'd earned some status in the slowly expanding pocket universe of British cage fighting.

By now I'd realised the UK MMA scene was the plaything of a few unsavoury characters. A lot of the promotions back then were run by gangsters or bench-pressing mobster wannabes. They'd all seen *UFC 38* sell out the Royal Albert Hall and concluded pound notes were to be made in 'cage fighting'. And with the UFC having to postpone plans for regular UK events to focus fully on its home US market, *UFC 38* had created a market the UFC currently couldn't service.

British MMA, circa 2004, was a subculture: 99.9 per cent of people had no clue it even existed, but the 0.1 per cent who did lived it. The vibe around the sport, in the gyms, in training, around the fight hotels and arenas, was edgy and cool. Years before social media was big, fans and fighters communicated directly with each other using insider terms on message boards, one of which is, to this day, called 'the Underground'. It wasn't unlike my DJing – it was more than an interest, it was a lifestyle and a tribe with its own language.

Of the dozen or so promotions who rushed to capitalise on that early interest, two in particular emerged as the big fish in the small pond. In the North of England there was Cage Warriors, and in the London area there was Cage Rage.

By 2004, Cage Rage was steaming ahead, scoring a TV deal with Sky Sports and attracting regular crowds of nearly 3,000 to shows known for flashing lights, gallons of dry ice, bad tattoos and creosoted bikini girls.

They had quality fights as well. Yeah, Cage Rage had its fair share of radioactive steroid doormen, but its main eventers were usually world-class talent including Freeman and other UFC veterans like Mark Weir, Matt Lindland and 'Babalu' Sobral.

It was Sobral that Cage Rage owners Andy Geer and Dave O'Donnell called Davies to talk about in June 2004. The Brazilian submission expert's opponent for their 10 July London event had pulled out, and they needed a replacement.

'Dat Bisping kid you got – duz 'ee fancy it?' O'Donnell wanted to know. The pay was a thousand quid. The fight was also for the newly created Cage Rage light heavyweight title and – a huge selling point – the main card of *Cage Rage 7* would be broadcast several times on Sky Sports.

Davies pitched it to me. 'Sobral is a big name, but I have confidence in you.'

I had confidence in me, too, and I took the fight. Of course, fighters are *supposed* to be brave and be willing to take on anyone, anywhere, anytime. It's the manager's job to be more circumspect.

Sobral was more than a big name. Babalu had beaten 25 of the 31 opponents he'd faced in his eight years as an MMA fighter, including a former UFC champion (Maurice Smith), a UFC title challenger (Jeremy Horn) and a future PRIDE and UFC champion (Shogun Rua). The only men to have beaten him were Chael Sonnen, Chuck Liddell, Kevin Randleman, Fedor Emelianenko, Valentijn Overeem and Dan Henderson. The Brazilian was as legit as it gets on the ground and had massive experience against the best fighters in the entire sport.

To match against that, I had six months of training in Nottingham and 100 seconds of MMA fight experience. It was probably for the best that Sobral himself pulled out just ten days before the event, and was replaced by Mark Epstein.

'The Beast' was the Cage Rage heavyweight champion and, maybe as a favour to his friends and training partners O'Donnell and Geer, he decided to drop down to the 205lb light heavy division.

'This is still a step up,' Davies told me when we met up after the weigh-in at the budget north London hotel. 'Epstein has had nine fights, some against good American competition. He's pals with the promoters – so don't expect the judges to necessarily do you any favours.'

I have great memories of *Cage Rage 7*. It was held at Wembley Conference Centre. The place is gone now, knocked down years ago, but to me on that night that 2,500-seat venue with its 1970s lighting was *the Wembley*. The place where real sports take place.

Somehow reporters from US-based websites like Sherdog and MMAWeekly got my mobile number and I did my first interviews with American media. On weigh-in day I did my first to-camera interview, which was both exciting and painfully awkward. Without warning, I'd been ushered in front of a big Cage Rage logo, had a camera shoved in my face and was asked: 'What's your message to Mark Epstein?' The very best line I could think of was, 'Good luck. You are going to need it.'

Dave O'Donnell was something to behold in his element. With his bald head squeezing out the top of a red shirt and black suit, and perpetually yelling and laughing in the thickest of cockney accents, Dave was the face and voice of Cage Rage. He absolutely loved MMA – he does to this day. On the afternoon of *Cage Rage 7* he was bolting around everywhere – front of house, backstage with fighters, taping interviews to be rolled in during the TV broadcast – he was on fire and loving every second of it. I immediately liked the guy.

For a lot of British MMA fighters, Cage Rage was the big show. They were almost physically aroused to be part of the UK's UFC cover band for four Saturday nights a year. It was extra money, a reason to train and – best of all for these guys – great for the hardman rep when working the doors of London nightclubs. But I wasn't like them, I was here to earn some money, get better and use the experience to go on to the world stage. Wembley or not, Cage Rage was not my World Cup Final.

It was time for my fight. The noise the fans were making was amazing. I'd be lying if I told you my heart wasn't pumping hard as I walked across the catwalk-like runway from the backstage area to the cage apron. I stepped into a cage for the first time ever. A few moments later, the cage emptied and I heard a bolt scrape shut. The door had been locked. It was just me, the referee and Epstein surrounded by a wire mesh and a wall of noise.

Oh, shit, I surprised myself thinking. I was literally locked in a cage with a man I was going to fight.

I felt adrenaline sharpening my senses. This one was a little different. I'd never even trained inside a cage, but in the few times we'd spoken about it, Paul and I agreed the best plan would be to stay in the middle and avoid getting pushed against the fence.

My opponent stood waiting for me in the centre of the cage. We were both wearing bright-red shorts. Even though he was Cage Rage's heavyweight champion, Epstein was squatter than me at 5ft 9in – but dense with muscle.

One report I read the week of the fight observed Epstein 'had the face of a murderer'. I'm not sure I'd go that far, but he certainly fit the bill of a 'cage fighter'.

Even so, there was no hesitation when it came to attacking him at the first bell. I hacked at him with straight punches and stunned him with a right. I gave chase across the cage – but ran into a solid counter. Epstein surged forward with leg kicks and power punches. He pressed me against the fence. For the first time in my life, I felt the skin on my shoulder pinch as the mesh stretched and contorted under our weight. I fought my way off the fence but then foolishly threw a front kick, which Epstein caught. With me stood on one leg, he took me down to the ground.

'The Beast' loved to ground and pound, I knew. I was a little worried he'd taken the fight precisely where he wanted it. The rest of the round was spent with Epstein on top of me but, as ref

Grant Waterman stood us up when the bell sounded, I realised I'd controlled the whole round. I'd stifled Epstein's aggression with an active and constantly moving guard, threatened him with submissions, and landed punches from the bottom. He'd not been able to hurt me even from his favourite position. I couldn't wait for round two and, as soon as it began, the bombardment started.

I blasted him with lefts, rights, hooks and knees. Mark was a tough guy and somehow had packed an Incredible Hulk's worth of muscle around his shoulders and neck. He absorbed a ton of punishment before the ref waved it off 87 seconds into the second round. The Cage Rage belt – my first in MMA – was handed over.

There was only one more fight after mine (Mark Weir lost to a quiet, respectful American fella named Jorge Rivera) so by the time I'd dried myself off from a quick shower Dave O'Donnell had put his commentator's microphone down and was once again bouncing around backstage doing a million things at once.

But he wasn't too busy to notice that I'd brought over 60 ticket-buying family and friends with me.

'Fackin' 'ell, yew are a popular laad, aintchya?' he boomed. ''Ere – 'ave a pint on me, mate.'

He handed me 600 quid in cash, on top of the grand I'd got for fighting. Then he slapped me on the shoulder and on Dave went, his bald head swivelling left and right, clearly having the time of his life.

A little while later I limped across the car park next to the Conference Centre. It was about midnight and the car park was almost empty. In the distance seven huge cranes loomed over a construction site which would, in a few years, be the new Wembley Stadium. I climbed aboard the packed 72-seater coach that had been waiting for me and it erupted in cheers. Then came the song:

There's only onnnne Mikey Bis-Ping!
Onnnnnnne Mikey Bis-Ping!
Walkin' along,
Singin' a song,
Walkin' in a Bisping Wonderland!

I cracked up as my family and friends sang a song of victory for me. They were standing and cheering and all looked so proud and happy. They'd had a great time at the fight.

'COME ON!' I shouted, yanking the title belt out of my bag to more cheers.

With a seven-hour drive north in front of him, the driver pulled off as I went up and down the coach hugging my dad, siblings and friends. Keeping my balance wasn't easy and I sat down next to Rebecca. I cracked open a lager as we settled in for a noisy ride home.

This was one of the best moments of my career. It's still so vivid I could describe the way the fabric of the seat made the middle of my back itch a little, and the grunting noise the coach made as it went from first to second gear. It's so vivid, but that night also seems an eternity ago.

CHAPTER FOUR

BEST IN BRITAIN

Twenty-eight days after winning the Cage Rage belt, I had my fourth fight. It was another Freeman-promoted *Pride and Glory* show in Newcastle and I knocked out Andy Bridges in 45 seconds.

The Machine began training with Davies's small group, driving down from Tyneside twice a week to spar. By this time my main accommodation was an array of Nottingham's cheapest B&B's, friends' couches or, more often than not, my car.

With a full-time job, a family and several paying strength-and-conditioning clients, Davies's ability to commit to me would ebb and flow. More than once, instead of meeting me at the gym, he would only have time to email me a weight-training session. I understood that Paul had a million other things to do – I really did – but this wasn't a side-project to me. This was my career; it was time away from my family. Rebecca and me were banking everything on this.

Determined to continue to improve as quickly as possible, I began networking like crazy, zigzagging the north of the country on a quest to become a better fighter. There was a Gracie Barra BJJ school in Bolton, so I went there to absorb submission defences. I trained in kickboxing at the well-respected Black Knights gym. There was a good group of MMA guys in the Birmingham area, I heard, so I drove down there one day only to arrive as the class ended. A guy called Marc Goddard, who'd go on to be a leading referee, took pity on me and invited me in for a roll. I sparred with pro-boxers, Thai fighters and kickboxers – anyone who had professional combat sport experience. All the while I trained and entered any jiu-jitsu tournament I could get to.

I laugh at young fighters today when I hear them saying things like, 'In my next camp, I want to work on such-and-such a thing.' What's wrong with them? They're young – they should be training every single day! They've no idea how lucky they are to have a striking coach, a BJJ coach, a wrestling coach, strength-and-conditioning experts and top-drawer sparring all under the same roof. If I'd had access to the training available today, I'd have been UFC-ready inside of one year, believe you me.

My cardio levels got a massive boost when an old-school strength and fitness expert called Jeff Rainbow took me under his wing. I can still remember groaning at the sound of his instructions at the bottom of Nottingham's Castle Hill: 'At the top of that hill there's a tree with a branch about nine foot above the ground – sprint up the hill to the tree, jump and touch the branch ten times with your right hand. Then ten times with your left hand. Then do ten push-ups and get back here. You've got five minutes. Go!'

Jeff was awesome. He helped forge one of the most effective weapons I used in my entire career – my cardio. He showed me how to weaponise it – to push through pain and keep working through exhaustion and take the fight where other athletes couldn't follow without falling apart. I kept on pushing my entire career and I credit my cardio with many of my biggest career wins.

With all the quality training I was getting, I underwent a physical transformation. I was beginning to look, feel and perform like the athlete I always should have been.

And I needed to. Epstein's supporters had bombarded the UK MMA forums like CageWarriors.com and SFUK with posts saying my Cage Rage title win was a fluke. That Mark took the call on short notice and, if he'd had a full camp, he'd have thumped me. Our *Cage Rage 7* fight was already considered to be one of the best in the short history of the British scene – and Dave O'Donnell had already seen I could do a bit of box office. The rematch was a no-brainer.

The return bout was set for *Cage Rage 9*, on 27 November 2004, back at Wembley. By the time it rolled around, I felt several levels above the fighter who'd faced Epstein in July. My body was trip-wire tight and my skillset was bigger and sharper. I'd been training full-time for 11 months, and felt I had an edge in talent, aggression and athleticism over any fighter in the UK. I was the best of the Brits, I wasn't shy of saying it.

The Wembley Conference Centre sold out on the night and Sky Sport's cameras were once again trained on the cage. It was still a niche sport, but the UK MMA scene was growing rapidly. You could feel it.

Just like in the first fight, I attacked Epstein from the opening bell. This time I found my range quicker and sensed Epstein's counters sooner. I dropped him for a split-second with a sustained attack and, later in the round, chopped him down with a jab + cross + left hook combo. The second knockdown hurt him. I pounced on top of him and rained shots from full mount for several minutes. Referee Waterman must have thought about stopping it.

In the second, I continued to exploit my height and reach advantages: cracking home lefts and rights in combinations while Epstein could only swing and miss. The only shot Epstein landed with any regularity was a leg kick. I hit him at will. By the end of the second round, Epstein had the face of a murder victim rather than a murderer.

He hurt me in the third, though, and I had to overcome the first difficult moments of my career. I'd not learned how to check a leg kick yet (the art of intercepting the oncoming strike on the shin, rather than allowing the impact to tenderise your leg muscles) and, unable to land much else, the Beast had continued to go for my lead left leg all night. Towards the end of the third and final round, Epstein slammed his shin into the flesh just above my left knee.

My entire leg locked stiff with pain. The London Massive went nuts as Epstein went after my leg again and again. Nothing hurts quite as vindictively as a solid kick to the leg – they are horrible – and with me not knowing how to defend against them, I took a few more than I would have liked. But, gradually, feeling returned to the limb and I re-engaged. Epstein's brief rally was over. I found the target for a big right hand to end it at 4:41 of the last round.

That's how my first year as a mixed martial artist ended, 5–0, with all five wins coming inside the distance. I'd not seen any life-changing money yet, but everything else Paul Davies had predicted before the previous Christmas was coming true. I now looked and felt like a real professional athlete. I had miles to go in terms of development, but at least I knew I was on the right road. I couldn't wait for 2005.

My left leg took a while to heal from the leg kicks. I watched the Epstein rematch back on tape TV over and over, partly because it was cool seeing myself on a Sky Sports broadcast but mainly because this was my first opportunity to take a detailed inventory of my progress as a mixed martial artist.

Each time I put the DVD in, I underlined the same conclusion in my mental notebook: I needed to improve my defence against leg kicks.

'We got to get you to Thailand,' Paul said. 'That's where the best strikers in the world are. That's where you are going next.'

The hotel I stayed in when I arrived two weeks later in the Ramkhamhaeng region of Thailand was next to a river that churned up the stench of human faeces whenever motor boats went by. There are many incredibly nice parts of Thailand – this wasn't one of them.

My small room had a low-laying bed, a table, a light bulb hanging by a wire and a tiny bathroom with bright blue tiles. All 12 square feet of it was infested with unreasonably sized insects. These bugs looked at you with eyes that took up half of each side of their face while waving these antennae around in the air as if they planned to lasso you. Some of these creeps had bodies the size of rounders bats. My skin crawled at the first sight of them but by the second week I was brushing them off my toothpaste in the morning like it was normal.

Thai food has become one of my favourites, but back then my palate hadn't travelled too far outside of England. I was okay eating dishes made with rice and eggs but I steered well clear of the food I dubbed 'dead things in water'. Some of the local favourites were dead scorpions in water, dead toads in water and – for snobs who insisted in messing around with a classic – dead spiders floating on water.

The training I received at a hardcore traditional Thai boxing gym made it all worthwhile. At first the trainers treated me like just another martial arts tourist acting out his Jean-Claude Van Damme fantasies, but after a day or so they realised this *farang* ('person from the white race') was actually a genuine fighter. From then on, the training they gave me was amazing.

The gym was exactly how Van Damme's movies portrayed, a huge space where 40 or 50 leather-skinned Thais sparred and whipped their shins into rows of sun-bleached heavy bags.

While other traditional martial arts had grown overly codified and isolated in their dojos, the techniques used in Muay Thai (literally 'boxing from Thailand') had been continuously sharpened in actual combat for at least 300 years. Thai fighters were typically trained from a young age, drilling twice a day – morning and evening – to avoid the worst of the wet heat. Unless the event was rained off, there were fights almost every day in the major towns. It was literally everyday entertainment, a place to go and gamble like people in England go to the bookies. Boxing-style gloves were only introduced in the twentieth century, although the bareknuckle variety was still widely practised just across the western border in Myanmar as Lethwei.

Having been accepted by the coaches and fighters, I began making significant progress not just on defending and countering leg kicks, but also everything else I could take from these masters of the 'Art of the Eight Limbs'.

Nobody spoke much English – not the fighters, the trainers or even the hotel staff – so I spent a lot of time inside my own head, reflecting on these people who had quickly accepted me into their community. I was impossibly wealthy in comparison to all of them. I was training so I could fight to get a bigger house, a better car and a better future for myself and my family. These guys kicking the bag next to me were fighting literally to win enough prize money to eat, to provide one meal for a loved one or maybe put a roof over their heads before the rainy season struck.

I'm sorry that I don't know their names to put down in this book. Thai names are hard to pronounce and even harder to spell. I do know I left Thailand a better fighter and humbled by the experience. Every young fighter should travel to Thailand and learn from these people. When I got home, I couldn't wait to use my new armaments. I took a K-1 rules kickboxing fight and a cage kickboxing bout and won them both by knockout.

My sixth MMA fight came in the Cage Warriors promotion on 30 April 2005. They, too, had created a light heavyweight championship and invited me to compete for it at their event at the Xscape Centre, Castleford. Opposing me for the inaugural title would be 35-year-old boxer Dave Radford.

Radford had once fought legendary boxer Roberto Duran on a few hours' notice. His eyes and cheeks were permanently puffy from years of bareknuckle fights. He was obviously a tough bastard. What he was not was a mixed martial artist. I knocked him out in 2 minutes and 46 seconds.

As the champion of Cage Rage and Cage Warriors, it was getting harder for the naysayers to deny I was the best light heavyweight fighter in Britain.

Paul casually mentioned to me that he'd been offered a good opportunity in sports science in New Zealand that he intended to pursue. He began selling the idea of me moving down there with him. I didn't know what to say. I still had this student/master relationship with him, just like I had since I was eight years old, so didn't feel it was appropriate to point out that I had a family, was the champion of several UK-based promotions and that there was no MMA scene at all in New Zealand. I found it easier to say, 'I'll talk to Rebecca about it,' rather than give him the obvious 'no'.

I knew something had to change but I was looking for Paul – my mentor and the man who had a sixth sense about martial arts – to suggest what that looked like.

Instead, a way forward sort of presented itself. There was a thread on the CageWarriors.com forum from a big new gym in Liverpool asking for sparring partners. 'Big guys only need apply' was written at the bottom of the post.

They replied to my message quickly and I drove down towards Liverpool a few days later. The building the new gym was housed in was a bland factory unit on an industrial estate directly next to the M62. Its windows were shuttered in metal and the painted door, reinforced with metal plating, looked like it could keep Robocop out.

I stepped inside and to the immediate left a door was open to a makeshift office. I introduced myself to the woman in there and said I was here for the sparring. Within a few minutes I had met Tony Quigley, a Sherman tank of a man with ginger hair and a well-groomed beard (also ginger). He was the boxing coach and I liked him immediately. He showed me the changing room opposite the office and, when I was gloved up, he took me into the gym to get warmed up.

The gym space was basically a 4,000-square-foot cube with training mats on the ground. A row of heavy bags hung from brackets in the wall on the right, and behind and to the left was a lonely weights bench and a few barbells. Music with a little too much bass was getting forced though stereo speakers mounted here and there. At the far side of the gym there was a decent-sized cage and full-sized boxing ring. The cage and ring were packed tightly next to each other. That far-left corner that the cage was pressed against had a rolling shutter door, a reminder this building had once been used as a sausage factory.

The place was one of the best-equipped MMA facilities in the UK, but in 2005 that was a pretty low bar to clear. The sparring I was there for was against an undefeated Brazilian super-heavyweight named Antonio Silva, a karateka and judoka whose size had, inevitably, resulted in him earning the name 'Bigfoot'.

Sharing a cage with the 6ft 6in, 20-stone future UFC heavyweight title challenger wasn't a particularly pleasant experience, but by then I had mad cardio and I'd always been a scrapper. I'd barely made the drive back home when the owner of the gym called me up. The charm offensive that came down that phone would have made Pepé Le Pew blush, if only he could have understood the thickest Scouse accent I'd ever heard.

There were appeals to my patriotism – did I want to be the British fighter who went on to fight and beat the Brazilians and Americans? There were appeals to my ego – I'm already the best in the UK, with better regular sparring I would be the best in the world. And, finally, an appeal to my wallet and common sense – did I really like being away from my family all week, sleeping in my car and on sofas? Wouldn't it be better to drive to this gym in the morning and be home in time to see my kids before they were in bed?

He also slipped in enough seemingly random information about his other businesses for me to receive the impression he was both a successful businessman and a passionate investor in the future of MMA.

What the Liverpool gym offered was a one-stop shop for all my training. After more than a year of ploughing up and down motorways going from gym to dojo, the idea of having boxing, kickboxing, grappling, a cage to practise in and quality sparring all in one place was very appealing. Especially as not only Freeman, but also Hardy and Daley were gone from the roster of training partners in Nottingham.

It turned out Hardy leaving (and Daley following him) had been on the cards since the moment I'd begun training in Nottingham. Dan is a smart guy with a lot of pride and, unbeknown to me, before I'd even arrived for my first training session with them, Paul Davies had been sermonising to all his students that 'the most naturally talented fighter in the country' would soon be joining them 'as the leader of the team'.

To their credit, none of them blamed me personally, but they all must have been pissed off that I got the lion's share of Davies's tuition. (I found a similar situation during *The Ultimate Fighter* season three infuriating – and said so after about one week.) Eventually, Dan had enough and informed Paul that he and Daley were moving on to train elsewhere.

Davies called up everyone in his extensive contacts book and told them not to train with Hardy or Daley. He infamously used the phrase that they'd been 'outlawed'. Hilariously, and so typical of him, Hardy adopted it as his official nickname as a 'fuck you' to Paul. Dan 'The Outlaw' Hardy would go all the way to challenge for a UFC world title while Paul 'Semtex' Daley would also fight in the UFC and other top promotions in the US.

I had no intention of leaving Paul – but I did need more training and better sparring than he could provide in Nottingham for now. Especially with his looming emigration to the other side of the planet, something had to change now. Basing my training in Liverpool seemed like the obvious move, and Davies was open to the idea. He drove up to see the gym, met the coaches and from there we all sat down together and worked out an arrangement. I'd train day-to-day in Liverpool, but Paul would still be the head coach and the Liverpool gym and Paul would split the commission.

'I'll still be your manager and coach, though,' Paul warned. 'I will still be in regular contact checking on your progress and you'll adhere to my training methods on a day-to-day basis. I will email you your workout regimes and what you are to do. Follow those instructions exactly. I will also be your chief cornerman during all your fights.'

As has been reported in the media, the relationship with the Liverpool gym ended bitterly and with lawsuits. I've no wish to be associated with these people, who I mistakenly trusted with managing my career from late 2005 to 2011. Nor do I want to give them undue credit for my success as a mixed martial artist. So, you'll have to forgive me when I refer to the gym and the owners/management generically.

There was a honeymoon period in Liverpool, for sure. Some of the coaches were glorified pad holders, but Tony Quigley was an outstanding boxing coach. When the place was full it was good training, especially as I had the chance to spar and roll with several different professional-level mixed martial artists and had a cage to practise in. I'd already met Bigfoot, of course, and there were several other Brazilians who lived and trained in the gym including José Nindo, Choco Nogueira and Mario 'Sukata' Neto. The character member of the place, and someone I immediately liked, was a chubby, freckled Scouser with a wicked sense of humour named Paul Kelly.

It was a relief to be able to spend less time on the motorway and more time with my kids, but I quickly noted the disconnect between what I'd been told the Liverpool gym would be and what it was in reality. For example, one of the resident coaches spent most of his time sat down reading newspapers.

One morning I saw him roll and do a superb escape and sweep. When I asked him to show me how to do it later that morning, he point-blank refused.

'You don't pay me,' he said, picking up his newspaper.

'But, the gym takes a percentage from my purses and sponsors,' I said. 'Then the gym pays you from that.'

He shook his head and mumbled something. He never showed me that sweep and this was one of many issues I encountered while training at this place. On more than one occasion, I'd make the hour-plus drive from home only to be told (in person or by an unopened metal door) that the gym was closed for the day. There were many other occasions where I'd be the only guy working out, my punches on the heavy bag sending echoes around an empty gym.

Nevertheless, Liverpool was a better option than Nottingham.

Maybe we were both naive thinking the physical distance wouldn't result in an emotional distance, too, but my relationship with Paul Davies began to decline. That was really difficult for me. I'd looked up to Paul since I was a child. I don't want to use the word 'love' because that's not quite it, but I had a ton of respect for him. I wanted him to be proud of me and to reward his belief in me.

We should have had a proper adult conversation about it – especially about the whole moving to New Zealand thing – but I was young, inexperienced in managing my own career and deferential to Paul. To be fair to Paul, I think maybe he felt he was losing me to the Liverpool people and didn't want to come out and have the talk we needed to have. Instead, we kept up a forced politeness as things became more and more tense.

I was getting dismayed by the lack of support during fight weeks. I was left to do my weight-cut and travel to whatever town I was competing in by myself. I wouldn't see Paul until a few hours before I actually fought.

Things came to a bit of a head for my 18 June challenge for Alex Cook's FX3 organisational title on a show in Reading. Not knowing any better – and with no one to teach me any better – I did the weight-cut at home in Clitheroe and then made the drive to Reading for the weigh-in by myself. Anyone who knows anything about weight-making will understand how crazy it was for me to get behind the wheel of a car at all, much less for a six-hour drive down the M6.

Back then, my week-to-week weight hovered around 15 stone. I would then subject my body to a combination of extreme sweating and starvation, dehydrating it until I weighed the 14st 4lb maximum allowed for light heavyweights. The dehydration plays havoc with body and mind.

I was so weight-drained during the six-hour drive I actually slammed on the brakes on the M6 to avoid a pack of dogs I hallucinated. I shudder at the memory.

I weighed in, ate alone and went to bed in the Reading hotel. The next day I ate breakfast and a light lunch alone too. Neither Paul nor the Liverpool group were anywhere to be seen. Finally, about an hour before I was due to travel to the fight venue in the late afternoon, I clocked Paul sipping a pint at the bar with a random mate.

'You got handwraps?' Paul asked me.

No, I hadn't brought handwraps. I easily could have but that wasn't how we'd operated for the previous six fights. Our separation of responsibilities placed Paul, as head coach, in charge of my training and equipment needs.

I said, 'Sorry, I didn't think I needed to bring any.'

'It's okay, I forgot to bring any with me also. Don't worry – I'll go speak to the front desk. They'll have some sort of bandages in the hotel's first-aid kit.'

Wrapping hands in combat sports is an art form. Like the gloves used in boxing, kickboxing or MMA, the purpose of the wraps is to protect your hands, not your opponent's face. With the fingerless style of gloves used in MMA weighing only 4 ounces, there's only so much wrapping that is allowed or even practical but all 27 bones in your hand have to be equally well fortified. Damage to any one of them renders a pro-fighter unable to use one of his main weapons during a fight and, if the injury is serious, potentially unable to work.

With only cheap first-aid bandages available I asked Tony Quigley, who'd bound thousands of fists in his boxing career, to wrap my hands once we got to the fight venue. That pushed Paul further into a dark mood in the dressing room, but I had a fight to win. Paul's ego wasn't something I had the luxury of worrying about at that time.

I beat Alex Cook in 3 minutes 21 seconds of the first round. I softened him up with strikes and then choked him to take the FX3 light heavyweight title. It was my third championship belt in my short MMA career.

The win didn't cheer Paul up. I'd looked up to this man since I was eight years old but it was now impossible to ignore the fact that, visionary though he was, Paul was learning about professional combat sports just like I was.

My first defence of my Cage Warriors title was up next, less than a month later in Coventry. The opponent was Miika Mehmet, a polar-bear-sized European buzzcut. A few weeks before the 16 July 2005 event, Paul called, insisting I drive down to see him.

I drove the familiar M62–M1 route from Clitheroe to Nottingham without nostalgia. When I pulled up outside Paul's semi-detached house, he was in the front window waiting for me. His family was out somewhere. My childhood mentor and I spoke over his kitchen table. He got right into why we couldn't have had this conversation over the phone.

'Michael, for you to prove your loyalty to me – today – you will sign this contract.'

'I am loyal, Paul,' I said.

'If that's true – sign this document.'

He pushed a typed-up agreement across the table to me. The pupil/sensei dynamic kicked in, and I didn't feel like it was appropriate to read every single line on each page. This was my mentor and I was loyal and grateful for the opportunities that were now becoming a reality. Even if I had read every word, it was written in the intentionally protracted manner of practised legal jargon. Among his many talents, Paul Davies was a lawyer.

'You either trust me, or you don't,' he pressed. 'You will sign that now, or you won't. You will prove to me that you are loyal right now or you tell me that you aren't loyal.'

He didn't expect me to sign it in blood, but he wanted it signed there and then.

'Of course I'm loyal,' I stressed. 'I'll prove that right now.'

But he wanted a witness. Paul virtually frog-marched me next door to his neighbour's house, where a baffled fella who clearly had never met Davies served as a witness to me putting my signature on paper. That crazy piece of business completed, I began trying to talk to Paul about my upcoming fight. Paul demurred and said that he'd be moving to New Zealand reasonably soon.

I shook hands with the man who'd coached me off and on since I was a child. I climbed back in my car for the journey back to Clitheroe and put my seatbelt on. I waved as I pulled away, but he didn't.

I wouldn't hear from Paul Davies again for five years.

In my first fight without Paul in my corner, I defeated Miika Mehmet in the first round (strikes) to defend my Cage Warriors title. After three minutes and one second of fighting, I was declared the winner and was now 8–0 as a professional mixed martial artist.

But I didn't get the chance to defend my Cage Rage title again. The promotion had a major falling-out with the Liverpool gym over a payout for Bigfoot Silva's purse. Threats were exchanged and Cage Rage immediately banned all fighters associated with the gym from competing on their shows. With Paul Davies having left the hemisphere, that meant I was also a banned fighter from Liverpool, too.

I was bummed out. Cage Warriors wasn't yet at the level of Cage Rage and, of course, I wanted to appear on Sky Sports rather than on taped delay on the Wrestling Channel or whatever rinky-dink station Cage Warriors was on at the time. Andy Geer – Dave O'Donnell's business partner – was the one who called to tell me I was no longer the Cage Rage champion. Geer sounded positively thrilled about taking a title off a northern fighter and, for years afterwards, I couldn't stand anyone associated with Cage Rage.

But my time on the UK circuit was coming to a natural end anyway. I made two more defences of my Cage Warriors belt, beating Jakob Lovstad and then Ross Pointon in one round apiece on shows in Coventry.

I was 10–0 with all ten fights coming inside the distance. And that's when the UFC came calling.

CHAPTER FIVE

THE ULTIMATE FIGHTER

While I was fighting for recognition in the UK, UFC boss Dana White and his team hit upon a Trojan Horse approach to get UFC fights on American television.

Part *Big Brother*, part the best bits of *Rocky*, *The Ultimate Fighter* took 16 of the best unsigned fighters in the US and put them in a Las Vegas mansion together before dividing them into two teams of eight. The two teams were coached by an established UFC star and his staff, giving the contestants access to world-class training. In every episode, a fight would take place in the gym, with the losers eliminated from the show. The final two fought on an actual UFC event in Las Vegas and the winner would be awarded a life-altering contract with the UFC.

The show attracted a huge audience, mostly comprised of people who were seeing the amazing sport of mixed martial arts for the first time.

What *TUF* had done for the sport on US television, the UFC reasoned, it could do on British TV, too.

Everyone and anyone connected with combat sport in the UK got the email from UFC matchmaker Joe Silva: an open audition for *The Ultimate Fighter* season three would take place in London in December 2005. Prospective fighters needed to have had at least one professional fight, be able to fight as a middleweight or a light heavyweight, own a valid passport and be able to travel to the United States for one week immediately to complete the final audition process.

The entire UK scene was buzzing on the day of the audition inside a leisure centre in central London. About 30 hopefuls, plus their trainers, piled into a large hall and soon the gunshot sounds of Thai pads getting kicked bounced off the wooden floor and into the air. Rumour had it the UFC were going to take only one light heavyweight and one middleweight, so we were all sizing each other up, big time.

An American woman stepped into the middle of the mat, welcomed us and informed everyone that Joe Silva and the UFC President himself, Dana White, would be there shortly along with the producers of *The Ultimate Fighter*. She directed us to the other side of the floor, where there was paperwork to be filled in. I took especial care to boldly and cleanly list my undefeated record and titles won.

Then the lady told us to warm up and be prepared to grapple soon.

The doors opened again, and in walked Dana, Joe Silva and several others. A cyclone of energy and swearing, Dana wasted no time letting us all know what an opportunity we had in front of us. As if to demonstrate just how much winning *TUF* could change our lives, the UFC boss had brought Forrest Griffin and Stephan Bonnar with him. The two light heavyweight Americans had fought in the finale of season one of *TUF* earlier in the year and were already superstars of the sport.

'These two guys are now two of the hottest fighters in the sport,' White roared. 'This is it! You guys over here have been asking, when's the UFC coming back? How do I get into the UFC? How do I get the UFC to notice me in England? We are here! You have our attention right now! This is fucking it! Show us what you fucking got!'

Then Joe Silva, a short guy whose jet-black hair hinted at his Puerto Rican ancestry, reiterated what they were looking for. He said he was familiar with who most of us were and our records, but we shouldn't assume that. 'Tell us why we should pick you and not someone else here today.'

The final big decision-maker was the tall and artificially tanned Craig Piligian. He was the executive producer of the series.

'Dana and Joe care about finding the next UFC champion,' he said in the most American of accents. 'I'd like to see that happen, too, but what I care most about is making great television. After Dana and the guys look at your fight skills, we will sit you down and interview you – but I don't want to hear "yes, sir – no sir" answers. I want to see personality.'

I took note.

Piligian, Dana and Silva sat down behind a desk while Forrest and Bonnar walked around as smaller groups of us were paired off to grapple. Then they held target and kick pads for us. Forrest held pads for me.

I heard Forrest speaking to Joe Silva a few minutes later, saying something to the effect of 'That guy over there is the best one here,' and Joe, who prides himself on a) knowing more about every fighter in the planet than anyone else and b) letting everyone know he knows more, replied with something like: 'No shit. He's the champion of every promotion in the country.'

Those that got through to the next round were all then invited back inside the hall individually for an interview.

This was Piligian's forte. He opened up with: 'It says here your name is Michael *Galen* Bisping —'

'Yeah, you can keep your gay jokes to yourself, mate,' I shot from the hip, 'I've heard 'em all before.'

Dana let out a chuckle and Craig smiled before pressing: 'You've not heard my jokes before …'

'Oh, yeah, I'm sorry. I'm sure they will be *completely* original and *absolutely* hilarious. I mean, you do look like a *very* funny guy …'

Everyone laughed. My gambit of insulting the exec producer had paid off.

Dana then asked what I thought about 'my competition' – the other guys who'd shown up looking for a spot on *TUF 3* that day.

'I'm so happy they are here,' I answered. 'Thrilled, really.'

'Yeah? Why?'

'Because I've beaten every single one of 'em in MMA, kickboxing or BJJ,' I stated to laughs from Dana and Piligian. Dana turned to Joe to confirm my record.

'He's ten and zero with all ten by stoppage. He's won the Cage Rage and Cage Warriors belts.' Joe Silva seemed to be a 'yes' vote for me. (When I got to know Joe over the years, he'd tell me I was about to be called up to the UFC anyway, based on my record alone, but he and Dana thought I'd be perfect for the *TUF* series.)

'Who's here today that you beat?' Dana asked.

I rattled off Alex Cook, Ross Pointon and several other names and added, 'I'll beat everyone you've got waiting for me in America, too.'

'See,' Dana said to Piligian. 'What did I tell you about this guy?'

We were told our flights to Las Vegas for the final interview would be booked that night, and we should report to Heathrow Terminal

1 the following morning at 8am sharp. Paul Kelly and Ross Pointon were among the six or seven of us who'd made it through to the final interview process in Las Vegas.

As soon as you land in Las Vegas, it bombards your senses and reaches for your wallet. The airport hummed with the noise of big-screen commercials for the Blue Man Group, Penn & Teller, and nightclubs open until 9am.

We were staying in a smaller hotel a few miles away from the Strip. When in the hotel we were told to not leave our rooms, full stop, unless we were sent for – or we'd be disqualified from consideration for the show.

'So ... we're like prisoners, yeah?' Ross asked.

'Pretty much,' said one of the UFC producers. 'We don't want you guys seeing who the American fighters are – if that leaks out, it hurts the show. Plus, if you make it to the show, you aren't allowed to leave the *TUF* house during the entire seven weeks of filming. You will be driven to the *TUF* gym to train and back twice a day. It is not for everyone. We need to see if you guys can hack it. But that's to come – tomorrow you'll be driven together to do your medical.'

Even though 'doing medicals' doesn't sound thrilling, the first day in Vegas was a blast. We weren't on holiday, but you couldn't have known it from how we were acting. We clowned around in the doctors' offices, in the van and in the restaurants we ate in.

After the blood tests (Hep B, HIV etc. – anything that can be transmitted by blood during a fight), eye tests and the rest were done we were taken back to the hotel and sent to our rooms like naughty kids.

Halfway through the next day I was so bored. The hotel room was closer to what I'd seen in *Leaving Las Vegas* than *Casino*. The television was unwatchable – there are so many adverts on American TV you actually forget what it is you're watching. My sweaty, bland meals were delivered three times a day in black plastic boxes that creaked.

On day three I was so bored I sneaked out for a walk. I was still bored when I got back, so I decided to have a little fun with Ross and Paul.

'Mate,' I began the call to both their rooms, 'the UFC producers are here in my room and they want to film us sparring. You've gotta come here in fifteen minutes – they will take us together to a ballroom or something where we'll spar.'

I pretended to be talking to someone in my room for a second, then added, 'Mate – the producer says warm up in your room so you look sweaty for the camera. They are pretending we've been working out in a gym or something. You've got to come in wearing your fit gear. Shorts, gloves, no shirt, barefoot – and ready to spar right away. Fifteen minutes, mate, be ready!'

Both Ross and Paul showed at my room up 15 minutes after I called. They'd both walked the hallways and rode the elevator with beads of sweat rolling over their stomach tattoos, looking like proper dickheads.

'No way, man, no way,' Ross protested when he found out he'd been had. 'I was in the lift with a mum and her two kids. Daughters, like. She was pulling them close to her like I was gonna kidnap one of 'em. I was trying to tell 'em I was a UFC fighter, like, but I was too out of breath to talk proper. I just sorta breathed at 'em like a horny bull. That really freaked her out, man.'

On the fourth day of captivity, there was a phone call to be ready for the final interview. An hour later came a knock on my door and I followed the producer down the hall, a few floors up in the elevator and into a suite.

There was a circular wooden table with chairs around it. I sat on one side; Dana and the producers were on the other. The final interview went pretty much like the first one, with me giving the producers as good as – or better than – I got.

'Get the fuck outta here!' Dana laughed, telling me I'd aced the final hurdle and was now going to be on season three of *The Ultimate Fighter*.

I went back to my room and called Rebecca.

'I'm in,' I told her. 'Fighting on American TV to get a UFC contract!'

'I knew it,' she said. 'I knew you'd get in – but I'm not sure America is ready for you.'

Paul Kelly didn't make the show. Dana knew he wasn't a real middleweight and the producers didn't know what the hell he was saying in that Scouse accent. He was told to keep winning – as a welterweight – and he'd be in the UFC sooner or later. Paul seemed happy enough with that.

Ross, though, did make the selection. He was told to report back to Vegas as a middleweight. He was childlike in his excitement.

I spent Christmas 2005 at home and trained like a maniac. I was going to be ready to fight on day one of filming. I made the return journey to Vegas just a few days into 2006.

You've probably seen on the show that I was dropped off outside the big Vegas mansion. Most of the other fighters were already in the house and overcome with excitement to be unpacked at a $5million, seven-bedroom house with a snooker table and swimming pool.

My opponents – and that's exactly what I viewed them as – hadn't showed up with the mentality I had. Some of them weren't in condition to spar, much less fight. Others were more impressed by getting on TV than the chance to break into the big leagues of mixed martial arts. We weren't there to 'help each other get better' or 'push ourselves to be the best martial artists we could be', as I heard some of them repeating back and forth to each other like they were in a Nike commercial.

This was *prize*-fighting! And the prize was a literally life-changing contract with the number-one organisation in the sport. There was one of those for the light heavyweights to fight over and one for the middleweights – and the light heavyweight one was going to be mine.

The ones who were there to actually fight stood out. Ross, of course, is the epitome of a scrapper. Then there was Kendall Grove, a 6ft 6in tattooed Hawaiian with a great sense of humour who, somehow, fought as a middleweight. Ed Herman, also a middleweight with a neck as red as his hair, wasn't there to make friends either.

The one light heavyweight I noticed was Matt Hamill, an ox of a man from Ohio with menacing physical strength and impressive wrestling credentials. Hamill was profoundly deaf and clearly used to smashing through life's obstacles.

The other 15 contestants and I were driven early the next morning to the *TUF* gym. We were told to bring our gear. The gym was located at the end of a long cul-de-sac about a ten-minute drive around the I-15 freeway that orbits Las Vegas and its surrounding suburbs.

From watching the first two seasons on British television, I thought the *TUF* gym was right next to the Palms Casino. It was actually over a mile away, at the end of a lane in a business sector.

Were it not for the big production truck parked outside, the *TUF* gym would not have stood out at all from the rest of the white commercial units that surrounded it. Inside, though, was a different story.

The main space was part TV studio with rigs throwing dramatic light and shadows from the rafters 30ft up; part high-tech MMA training facility with rubber-covered mats, brand-new punching bags lined against one wall along with raised platform treadmills, bikes and stepmasters; and, finally, part fight arena – the Octagon, the real, UFC-approved Octagon – was at the far end of the rectangular room.

The walls were stark yellows and deep blues – colours that 'pop' for the cameras. There were banners hung from the walls featuring images of legendary UFC fighters past and present.

There were cameramen pointing metal and glass tubes at us from every angle. The producers needed to capture every interaction and word spoke by all 16 of us.

Dana was there and gestured to two men walking towards us: 'Meet your coaches, Tito Ortiz and Ken Shamrock.'

Dana informed us that light heavyweights would immediately train with Shamrock and his coaching team. Then we'd be back the day after to train with Tito and his people. From those two evaluation sessions, Shamrock and Tito would get an idea of who they wanted on their specific teams.

'Middleweights? Get outta here!' Dana yelled. 'Light heavyweights – warm up!'

Ken Shamrock was one of the OGs of the sport. Already a UFC Hall of Famer, he had competed at the very first UFC event in November 1993. He was action-movie muscular and had parlayed his early-era Octagon success into a big-money run with the WWF pro-wrestling circus. He'd yo-yoed between wrasslin' and MMA for the next decade, absorbing the worst kind of injuries associated with both. By the time of his fourth – and final – return to the UFC in 2006, he was 40-something. A faded force as a fighter, out of touch as a trainer.

'I don't do no BJJ stuff,' he said, with the complacency of a man who'd decided there was nothing more to learn. 'I am a brawler and a leg-lock guy.'

Team Shamrock's evaluation process consisted of a bunch of unstructured sparring that Ken watched dispassionately from afar, then 300 press-ups, 300 sit-ups and 300 squats followed by 'feats of strength' tests that had no relevance to the sport of MMA.

The contrast with Tito's evaluation session the next day couldn't have been more pronounced. Tito was 11 years younger than his bitter rival and only two years removed from his record-setting reign as UFC light heavyweight champion. Anxious to get first-hand intel on our abilities, Tito rolled with each and every one of us.

I made an impression by catching him with an old-school armlock I'd used since I was a child. Tito tapped and we continued to roll. He used a great sweep on me and, after we'd finished, made sure to demonstrate it at half-pace. That was training with Tito Ortiz – no ego, just a guy with a ton of knowledge he clearly intended to share with whoever made it onto his team.

And Ortiz's assistant coaches were also amazing to work with. Dean Lister, I knew, was a BJJ world champion who had won several MMA titles and recently signed to the UFC. The chance to spend almost two months training with Lister alone was an amazing opportunity. The third man on 'Team Punishment' (named after Tito's branded clothing line) was a hugely respected striking coach named Saul Soliz. I completely 'clicked' with Saul during my 15 minutes on the pads with him.

After a day of training with each coach, there was no doubt in my mind that I wanted to be picked for Tito's team.

On the third day of filming, that's what happened. Ortiz won the coin toss to get first pick and went for Matt Hamill. I was the second pick, but was happy enough to leave there safely on Ortiz's team.

Team Punishment began training twice a day the next morning. We were picked up at 9:15am and all driven together to the *TUF* gym for a 10am session. Team Shamrock would be arriving as we left at noon and trained until 2pm. We'd go back to the house to eat and rest up and then be back at the gym at 4pm for another two hours. Team Shamrock's second session was 6pm to 8pm.

We trained seven days a week. For the entire seven weeks of filming, I think Tito gave us maybe three afternoons off. It was intense but I'm immensely grateful to have been given that opportunity – it was transformative for me as an athlete and fighter.

The level of the tuition, the precision of the drills we were put through and the knowledge Tito, Dean and Saul were sharing was a revelation to me.

Broadly, Saul was the striking coach, Dean was the submission coach while Tito was the wrestling coach and handled most of the strength and conditioning. All three knew where their speciality intersected with the others and how best the different aspects of MMA could be welded together in the strongest way.

I became aware there was a stigma of sorts about British MMA fighters. There was no denying British MMA was years behind the US, but some of the Team Shamrock light heavyweights were quietly dismissive of my chances.

Then Kendall beat Ross pretty easily in their quarter-final fight.

See, see? guys like Mike Nickels and Kristian Rothaermel snickered. *These British guys can't get it done in America. Bisping is just cocky – that's not real confidence.*

I just sort of looked at them and smiled. I wasn't Ross. Kristian Rothaermel would find that out himself – he was my quarter-final opponent.

The day of my quarter-final arrived and I couldn't wait to get to the *TUF* gym. To encourage the flow of conversation for the cameras, the producers had the two fighters who'd be in action travel to the gym with just one teammate. Kendall and I had quickly become mates and so I chose him to drive with me.

'Five grand, coming my way,' I told him in reference to the $5,000 bonus which was paid for every stoppage victory scored on the series.

'You got this,' he said.

The rest of Team Punishment and our coaches were already at the gym. Saul taped my hands in our team dressing room. The referee came in and reminded us that, during this season of *TUF*, the fights in the gym were scheduled for two five-minute rounds. 'In case of a draw after those two rounds, you will be returned to your corners and commence a third round fought under sudden victory rules.'

The clunky term 'sudden victory' was used in place of the actual name of such a sporting situation – sudden death. There hadn't been a serious injury in MMA to that point, but no one was looking to tempt fate.

Tito reiterated the plan: 'Get him tired, then get him outta there.'

On Tuesday, 17 January 2006, at *The Ultimate Fighter* gym, 19–21 Complex Drive, Las Vegas, Nevada, I stepped inside a UFC Octagon for the first time for a fight.

To ensure bouts could fit into *TUF* episodes uncut, most of the ceremonies associated with professional fights were stripped down or cut out completely. There was no MC, no walk-out music and, the biggest difference, no crowd except for the two teams, coaches, Dana and a few UFC staff and the production team.

I stormed out of the dressing room to the Octagon first. Tito and the coaches kept pace a few steps behind me. My teammates shouted and clapped encouragement as they took positions on one side of the cage. Then Rothaermel entered the Octagon. He looked like he didn't want to be there.

I'll soon get you outta here, mate.

I knew from the Shamrock evaluation that I would have a big edge in stamina so set a fast pace. He took me down a couple of times and went for the submissions he favoured. But I'd escape, and he couldn't match my striking. Two minutes in, Rothaermel was hurt, bleeding and tired. I could hear him snatching for air as I spiked elbows in him on the ground. I stepped away, forcing him to use his last ounce of energy to climb back to his feet. Then I slammed home a right cross that ended the fight. The cheers from Tito and Team Punishment were immediate and loud.

'As usual!' I made the point of saying loud enough for the light heavyweights to hear. American opponent? American soil? Didn't matter – same result.

CHAPTER SIX

TUF TIMES

There was a difference in the house after that fight. I didn't hear any more whispers about how being the best in the UK 'don't mean shit in America'. The relentless aggression I'd showed against Rothaermel spooked the Team Shamrock light heavies. The gossip in the house was now that the 205lb contract would be going to whoever won the inevitable clash between me and Matt Hamill.

Having trained with and against Hamill for several weeks, I'd already reached that conclusion.

After twenty years of training and a desk drawer of gold medals in both Greco-Roman and Freestyle, Hamill's wrestling ability was substantial. During the first weeks of filming, he'd been able to literally shrug off the rest of Team Punishment's takedown attempts without using his hands.

Ortiz obviously expected Hamill to win the light heavyweight tournament. Before adding me to his team Tito had said, 'Every great champion needs a great training partner.' That was hurtful to a young fighter like I was – a mess of pride and insecurity. It's easy to recognise now: I was jealous. I looked up to Tito – he was the man – and it stung that Hamill was getting more one-on-one time than me.

Hamill was also dangerously aggressive in training. He recklessly injured several teammates by going much harder than was prudent for guys hoping to fight twice inside six weeks. And it wasn't Matt's deafness – even after the producers hired a full sign-language interpreter, he would still go 100 per cent when we'd all clearly been instructed to go 40 per cent.

The producers of the show need to craft narratives, of course, but the reality was Hamill was roughed up in sparring, too. Kendall rocking him with a right had made the final cut but there were several occasions where myself and others would give Matt a receipt for an earlier transgression of training etiquette.

Then there was the incident where Matt and I were drilling armbar escapes. Matt – again refusing to acknowledge the difference between drilling and fighting – refused to concede he couldn't escape and instead yanked his arm out at a crazy angle.

The resulting injury to his right elbow was a factor in Matt's unimpressive points win over Mike Nickels. Matt's kickboxing had remained battering-ram crude and he didn't seem to be improving his striking at the rate I was advancing my wrestling. Nevertheless, I had no doubt in my mind Hamill was the only guy who could stop me from winning the whole thing.

Then came the news that the medical team wouldn't clear Matt to fight in the semis. Hamill was out of the competition.

With Matt medically prevented from competing, the UFC needed to bring back one of the eliminated Team Shamrock light heavyweights. As shown on the series, Tait Fletcher and Kristian Rothaermel both refused the opportunity to fight me.

The identity of my new semi-final opponent was revealed to me on the floor of the gym. Both teams were in line-up along the outside of the blue mats like every other fight pick. I was stood next to Team Punishment's Josh Haynes, who'd reached the semis by out-willing Fletcher; across from us stood Jesse Forbes, Mike Nickels, Fletcher and Rothaermel.

All four of Team Shamrock's 205ers had lost their quarter-finals, but two would be invited back to replace Hamill and Team Punishment's Noah Inhofer, who quit the show because of some girlfriend nonsense.

Dana and the coaches walked to the centre of the mat and we got the full story from the UFC president. One part motivation discourse, two parts full-on bollocking, Dana launched into one of his patented speeches:

'Alright, we're in a situation where Matt Hamill can't return. Mike [Nickels], unfortunately you have a broken nose so you can't return to the competition. I'd be lying if I said I wasn't disappointed with what I heard today [Fletcher and Rothaermel refused to fight me]. I'm fucking shocked and disappointed. But I know somebody who'll take this fight with Bisping. I know someone who'll come in and give his all.

'The first fight on Thursday will be Jesse and Josh ... And the second fight will be on Friday ... and all I got to say is, thank God for fucking England.'

The door opened and there he was.

This guy! This crazy, utterly fearless fucking nutter!

'COME ON, ROSS!' I shouted, and I grabbed and hugged Pointon like a long-lost brother. 'You've got some fucking balls, mate!'

His big smile flashed his gold tooth. He flexed his arm tattoos.

Everyone in the room – me, Dana, Shamrock, Tito, Jesse, Josh and the production people you can't see when you watch this episode back – were smiling and laughing. Ross's excitement to be back was infectious. All of us were so happy for him, a guy who genuinely, passionately loved the sport and whose blind courage was really easy to admire.

My pride and excitement for Ross wore off in the van ride home. It was me he was fighting, and me who was going to have to break his heart.

Can you imagine being so mind-numbingly bored that a visit to the doctor's sounded like almost hedonistic debauchery? Neither could I, until the fifth week of filming *TUF*.

I'd become good friends with Kendall – we are close mates to this day – but we'd all run out of things we wanted to say to each other after a month of living in each other's pockets. Cabin fever had set in. Our communication had become limited to points, nods and the occasional inarticulate grunt. It was like we'd been poisoned and were slowly turning into Yoel Romero.

Being unable to contact my family was really taking a toll on me as well.

So, I concocted a little scheme. Fighters who complained of injuries were quickly taken out of the house and to whatever Las Vegas doctor specialised in the type of injury they had. Not wanting to alarm the producers, I claimed I had sprained my ankle and would like it medically checked out.

The show took zero chances with fighter health, and I was booked an appointment the very next morning. As I hoped and suspected, no camera crew was assigned to my little day trip. It was just me and a driver. I softened the poor guy up with a couple of jokes and small talk about his own family and then: 'It's killing me, not been able to speak to my family for this long. Could – could you give me your cellphone so I can call home? Just one minute, just to hear my kids' voices this once.'

The driver eventually relented. 'One minute!' he said. 'I'll be in deep shit if anyone finds out this happened.'

I dialled Rebecca. She picked up and was thrilled to hear from me. Having already broken one of the clauses on my *TUF* contract, I went right ahead and broke another.

'I won my first fight two weeks ago and I'm fighting in the semi-final in four days,' I told her. 'Get this – I'm fighting Ross! Ross Pointon!'

She knew what that meant.

'You've got this,' she said.

I got the chance to hear Callum and Ellie's voices. It was a huge boost for me. A reminder of why I was actually lucky to be going stir-crazy 6,000 miles away.

Whatever Tito Ortiz said when he picked me, after working with me twice a day, every day, for six weeks the UFC legend had this to say: 'Michael Bisping has a huge opportunity to be a great fighter.'

I believed it more than ever. I'd reported to the *TUF* gym in January in the best shape of my life. Six weeks later, I was three times fitter than that. I'd added a dimension to my cardio that I barely knew existed. My striking had improved, my submissions too, and I'd gained a solid foundation to build a wrestling base upon. More than any of that, I'd worked with the best of the best and confirmed to myself there was no massive gulf between them and me. I was ready to leave the UK scene behind and fight my way through the UFC ranks.

Ross was four inches shorter than me, had a shorter reach and, since his loss to Kendall three weeks before, had barely trained. He would be short and static in the Octagon – so I drilled flying knees for three days straight.

Referee Big John McCarthy signalled the fight to start and I went after my place in the final, firing a kick to the body and punches to the face. I ran into a hard right-cross counter from Ross. It snapped the back of my head into my shoulders at a weird angle. I disengaged, shook it off and calmed myself down.

'That's the last one you're getting,' I told Ross.

Shamrock was yelling for Ross to move around but my mate had the right idea: he stayed put, planted his feet and conserved what energy he had until I got close – then he swung for my face with all his might. He missed – by miles – with almost everything as I tore away at him with bursts of punches and kicks to the body. Then I launched into a flying knee – it thudded against Ross's chin.

He tried frantically to escape my follow-up attacks. He absorbed everything he could – but it was all over. I'd done it. I was in the final. I celebrated with my coaches as the reality of reaching the finale sank in.

Across the other side of the Octagon, Ross's heart was breaking clean in two. As I knew it had to.

'Come here,' I said, embracing him.

'I wannabe a fighter,' he cried into my shoulder. 'I ... I just wannabe a fighter.'

I peeled him off my shoulder just far enough that I could look him in his eyes. 'Ross! Ross, listen! Listen to me ... you *are* a fighter!'

Tito joined me in consoling my countryman. 'No one else had the balls to step up! Head up – be proud! You are a fucking warrior!'

Ross's courage earned him two fights on the official UFC roster. He retired years later with a 6–17 MMA record. Ross had dreamed bigger than fighting on the UK circuit – his life's ambition was to be a UFC fighter. No one can ever take away that he was exactly that.

My own ambition was bigger. I'd left the Rosses and cage rage warriors behind me and was about to step onto the biggest stage in the sport.

It seemed like I'd only been back in the UK for five minutes when a UFC camera was trained on me once again, this time following me, Rebecca and the kids around for three days, getting 'day in the life' footage that is so vital in connecting fighters with their audience. Then a British TV crew began filming a documentary for the UFC's UK broadcast partner Bravo (remember that channel?).

As the episodes of *TUF 3* began to air on both sides of the Atlantic, I began to see glimpses of what life as a UFC star would look like: an interview with an American magazine here, a photoshoot for a sponsor, the occasional request to sign an autograph while shopping in Manchester. That was all nice, but the doors opening in front of me would be slammed shut if I didn't beat Josh Haynes on 24 June back in Las Vegas.

I applied everything Team Punishment had taught me while training at the Liverpool gym, which I now knew for sure was leagues below the type of training Josh was getting at the famed Team Quest in his native Portland, Oregon.

In early June I was back in Vegas. I was training with Paul Kelly and a few others from Liverpool along with Canadian Sam Stout and Georges St-Pierre. Stout was headlining the 24 June finale event at the Hard Rock Casino while 'GSP' – already considered one of the sport's super-talents – was helping his friend prepare. I got several useful sessions of grappling with both.

Less useful was the torn ligament in my left knee I suffered 14 days before the showdown with Haynes. I was in front of a sports doctor the next day, who assured me that despite the pain, the only performance impact would be a slight decrease in stability on that leg. It was gonna take more than that to stop me.

Besides, the documentary show had hired out a 1956 Cadillac convertible for me to drive and I was due to pick Rebecca up at the airport. She loved it. I threw her bag in the back seat and my arm around her shoulder on the big wide seat and we cruised down the Strip like we were in a movie.

It's all coming right, I was showing her.

Josh Haynes was a tough, determined guy who was fighting, not unlike me, to provide a better life for his family. While I meticulously refused to underestimate him, I'd gotten the better of him every single time we'd sparred as part of Team Punishment.

Those memories buoyed my confidence ... until the day of the fight.

The pressure to win locked my shoulders tight. The dressing room at the Joint in the Hard Rock Hotel was tiny, airless. The walk from backstage to the Octagon was short. The TV lights above the cage were startlingly bright and hot. I felt I was going to faint. I paced the canvas, searching for breath.

My coach yelled through the fence, 'Deep breath! Take a deep breath!'

I did. I drew in several long draughts of air and on each exhale I felt a little of the tension ease out of my upper body. The fight was only seconds away but I was almost ready.

Then someone from my corner shouted, 'Remember! Everything you want in life depends on this fight!'

My stomach churned. Referee John McCarthy gave final instructions. The fight began.

Haynes surged forward with a right. I threw him over my right hip and followed him to the ground. I roughed him up with ground and pound, which settled my nerves. He used the cage to get back to his feet and I shot a knee into his gut. Josh swung another right hand. I landed a cross of my own. And another. We brawled against the fence and a battle of skill and will began.

Josh was willing – but he lacked the variety of skills I'd developed. I Thai-clinched his skull and sailed my right knee into his chin, dropping him hard on the seat of his pants. In a massive rookie mistake, I wasted two halves of a second waiting for the ref to stop it. He didn't – and instead Josh had time to scramble forward with a desperate takedown attempt. I kneed him again – but his hand was on the floor. The second knee had been illegal.

Big John directed me to a neutral corner to admonish me.

'You kneed him when he had a hand down – that's illegal.'

'He was out!' I wasted energy protesting.

'He wasn't out. Don't do that again.'

Haynes was recovering across the cage. I had to shake my head clear of thoughts of having won the fight.

The fight restarted and I went after my opponent with knees, elbows, big right hands, kicks, slams. Josh Haynes's face was red with blood, a strange contrast with his pale skin and neon-blue Mohawk. But he was still game. This was a man inspired to fight after his young son had defeated cancer – he had no quit in him.

In between rounds Josh's right eye had closed and he was noticeably more tired than the previous round. He was easier to control in the clinch and I could get him to the ground at will. He refused to tap to several close submission attempts – but fighting me off leached energy out of him. Three minutes into the second round I beat him in a scramble and began a hailstorm of strikes while he was on the ground. He desperately got to his feet and I dropped him again with a left uppercut. I poured on the punishment but Josh still wouldn't signal surrender. I let him get up and decked him again. This wasn't defiance, this was denial. It was now the referee I was appealing to. I was unrelenting and, with 47 seconds left, McCarthy finally rescued my opponent from his own courage.

I collapsed with a smile on my face. I was the Ultimate Fighter.

In the crowd of 3,800 fans, my dad and Rebecca were hugging and celebrating with 20 more family and friends who'd flown ten hours to support me.

Doing guest commentary on the broadcast, Tito Ortiz said, 'Bisping was the most vicious 205er, the most technical and the most skilled out of all of them. Too bad I didn't see that when we first got a chance to train – but he is *The Ultimate Fighter* light heavyweight champion.'

For the first time in my life, Bruce Buffer, known then and now as the Voice of the Octagon, announced that I'd won an official UFC fight for the very first time. '… for the winner by TKO – and now – the new Ultimate Fighter to receive a six-figure contract with the UFC – MICHAEL "THE COUNT" BIS-PING!'

Then another first. Joe Rogan, the UFC's colour commentator, conducted an interview with me. 'This is an absolute dream come true. Josh showed great heart. The first round – the knee – I thought he was out cold. I stood back to admire my work. My mistake. The guy's got phenomenal heart.'

'I think we're gonna need some subtitles,' Joe said, referring to the text that accompanied every utterance I'd made on the series.

Then Dana White was on the microphone to present me with my trophy.

'Michael Bisping, on behalf of your coaches, Lorenzo Fertitta, Frank Fertitta, myself, congratulations! You are the Ultimate Fighter! You get the six-figure contract with the Ultimate Fighting Champions and you also get this Breitling watch.'

The glass trophy was nice but the watch – called a Breitling Avenger Seawolf – was a profound physical representation of what I'd achieved. It cost more than any car I'd ever owned. It was a token that the sacrifices we'd made as a family were paying off, and a promise there was more to come.

Rebecca and I took the kids on a holiday in the summer of 2006. It felt earned, a reward for all the time we'd spent apart. The UFC contacted me about fighting a BJJ expert, Eric Shafer, in early November and I began to train for that. Life began to settle into a rhythm as a UFC fighter.

Then a letter from United States Citizenship and Immigration Service dropped on my doormat like an atomic bomb.

Under INA section 212(a)(2)(A)(i)(I), 'previously convicted of a crime involving moral turpitude', my request for a US Employment Authorization Document works visa had been declined. In fact, I was banned from ever travelling to the United States again.

I fell apart in the hallway. My UFC career was over.

CHAPTER SEVEN

VISA PROBLEMS ... AND SOME OTHER THINGS

Rebecca had retrieved the US Immigration letter from where I'd flung it. She read all of it – which I clearly had not – and showed me the line where it clearly stated I was able to appeal the decision.

Two months later I was sat at the kitchen table. It was about 10:30 on the night of 2 November 2006. The kids and Rebecca were all upstairs asleep and I was left with a cup of tea for company. I've never been a worrier, but the US works visa situation was obviously on my mind. There had been no updates from the immigration attorney I'd hired and nothing from the American Embassy.

My management and I had not heard from the UFC in several weeks, either. I imagined they were pretty unhappy their new *Ultimate Fighter* winner was in limbo. After all, what's the point in an American fight promotion promoting a fighter banned from America?

This waiting around and uncertainty was draining. I'd had no real income since June. That evening, I'd broken the glass and used the 'emergency only' credit card to pay for another week's petrol to get to the Liverpool gym and back. We were on our way to being broke again. After all that training, 13 fights (13 wins! all inside the distance!) and giving up months of time with my family– after all of that – we were falling backwards to square one.

The Breitling Avenger Seawolf was on my wrist. I'd barely taken it off since June. I had daydreams of giving it to Callum when he grew up, and him giving it to his son or daughter. Maybe my grandchild would feel something of the sort of pride I felt when my old man first told me about Grandad Andrzej riding out to face the Russian invaders.

I wondered if I'd have to sell it.

As if to answer that gloomy thought, my phone began buzzing. It was a '001-702' number. A Las Vegas number. If I was nervous when I answered, my heart skipped a beat when I heard the voice speaking from the other side of the world.

'Bisping? Dana.'

Oh, shit. This is it.

'Hi, Dana. How … how's it going, okay?'

'Good, buddy. Listen, we haven't been able to book you a fight since June …'

Oh, here we fucking go …

'… so how are you doing for money?'

Huh?

'Money? Err, yeah, things are tight. I'll be happy when I fight again, that's for sure. But, yeah, no, I'm doing alright.'

Dana said as soon as I was able to come to the US, Joe Silva would be arranging a fight on a 'big show'. Then we had a brief chat about the upcoming *UFC 65* fight with Georges St-Pierre challenging Matt Hughes, the dominant UFC welterweight king who'd repelled GSPs challenge before. I was again struck by how much Dana sounded like an everyday fan when he talked about the big fights.

There was a pause in the conversation.

'Listen, I'm sorry about all this, Dana.'

'What you talking about?'

'Y'know, the visa and everything ...'

'Don't worry about that,' he said. 'We all do stupid shit when we are kids.'

Three days after the call from Dana, a thin US cheque for $10,000 was delivered to my home. Paper-clipped to the front was a handwritten note:

Get your kids something for Christmas. See you soon – Dana.

That cheque was a turning point. I felt supported and understood by the people I worked for. The cheque had barely cleared when the postman delivered more good news: upon appeal, the American Embassy had approved my visa to travel and work in the United States. The relief I felt with that piece of paper in my hand was unreal.

There was more good news – I would be fighting again in 2006. The UFC rapidly rebooked the Schafer showdown as the opening bout on the massive five-fight *UFC 66* pay-per-view event. Scheduled for 30 December in the 16,000-seater MGM Grand Garden arena inside the city-like MGM Grand hotel, the end-of-year bonanza was going to be headlined by the long-awaited rematch between Chuck Liddell and Tito Ortiz.

Moving from the *Ultimate Fighter 3 Finale* to the main card of *UFC 66: Liddell vs Ortiz II* was like going from a town-hall gig to opening up a stadium for Guns N' Roses. Tito had wiped the floor with Shamrock over the summer and was now rematching Liddell in a fight that had captured the imagination of fans and media far outside the Sherdog.coms of the world. *UFC 66* was going to be a massive, pivotal night for the entire sport – and I was going to be part of it.

After taking off from Manchester at 10am I spent ten hours on a packed Virgin Atlantic Boeing 747 before landing in Las Vegas at 2pm, local time, on Sunday, 17 December 2006. As predicted by my lawyer, rather than getting rubber-stamped through customs like everyone else, I spent over 90 minutes in the company of the thorough officers of America's largest law enforcement agency, the Customs and Border Protection (CBP). Who cared, though? I was just relieved to be back in America and the Fight Capital of the World.

There was no information as to which carousel my suitcases would have come out on, so I had to stomp around the entire Baggage Claim – while under heavy audio/visual bombardment from commercials to go see a Céline Dion concert – until I located them. Snatching the handles, I dragged them out backwards through the doors before my ears could again be molested by the shrieks of that fucking sinking-boat song.

Few people who've been caught outside in the furious sunrays of Las Vegas's summer can believe it, but it gets surprisingly cold there in the winter. I pulled my hoodie up as I stood in line for a taxi. The neon lights of America's playground for grown-ups flashed off the cab's roof. I wasn't heading towards all the action for another week, though. I directed the driver to drive right through the strip and four miles along the Interstate 15.

The UFC provides rooms for fighters and cornermen during fight week, but my team and I agreed we needed to get out here a week before that to fully acclimatise. My manager would be arriving two days later along with my striking coach Tony and a much-needed sparring and running partner. A California jiu-jitsu world champion named Kazeka Muniz had been drafted in to help sharpen my submission defence. He was to meet me at the hotel right away.

The hotel we were staying in until 26 December was located off Interstate 15 on Sahara Avenue. Set among petrol stations and plain office buildings, the Palace Station had offered bingo and a buffet to Vegas locals since 1976. It was the oldest of the Fertitta family's 16 casinos, but was literally walking distance from the basement gym under the UFC offices. That gym would be my training camp until I could move to the MGM Grand the day after Christmas.

Muniz had arrived before me and checked into the twin room we'd be sharing. He was a smaller guy, with an accent drifting between Brazilian and Californian, sometimes within the same sentence. He was an outstanding BJJ coach but soon revealed himself prone to mood swings. We were total strangers, thrown together: working out, eating together and sharing a small hotel room ... I could have done without him making it even weirder.

After 48 hours glued together, we both were looking forward to the Liverpool team arriving so we had other people to talk to – and I could bunk in with Tony.

But I didn't see the Liverpool crew that week. Instead I'd get a daily text or telephone call from my manager stuffed with 'dog ate my homework' excuses. Every day, Mr Liverpool would insist flights were booked. The day after he'd admit they weren't – but they would be booked that day.

Miffed, I took full charge of my own training. I ran the hotel's 16-storey staircase every morning, repeating the lung-busting drills

Tito had put me and Team Punishment through six months before. I made full use of the basement UFC office gym, hitting the UFC logo on the black heavy bag with jabs, hooks and crosses at a pace I knew would overwhelm Shafer.

Then, luckily, Forrest Griffin appeared in the UFC office gym. We were having a bit of a chat when he asked why I was training alone. In no mood to bullshit the guy on behalf of a bullshitter, I told him.

'I've had no sparring since I left England,' I finished.

'Wanna spar? I'm going to Xyience now,' Griffin said. 'There's a few guys, Mike Whitehead, Jay Hieron. Decent group. I'll drive.'

He didn't need to ask me twice.

The Xyience Training Center was a small gym in a strip mall on South Tenaya Way. (A strip mall, to the disappointment of many pervy tourists, is what Americans call a row of shops.) The rectangular space could easily have been used as a DVD store, a grocery, a shoe shop or anything else. It's long since shut down, and is probably now a Starbucks.

Forrest was fighting Keith Jardine at *UFC 66*. He and I were both competing on the night as light heavyweights but Griffin was enormous compared to me. He was also a very hard worker in the gym and our sparring session (in the middle of the mats – the gym had no cage or ring) was intense. Some of the guys working out stopped to watch us go at it, but we kept it professional and well under control.

Afterwards, we grabbed lunch together and Forrest then dropped me off at the Palace Station.

As happy as I was to have had some great sparring finally, at the same time I was even more pissed off that my own team was AWOL. I dialled England again. 'When are you going to get here?'

I demanded of my manager, who was still at home in Liverpool on the Saturday before *UFC 66*.

'It is Christmas Eve tomorrow, so, y'know ...' my manager began as if the steady progression from 17 December to 24 December was both unanticipated and personally inconvenient. 'We'll have Christmas here and be in Vegas on Boxing Day. The flights are all booked, nice and cushy. We land early afternoon and we'll train yer that night.'

'I've been here six days without a proper striking coach to hold pads,' I said. 'The fight's just a week away now. I should have been sparring all week.'

'Don't worry. It'll be cushy. We will be there on Tuesday.'

Christmas Day 2006 was thoroughly depressing. I never thought I'd spend Christmas away from my kids, but instead of watching the excitement on Callum and Ellie's faces and having a turkey dinner with my loved ones I was alone in an aging casino, watching the dregs of Las Vegas stuff banknotes into slot machines.

Everything changed on Boxing Day.

As the official host hotel for *UFC 66*, the MGM Grand was already buzzing when we took a cab over in mid-morning. *UFC 66* had taken over the place. There were Liddell and Ortiz banners hanging from the tall ceilings of the busy lobby. UFC T-shirts were flying out of gift shops and onto the backs of every third guy you laid eyes on. The giant 25ft screens behind the jet-wing-sized front desks pumped out a *UFC 66* ticket commercial into the eyes and ears of everyone checking in. And Chuck and Tito's images glared at each other across customised velvet poker tables.

If you include the surrounding hamlets and farms, Clitheroe has about 14,000 residents. The MGM Grand in Las Vegas has just under 7,000 hotel rooms, average occupancy of which is 1.8 people. Add the hundreds of hotel staff, restaurant workers and an army of maids and cleaners, and the MGM can easily house the entire population of the town I'm from. And next door is another hotel almost as big. And next door to that another one. And another. And another. I've never got used to Las Vegas.

My comp'd room on the 17th floor had a walk-in shower, a king-size bed, a three-seater couch, a leather-topped writing desk and a dresser that contained a 70-inch TV. After eight nights sleeping a side table away from a sourpuss submission instructor, I'd have been happy with a mattress and a sleeping bag – but this was more like it!

As instructed, I reported to the temporary UFC office to pick up my per diem and fight-week schedule. The office had been set up in a large function room just yards away from the entrance to the Grand Garden Arena itself.

I couldn't resist it – I ducked into the arena and walked into the centre of the floor where the Octagon would stand four days later. I turned around slowly. Every one of the 16,800 emerald-green seats that stretched out from the floor to the rafters would have a person in it when I fought.

Beyond excited, I rushed back to my room. I was bursting with nervous energy and wanted to train as soon as Tony and the others were ready. I tried to call their rooms. The hotel switchboard operator insisted no such people were checked in.

'Sir, I have no record of any bookings for any of the names you've provided me,' the nice American lady on the phone said. 'I've searched as far as January fifteenth – nothing. Is it possible your friends are in another Las Vegas property?'

'No,' I said. 'Thank you, though.'

'You're welcome, sir. Is there anything else I can help you with today?'

Unless she weighed 200lb and could hold pads, there really wasn't.

In disbelief, I called my manager's mobile, fully expecting another blizzard of bullshit from him. The dial tone confirmed he was still in England. Then it went to voicemail.

My manager didn't call or return texts until several days after I got back from America.

But Rebecca arrived on 28 December. She was all the support I needed.

The *UFC 66* weigh-in was attended by more fans than had ever attended any of my fights. Over 4,000 fans piled into one half of the Grand Garden Arena to see the 18 fighters hit their poundage mark and pose in their shorts.

The other half of the arena was kept out of the fans' view, behind a giant curtain. UFC floor manager Burt Watson directed me and Kazeka through a partition in the curtain and to a section of seats.

'Sit here until called for, baby,' said Watson. He was an African-American who'd gone from the military to managing boxer Joe Frazier. He described the job he did for the UFC as 'babysitter to the stars'.

In contrast to the noise and brightness of the stage area, backstage was so dark the Nevada Athletic Commission had bankers' table lights set up so they could see the paperwork every fighter had to complete. Next to the paperwork desk was a small curtained-off booth where each fighter was taken one by one for a final medical and eye exam. Next to that was another table with bankers' lights where we chose the gloves we would fight in.

The emerald seats all around us looked black in the dimness. And finally, in the middle of the floor like it was waiting in the shadows, was the Octagon.

At 4pm Joe Rogan, live mic in hand, burst into view of the fans and skipped up the stairs to the stage. 'LADIES AND GENTLE-MEN, WELCOME TO THE OFFICAL U-F-C SIX-TEE-SIX WEIGH-INS!'

He was joined on the stage by Watson, Joe Silva, the Octagon Girls and the Nevada Athletic Commission boss Keith Kizer. One fighter after the other walked out, weighed in, and hammed it up with his opponent for the cameras.

This ritual repeated with a rising sense of anticipation until, 15 minutes in, Rogan announced, 'NOW FOR THE MAIN CARD OF *UFC 66* – LIVE ON PAY-PER-VIEW ...'

It was Eric Shafer's turn. My opponent was wearing green shorts that, with his bright-red hair, made him look very festive indeed. The biggest stars in the sport – Andrei Arlovski, Forrest, Tito and Liddell – were in line behind me but my eyes lasered on Shafer's back. He looked big, strong. And then he was told to walk and disappeared through the curtain.

Rogan's voice boomed again: 'TWO-OH-FIVE FOR ERIC SHAFER! AND ... HIS OPPONENT FROM THE ULTIMATE FIGHTER ... MICHAEL "THE COUNT" BISPING!'

'Go, Bisping,' said UFC staffer Liz Hedges. I stepped through the parting in the curtains – into a shower of cheers. I was taken aback for a second. I wasn't expecting that sort of response. The previous nine athletes hadn't got those sort of cheers – but that was the power of *The Ultimate Fighter*. The show had placed me in the fans' living rooms every week for three months.

They hadn't merely seen me win fights, they'd seen me miss my family, tell anecdotes and jokes to pass the time and even make a bit of an arse of myself. They'd seen enough of me to know a little of who I was as a person – and they'd decided they liked me.

I managed the walk up the stairs to the stage without tripping but I'd made a rookie mistake in electing to wear a sweater, tracky bottoms, trainers and, who knows why, even a baseball cap. It took me forever to strip down. I'd noticed the other fighters would hand their clothes to their cornerman – which is the whole reason we go up there with a cornerman – but Muniz stood there with his hands in his pockets. I rushed to pile my clothes up on the floor while Dana, the Who's Who of the UFC and 4,000 strangers watched me.

Exhaling and stretching out my arms, I stepped on the scale.

'Two-oh-five!' Kizer said.

'TWO-OH-FIVE FOR MICHAEL BISPING!' yelled Rogan.

Stood there in only my underwear, I scrambled to pick up some of my garments from the ground (Muniz's hands remained pocketed), but apparently I'd already held the show up too long already.

'Mike!' Dana shouted.

I dropped my tracksuit bottoms and posed off with Shafer in my underwear. You'll forgive me, but I didn't attempt any sort of banter or intimidation tactics on account I felt kinda awkward with my arse squeezed into compression shorts. Shafer and I shook hands and the formalities were over. He exited stage right while I gathered up my garments.

After reaching the backstage area I retook my seat. I vaguely noted every other fighter was ecstatically excited to be drinking and eating.

'Dana will be here in thirty minutes for the fighter meeting,' UFC vice president Donna Marcolini shouted to all the fighters. 'All fighters and camps – remain here for the fighter meeting.'

Then Donna approached me and asked if I had a CD with me. I looked at her like she had two heads.

'A CD,' she repeated. 'For your walk-out music? Your manager would have been told to bring one with whatever song you want played as you walk out to fight.'

It was the first I'd heard of it, I had to tell her. My managers hadn't shown up for two weeks. I'd not given a second's thought to walk-out music. I was brand new to all of this, sorry.

'Dana will pick something for you,' Donna said. 'Don't worry.'

The *UFC 66* fighter meeting was held about half an hour after Chuck and Tito had weighed in. All the fans and most of the staff had left and the arena was even darker, and quiet except for the periodic *Beep! Beep! Beep!* of an articulated crane slowly carrying large spotlights into the rafters above the Octagon.

The other 17 fighters who'd be fighting the following night all sat in the first six or seven rows of the risers. Most fighters had one or two coaches with them, and each mini-team was spread out from the others. Particular care had been taken to avoid close proximity with opponents.

The new kid in class, I sat right at the front. Rory Singer apparently wanted to make a similarly good impression and sat right next to me. After a few minutes, Dana and Joe Silva came over to us. They went over a couple of house-keeping regulations (a holdover, probably, of the days when different MMA organisations had slightly different rules) before getting into the real reason for the gathering.

Dana put both fists down on the long table the Commission had used an hour earlier. The UFC president leaned forward and began to fire us up.

'Tomorrow night's your night,' he said to one and all of us. 'Go out and fucking shine. Win! Fucking win – but win exciting! Let it go! Don't be sitting at home next week and be going, "Oh, fuck! I should have let it all hang out – I should have let it go." Let it go!'

I was already nodding away – but Dana wasn't done.

'Do it! And for that ... I'm gonna give twenty thousand dollars to the two guys in the best fight of the night. That's twenty thousand dollars! Each! And twenty thousand dollars for the best knockout and twenty thousand dollars for the best submission ...'

Almost interrupting himself, he added, 'Fuck it! Make it twenty-five thousand dollars for the best fight, best knockout and best submission!'

'Make it thirty!' I shouted.

Rory liked my suggestion. 'MAKE IT THIRTY!' he yelled, as if, together, we could peer pressure the UFC president. But then Joe Silva was heard from: 'Remember, you can get two bonuses. You can get Fight of the Night and either Knockout or Submission of the Night in the same fight. It's happened.'

I hadn't thought of that. Quickly, I calculated how much money that would be in British pounds: more than I'd seen in my life.

I looked over my right shoulder and found Eric Schafer. *Sorry, buddy, but I'm gonna smash you tomorrow.*

UFC 66, fight day, was here. In the morning I took Rebecca shopping for something nice for her to wear to the fights but – not knowing enough to go to one of the off-Strip malls – we couldn't find anything within our budget. Still, we had a great few hours; neither of us had done much travelling and it was a relaxing way to spend the last few hours before the fight. When we got back to the hotel we had a light lunch in the MGM Grand buffet before heading back up to our hotel room to wait out the final few hours before the fight.

The information packet the UFC had given me at Tuesday's check-in said I needed to be at the arena by 4pm. That was about three hours and ten minutes before I would be gloved up and making the walk. Muniz had promised to arrive a little before me. He would make sure the room was set up correctly, that we had towels, water, a spit bucket and the other tiny details that became vitally important the instant you needed them. He would be joined by Walter, another friend of my amazing manager, who had been recruited – by text, no doubt – to also work my corner.

Around 3:30pm, I put on a pair of tracksuit bottoms, trainers and a UFC-branded hoodie. Rebecca looked on with pride.

'I love you,' she said.

'I love you,' I pulled her close into a big hug. 'Don't worry. I've got this, babe.'

With that, I set off from my hotel room.

As soon as the elevator doors opened to the ground floor I felt it – the MGM was blazing with energy. Nothing compares to a big-fight night in Las Vegas. The tables and slots were doing noisy business, the restaurants and bars were buzzing and everywhere you looked there were hordes of fans in UFC, Tapout and Affliction gear.

As I got closer to the entrance to the Grand Garden Arena itself, I ran into a wall of maybe 2,000 fans anxiously waiting for the doors to open. These were the hardcore of the fanbase; the ones who absolutely had to see every single fight on the card.

They were locked shoulder to shoulder like a Viking shield wall. *How are UFC fighters supposed to get to the arena?* I asked myself.

The Bisping family. Back row, left to right: Dad, Konrad, Stephen and me. Front row, left to right: Adam, Maxine, Mum and Shireen.

Me as British kickboxing champion, aged 16, circa 1995.

At a martial arts tournament somewhere in the UK with early training partners Andy Harby and Dan Hardy, early 2004.

Beating Ross Pointon on 26 November 2005, in Coventry at a Cage Warriors event. We'd meet again two months later during *The Ultimate Fighter*.

Hitting the big time, beating Josh Haynes to win The Ultimate Fighter, June 24 2006 in Las Vegas, Nevada.

Finishing Eric Schafer at UFC 66 at the MGM Grand Garden Arena on
December 30 2006 in Las Vegas.

Me and UFC President Dana White, Octagonside at an event in 2007.

My unforgettable first UFC win on British soil, vs Elvis Sinosic, UFC 70: Nations Collide, April 21 2007.

UFC co-owner Lorenzo Fertitta, Rebecca, UFC President Dana White and me backstage at an event in 2008.

Hugging Callum moments after the emotional comeback win vs Denis Kang, UFC 105, Manchester, England, November 14 2009.

I always look for Rebecca immediately before stepping onto the Octagon, for a kiss. On the few occasions she hasn't been at my fights, I think of her and kiss my glove. (December 3 2011, Las Vegas before my Jason Miller fight.)

Rebecca and me on our big
day, Rancho Las Lomas,
Southern California, May 2014.

I was always fired up at the weigh-ins for UFC fights in the UK, and the July 17 2015 ceremony in Glasgow, Scotland, ahead of the Thales Leites fight was no different.

With Anderson Silva in front of Tower Bridge on February 25 2016, ahead of our fight in London.

Decking Anderson Silva in the second round with this left hook was a huge moment in the fight for me.

The fourth round against Anderson Silva was the most important of my entire career. I was hurt, bloody and tired but I knew I had to win that round.

Their managers probably figured that out for them, I answered, *and your manager is in Liverpool.*

With no clue what to do, I approached a pair of security guards in purple blazers. Trying very hard not to say, 'Do you know who I am?' I explained why I needed their help. They looked at my UFC hoodie and exchanged glances.

'You're a fighter, sir?' one asked. 'Where's your wristband? Where's your team? Why don't you have any bags, sir?'

I didn't know I'd had three days to collect a wristband from the UFC. Apparently it was written in my fighter packet somewhere but I'd missed it. If only I'd paid someone, let's say 20 per cent of my purse, to take care of all this for me.

'I'm sorry, I didn't know about the wristbands,' I said. 'I really am a UFC fighter. My name is Michael Bisping. My team are waiting for me in the arena.'

A throng of fans managed to convince the security guys to escort me through the crowd, through the metal detectors, down the escalators, into the Grand Garden Arena and into the backstage hallways.

From there I picked my way by the commissioners, UFC staff and camera crews until I reached my dressing room.

MICHAEL
BISPING

was printed out on a sheet of A4 and taped to the outside of the door. I stepped into a room about the size of my bedroom back in Clitheroe. There were two foldout chairs and a massage bench against the walls; a bathroom off to the left and two mats on the floor. A TV crew from the British channel Bravo was waiting to capture the shot. Muniz and this Walter were nowhere to be seen.

'Where's your team?' the British producer asked.

'Good question.'

Ten minutes later there was a knock on the door and Mario Yamasaki stepped inside to touch base. The referee assigned to officiate my fight, he went over the rules (in 2006, rules varied slightly from promotion to promotion). He wished me luck and left. I waited another 15 minutes and then stood up and went back into the corridor to stretch my legs – only to be asked to clear the way as gloved-up fighters and their cornermen stormed by towards the entrances to the arena floor. Just then, Tito Ortiz came bouncing by on the way to his dressing room. He was flanked by five members of his world-class team and they all wore uniformed 'Team Punishment' gear.

I went back inside my room and took a piss.

Around 5:15pm Muniz and Walter showed up. Almost 90 minutes late. At least they had my gear with them. I got changed into my army camo-coloured shorts. I laid my civilian clothes out on a chair and placed my trainers side by side underneath. An official came in to wrap my hands. Then he helped me squeeze my fists into the gloves I'd selected the day before. He then left. It was still only 5:45pm and time was slowing down.

'Let's warm up,' I said. I stretched until I felt limber enough to drill some submissions with Muniz. Then I shadowboxed up a sweat. I felt solid and fast; 6:40pm was here. Good. It wouldn't be long now.

'FIFTEEN MINUTES, BISPING!' boomed Burt Watson from the doorway.

I continued bobbing up and down on the mat. I threw jabs and hooks at two-thirds pace, visualising.

'FIVE MINUTES! FIVE MINUTES, BISPING, AND WE ROOOOOOLLING!

The UFC's theme music could be heard from the monitors. Mike 'Goldie' Goldberg and Rogan were talking into the camera. *UFC 66: Liddell vs Ortiz II* was live on pay-per-view.

Watson and two other staff were at the door.

'TIME TO ROLL, BABY! LET'S DO THIS! THIS IS WHAT WE DO! ALL NIGHT LONG! ALL NIGHT LONG! WE'RE ROLLING!'

Burt led me to the lip of the arena tunnel. There was only a black curtain between me and *UFC 66* now. Shafer was already in the Octagon, waiting. I heard the first few bars of 'London's Calling' by The Clash over the speaker banks. Nice choice.

'LET'S GO!' Burt threw back the curtain. I could literally feel the body heat of 13,761 people as I plunged into the MGM Grand Garden.

The arena had transformed yet again. Lit up in blue and gold, and noise in every direction. Fans were cheering, reaching out for fist bumps. I reached back. I caught sight of Rebecca for a second.

I got this, babe.

I quickened my pace and turned left to the Octagon. The nerves caught me again as I stopped to have Vaseline applied to my face. They fell away for good as I leapt up the step to the Octagon. I felt the texture of the canvas under my feet as I did a lap around the cage.

Buffer introduced us. The referee gave us our final instructions. One last roar from the crowd. The fight was happening.

Schafer had a tense, straight-up gait about him in the Octagon. He was stalking forwards but not in a stance that offered much defence. I cracked him with a lead right cross. The shot stunned him for a second. I followed up by pressing him against the cage and digging a knee into his midsection. I then stepped back and disengaged. It was early days. I wanted him in the Octagon centre.

Now he followed with his hands tight by his eyes so I flicked a kick to his lower leg. He caught it but I managed to scramble to my feet. Nevertheless, I was surprised how fast his hands had gone from guarding his head to grabbing my ankle.

Resetting myself, I shot another arrow of a right hand and it also hit the mark. Then my jab landed. But then I again followed up the punch with another left-leg kick to Schafer's mid-section. This time he not only caught it, but made sure he completed the takedown. I landed in the centre of the Octagon with a thud. A split-second later my opponent's full weight crashed on my chest.

This was exactly where Shafer wanted the fight. He set to work, trapping my right arm under his knee and working to land strikes to my face. I didn't panic. I pulled my arm free and claimed half-guard. Schafer passed, though, and locked in an arm-triangle. He squeezed – hard – but the pressure was in the wrong place. I escaped and climbed to my feet. He jumped on my back. His grip was tightening around my neck but from the feel of his weight I knew his head was higher in the air than mine. I leapt up into the air before arching down towards in a swan dive to the canvas. Schafer's skull bore the impact of over 410lbs of fighter hitting the Octagon. Rattled, Schafer lost his grip and I used the fence to get back to my feet, threatening him with a guillotine to keep him thinking as I did.

He dived for a takedown. It was slow. My left knee thudded into his jaw. We grappled again – Eric the Red's strength was evaporating. He was now impossible to miss with punches. Blood was pumping from his open mouth as he lay on the floor. He was tired and open-mouthed. An open mouth makes the jaw even less adept at absorbing punches; every time I saw the black of his mouthpiece I threw a punch.

Schafer rolled over to his side – a clear signal to the referee that his ambitions had ended.

The referee waved it off at 4 minutes and 24 seconds of the very first round.

Lying on the Octagon, with the cameras catching every inch of my smile, I caught my breath. The Octagon door swung open. Medics rushed in to tend to my defeated opponent. My corner, Schafer's corner, Dana and Rogan, all followed.

Thank you, I said to Kazeka. I tried to hand him my mouthpiece to put in his bucket, but he was celebrating like we'd won the lottery.

Buffer announced me for the second time in six minutes. While interviewing me in the Octagon, Rogan volunteered the information I'd had 'visa problems and some other things'.

'I'd like to fight a lot more regularly,' I said. 'I could not wait to get in here ... somebody – everybody – better watch their fucking back.'

Yeah, alright, the smack talk still needed some practice. A lot of things did but, for now, it was finally a time for a celebration. After the 'visa issue and some other things', I could finally relax and let myself enjoy some of the fruits of my hard work. I showered and dressed quickly and joined Rebecca, who'd watched my fight all by herself from the stands, to see the rest of the fights.

I'd been sat down for less than five minutes when Donna found me. She gave me and Rebecca tickets for Octagonside seats but then added, 'Michael – Dana and Lorenzo need to see you.' She didn't say 'now' but she meant it.

Leaving Rebecca alone again, I was taken backstage and ushered into a dressing room which the UFC owners had turned into a command centre of sorts for the night. There were monitors and headsets set up on tables in front of leather sofas, and a choice of several suits still hung in plush dry-cleaning bags next to the vanity dressers. The room was empty and I couldn't resist helping myself to some of the food that was laid out on a black table at the back.

I had a gob full of cheese and crackers when the UFC owners – Dana and Lorenzo – came through the door. They both slapped hands and hugged me.

'Awesome performance,' Lorenzo smiled.

'Great fight,' Dana added. 'Fucking great.'

I was handed an envelope. It was the same size and shape as the one that had been delivered to my door in Clitheroe.

'Open it,' Dana said.

It was another cheque, fifty thousand dollars with the tax already paid – a gift for a job well done. The mental calculation I'd done at the fighter rules meeting was still fresh in my brain. I knew exactly how much money that was in British pounds.

A quiet pride swelled up as I sprinted back to Rebecca. I hugged her and told her and showed her all about the cheque all at the same time, but she understood what I was saying, like always.

I woke up in my room on the 17th floor of the MGM Grand on New Year's Eve, 2006. My face was a little sore from the four minutes I'd spent with Eric Shafer the previous evening. My head was *very* sore from the four-plus hours I'd spent enjoying the Las Vegas nightlife.

Before I'd crashed asleep five or six hours beforehand, I'd apparently had the foresight to leave a bottle of water on the elaborate side table next to the bed. I sat up and guzzled it down a dry throat. Rebecca was next to me, sound asleep.

The beds in the best Las Vegas hotels are much wider and longer than the beds I was used to. The mattresses are so deep you sink like a stone and almost have to climb out the next morning. I looked across the spacious room I'd stayed in for the last week. The dresser with the TV. The couch. The leather-topped writing table. And beyond the clothes and shoes I'd wrestled myself out of a few hours earlier there was a massive floor-to-ceiling window. I got out of bed and looked out of it.

Across the road, and 250ft below, the police were beginning to cordon off Las Vegas Boulevard. Every 31 December at about 2pm the streets around the Strip become pedestrianised so thousands of tourists can see in the New Year looking up at fireworks shooting off the roofs of these massive hotels.

A new year would arrive shortly with limitless possibilities. I was so ready for it. No one was going to work harder than me, I swore. I'd be the first in the gym, the last to leave, I'd fight my heart out each and every time. I'd say 'yes' to every opportunity that came my way outside the Octagon.

I couldn't wait for 2007 to start!

CHAPTER EIGHT

HOMECOMING

By Wednesday, 17 January 2007, I was already back in Las Vegas. Manchester's boxing world champ Ricky Hatton was having his first Vegas fight that weekend. To capitalise on the British sports press all being in town, the UFC had a big announcement at the *Ultimate Fighter* gym at 6pm. I was part of it.

The *TUF* gym was always overhauled between seasons. The red and green liveries of Team Punishment and Team Shamrock had long since been stripped away – a whole other series had been shot and aired between then and my UFC debut – and now yellow and blue, representing season-five coaches Jens Pulver and B.J. Penn, had been installed. The UFC had hired a gourmet hot dog and beer stand for the evening. The secret to a well-attended PR event, I was assured, is serving quality food.

About a dozen British boxing writers were bussed in from whatever hotel they were staying in to cover Hatton's fight. Dana White welcomed them, then stood on the apron of the Octagon and informed the room that the UFC was making a massive push in the UK. There would be a full-time office in London, a major TV deal had been signed, and there would be huge UFC events – stacked with the biggest names in the world – held in the British Isles each year.

It's probably difficult for newer fans to grasp just how world-changing this was for British MMA. From that point on, the biggest events in MMA wouldn't always take place on the other side of the world in the middle of the night when British fans were asleep. The summit of the sport wasn't remote and unreachable – it was an afternoon's drive away.

Then Dana introduced me to the British newspaper guys.

'You guys love fighting,' Dana said. 'We were always coming back to the UK. But it makes things easier that Bisping came along at exactly the right time. This guy is our Ricky Hatton.'

I spent an hour talking to the media, spending most of it trying to live down the Hatton comparison. Several of these guys were crusty old boxing types whose interest in the evening began at one end of a hotdog and finished at the other. But a handful – Gareth Davies from the *Telegraph*, Steve Bunce from the BBC and a few more – seemed genuinely interested in MMA, its rules, how I trained, and how far I thought I could go in the UFC.

I also met someone who'd become a major part of my career for the next few years and a good friend to this day. Marshall Zelaznik, a silver-haired 40-something from California, was the new president of the UFC's UK division and one of the smartest, most charismatic and funniest guys I know. We hit it off immediately.

'Did you hear what Dana said to the press guys?' I asked Marshall after the media left. 'The UFC are doing a big show at the Manchester Arena. That's thirty minutes from my front door. Do you know if I'll be on that card?'

A smile danced across Marshall's face. He said, 'Yeah, um, Mike ... you're the reason we are taking this first event back in the UK to Manchester.'

Oh, right.

UFC 70: Nations Collide was announced for 21 April 2007, at the mountainous Manchester Arena. The UFC weren't tiptoeing over the Atlantic this time. The company spent millions of pounds promoting the *UFC 70* event and its re-entry into the British sporting landscape. There were posters featuring *UFC 70* headliners Mirko Cro Cop and Gabriel Gonzaga, plus Andrei Arlovski and me, all over the country. My shaven head and face were plastered on bus stops in Manchester, train stations in the Midlands and taxis in London.

The event was constantly promoted with television and sports-radio adverts. You could feel a real sense of excitement build in British MMA as the days counted down. Over 15,000 tickets – £1.3million worth – had been sold. It was like the UFC had taken over Manchester.

My *UFC 70* opponent was Elvis Sinosic, a former UFC title challenger from Australia. The King of Rock 'n' Rumble, as he invited people to call him, was a legit BJJ black belt.

The UFC set up headquarters in the Lowry hotel in Manchester. In terms of the requirements of a UFC hotel, the five-star member of The Leading Hotels in the World™ with its health-spa lighting and original artwork galleries was a slight overkill.

On the day before the weigh-in, after my final sit-down interviews with the media (the UFC production crew's need for combative soundbites was sated when I said, 'Jiu-jitsu is great; doing jiu-jitsu when getting punched in the face isn't so great') I returned to my room to face the nightmare of sorting out tickets for my family and friends.

The moment *UFC 70* was announced I'd been inundated with requests for tickets. Most of the immediate asks came from the same people who'd travelled up and down the country to see my early fights, and I loved paying back that support by getting them seats to a massive show just a couple years later.

But the requests kept on coming and, not wanting to big-time anyone, I kept saying I'd take care of it. With 48 hours to go before the event, I had over 150 tickets sprawled all over my hotel-room floor needing to be sorted into specific envelopes with specific names written on the front. It took forever but I finally got it done.

Afterwards, I decided to drive home and spend the night in my own bed. I'd barely eaten all day, what with my media commitments and the stress of the tickets, so when a Burger King sign approached on the left, I turned in and joined the drive-thru line.

Sluurp!

Oh, fuck!

The medium Sprite in my hand had been drained down to the ice cubes. The Triple Whopper (with cheese and bacon) box was empty, too. The weigh-in to *UFC 70* was less than 23 hours away. I'd picked a great time to become a fast-food fan.

I needn't have worried. I hit the light heavyweight limit no problem.

The energy at the Manchester Arena on fight night made the hairs on the back of my neck tingle. It had been almost five years since welterweight legend Matt Hughes, a farmer from Middle America, had headlined in London, but those seeds had taken root. *UFC 38* had sold out the Royal Albert Hall's 3,800 seats – I would be fighting in front of a crowd of Brits four times that size.

The pressure to win for my family and for myself was as strong as ever but, as I warmed up backstage, I felt something else as well.

I wanted to win for the British fans.

This was UK MMA's coming-out party. Those thousands upon thousands of fans in the stands and those watching at home were counting on me to win. In a way, I was glad they were counting on me. If I had anything at all to do with it, I would not let them down. I felt the kind of pride I imagined my father and brothers felt when they put on their uniforms. I was going to represent my country and fight.

I stiffened my jaw and continued to hit Tony Quigley's mitted hands. The shots flowed. As the fight got closer, Tony had me running shuttles up and down the broad corridors underneath the arena. If the idea was for the sprints to burn off excess energy – that didn't happen. My brain had opened my adrenal glands and adrenaline was gushing through my body.

Finally, the call came: 'Bisping – let's roll!'

I'd picked my own walk-out music this time. I'd walked from the Lowry to the HMV store in Manchester town centre earlier in the week. I wanted something British, a song which would get the fans going. I picked Blur's 'Song 2'. It reminded me of the late 1990s, the days where I competed as a teenager with no pressure and purely for the love of the fight.

The space where the backstage area meets the walkway to the arena floor – usually a tunnel – is emptied of people in the minutes before a fighter is due to walk out towards the Octagon. Standing there, looking down the tunnel that cuts through two tiered sections of the crowd, is a nerve-racking moment.

You just want to get on with it. You've left your dressing room; you are on your way to fight ... and then you are told to stop by the UFC production floor manager. You are held in place for several minutes with a camera crew capturing every micro-emotion that crosses your face.

The lights had been dimmed out in the arena. Everyone's attention was on the 50ft screens that hung from the rafters. A video package was playing, hyping my fight. I heard my own voice echoing around the building: 'Jiu-jitsu is great; doing jiu-jitsu when getting punched in the face isn't so great.'

I focused on my breathing and waited for the lights and sound to come up.

The first few bars of 'Song 2' blasted out – and the Manchester Arena erupted. The place became unglued! The fans went mental! A BBC boxing report said it sounded like a pair of jet engines had been fired up. Nothing had prepared me for this reception. My adrenaline spiked sharply. I couldn't wait a second longer. I swerved passed the cameraman and sprinted towards the cage.

There were mobs of fans everywhere I looked. Everyone was going mental. The crowd noise shook the floor. It shook the roof. I had to be physically stopped from leaping up the stairs leading to the Octagon door with my trainers and hoodie on. I kicked my shoes halfway across the arena. I tore the hoodie off. I was almost sparking with energy as the cutman tried to apply Vaseline to my brow and face. When he was done, I stamped up the steps and burst into the Octagon.

It was like the world was in fast-forward. The introductions were over in another thunderous, rolling yell from the crowd and – at last – it was time to fight.

Sinosic was an inch taller than me but he fought taller than that. At the start of the fight he walked towards me with a straight-up stance and began firing leg kicks. He'd said in interviews that he would attack – he hadn't lied.

But I was a man possessed. I surged forward and caught his leg. I dumped him on the canvas. There was a rumble from the stands as

I began to ground and pound from inside his guard. As good as my word, I brushed aside an armbar attempt and continued to punch, hammerfist and elbow away. The reverberations in the place grew louder and louder. I could feel – physically feel – the soundwaves the fans were making. I speared my fists into Sinosic's ribs and head. I postured up to drop maximum weight into my elbow strikes.

Sinosic was trapped on his back. At the three-minute mark, my opponent's face was submerging into a pool of red. Elvis had several moments of influencing my posture or holding on to my wrists, but each time I'd rip away from his grip and resume my attacks.

'Overwhelming – an onslaught like we have rarely seen!' said commentator Mike Goldberg.

The referee appeared to be thinking about stopping it when the horn sounded to end the first round. The former UFC title challenger remained on the canvas for much of the rest period, attended to by his cornerman and checked out by the doctor, but – to his credit – Elvis came out for the second.

The round began with me landing hard punches and kicks. The crowd was screaming with all of their lungs. The finish! I wanted to give them that finish! Sinosic was desperate for a handhold in the fight. Momentarily, he grabbed a Thai clinch. High on adrenaline and with my brain racing ahead, I did the one thing you don't do to escape a Thai clinch. I ducked.

There was a flash.

Sinosic was on top of me. I was flat on my back. Holy shit – how did I get here? He had my left arm locked in a Kimura …

Pop! Pop! Pop!

I heard the sound of my elbow joint popping three times. Sinosic was cranking the double wristlock with every ounce of his strength. There was no way I was tapping. Not here. Not now. I broke out of the hold. I twisted into his guard and – from there – I unleashed a ferocious attack. Fourteen, fifteen, sixteen punches landed until the referee stopped the fight.

The whole arena went deranged. I lifted my arms as the house lights came up, revealing for the first time row after row of roaring fans stretching back and upwards almost as far as I could see. The British fans were going nuts as they celebrated our victory! They'd thrown and taken every shot – but the job was done! It was an intimate moment with 15,114 strangers.

I barely had chance to catch my breath as Bruce Buffer announced me the winner in 1 minute 40 seconds of the second round. Then Callum ran across the Octagon and into my arms. I picked him up and he took the first question from Joe Rogan.

'How great was it watching your daddy win?'

'Very good,' Callum answered.

That night spilled beyond my wildest dreams. I'd be awarded more Fight of the Night bonuses, I'd go on to fight on and headline huge UFC events around the world; I'd get the chance to do some amazing things outside the Octagon. But *UFC 70*, 21 April 2007, the Manchester Arena … that night will bring mist to my eyes for as long as I'm alive.

The UFC had proved popular enough to sell out the biggest arenas in the country, and it was becoming commonplace to see MMA magazines on the shelves of WHSmith and for a UFC fighter to guest star in a TV show here and there. But there was still a lot of work to do in terms of educating the British public and media about what the sport actually entailed.

Over the next few years the UFC PR team put Marshall Zelaznik and me in front of dozens of writers, reporters, TV and radio hosts, and editors to put the sport's best foot forward. It was an additional responsibility the UFC expected of me and one I took very seriously. Today, when I hear young fighters moan about having to do promotional work, I can't help but think they should be more grateful that there was a generation before them who did all the heavy lifting for them.

One well-known radio personality, a lady in her mid-fifties who'd squeezed herself into, I'm guessing, her daughter's leather miniskirt, began a live, in-studio interview by describing MMA as 'a sport for barbarians'.

I said, 'Well, I'm not a barbarian—'

'You look like a barbarian,' she insisted.

In those situations, when you find yourself live on air with someone only interested in manufacturing a Jeremy Kyle moment for their own purposes, I find fighting fire with fire a good strategy.

'I'll keep most of my thoughts on your appearance to myself,' I answered. 'Mutton dressed as lamb comes to mind, though.'

Despite a handful of interviews like that, the tide began to turn and the UFC became accepted, at worst, as an alternative combat sport to boxing. I'm proud to have helped lay the foundations for the sport in the UK and other places.

Don't get me wrong, I liked the media stuff most of the time. Some of the appearances were a lot of fun. Once me and Marshall were in a studio on Ian Wright's radio show in London. The former England footballer spoke to me as a fellow athlete, which was appreciated, and he mentioned the sport was rapidly growing.

Marshall agreed: 'A black-cab driver who brought us here was asking Mike about his next fight ...' Unfortuately Marshall's resoundingly American accent placed the emphasis on black – and I saw a great chance to troll the UFC exec live on air.

'A *black* cab driver?!' I exclaimed. 'Can you say things like that these days, Marshall?'

In his 15-year career as a striker, Wrighty had never been passed the ball so close to an open goal. As I knew he would, he whacked it into the back of the net.

'Did it surprise you that the driver was black?' the host asked a mortified Marshall with mock-seriousness. 'I guess I'm a *black* talk-radio host, am I?'

Marshall held his hands up in surrender and joined in the entire studio having a friendly laugh at his expense.

There were some fringe benefits to my unofficial role as a UFC UK spokesman. There was a lot of filet mignon at fancy restaurants (good food = media attendance, remember?) and I got to travel a bit while not having to worry about fighting.

Whenever UFC puts on an event, several 'guest fighters' are brought in to do the additional media appearances and fan meet-and-greets that athletes days and hours away from a fight can't be expected to do.

I attended *UFC 72* in Belfast in June 2007 as a guest fighter and used the trip to visit family. My cousin Tony picked me up from the hotel and drove me the 45 miles westward to Killylea, the tiny village where my mum's side of the family are from. The small pub we dropped into was ram-packed.

'This place must make a killing,' I said. 'You can barely move in here – and it's a Wednesday.'

Tony smiled. 'Michael – you are related to almost every single person in this bar.'

I had a great time having a drink with aunts, uncles and cousins I only knew from my mum's stories. I never billed myself as 'Irish

Mick Bisping' or anything, but I'm as proud of where my mother comes from as I am my heritage from my father's side of the family.

The next day I was eating breakfast at the *UFC 72* hotel when Dana bounced into the restaurant looking for me. He seemed like he'd been awake the whole flight over the Atlantic and was buzzing with the ideas he'd come up with.

'We're going to London in September,' Dana said. 'There will be a huge main event – biggest one on free TV in the US we've ever done. And we want you on the card in a big fight – in the co-main event.'

'Sounds good,' I said. 'Who's the opponent?'

CHAPTER NINE
MAIN EVENT

The 'big event in London' was, of course, *UFC 75*, which was announced and scheduled for 7 September 2007, in the gigantic O$_2$ Arena on the banks of the Thames. The biggest indoor arena in the UK, the O$_2$ is situated inside the spaceship-like white structure that used to be known as the Millennium Dome.

The huge main event Dana alluded to was Quinton 'Rampage' Jackson unifying the UFC light heavyweight title he'd recently ripped away from Chuck Liddell against newly signed PRIDE FC champion Dan Henderson. *UFC 75* was promoted as 'Champion vs Champion' and, just like *UFC 70*, the event would be broadcast on American cable-television station Spike, which would guarantee millions of viewers in the US alone.

When Joe Silva placed the official call to my management regarding my co-main event slot, my opponent was revealed as Matt Hamill.

The fight made sense from the UFC's perspective. Bisping vs Hamill had seemed destined to happen during *TUF 3* and there was plenty of footage of the pair of us together for video-hype packages etc. 'The ultimate grudge', as it was billed, was an easy story line for the fans to buy into.

The PR push when tickets go on sale for a big event (for UFC, typically three months or so before the fight night itself) is unimaginatively called the 'on-sale'. Rampage Jackson was flown into London to join me in doing the on-sale.

Although the same age as me, Rampage had been fighting half a decade longer. He'd fought his way around America's MMA circuit until making the leap to Japan's PRIDE FC in 2001 and becoming one of the biggest stars in the sport. He'd jumped back over the Pacific again to join the UFC in February 2007 and had repeated an earlier KO win over Chuck Liddell to win the UFC light heavyweight title.

Rampage was awesome, I decided very quickly. The African-American brawler from Memphis was hilarious. Self-deprecatingly hilarious, too, which was a rare thing for one of the most menacing fighters in the world. He was a proud dad. We had that in common, too. Rampage also had a big heart – while we were walking to the restaurant he slipped away and bought takeaways for two homeless men sitting in dirty green sleeping bags in an alleyway.

We really clicked over those few days.

'Come to Big Bear and train for this fight with me,' Rampage said over dinner. 'You look like the kinda guy who loves him some trainin'. My manager Juanito has a great camp in the California mountains. You should come.'

I felt obligated to clear it with my management, but they agreed a camp with the world's number-one light heavyweight – plus a host of other UFC contenders and MMA fighters – would be too good an opportunity to pass up.

In July, I was in California, on the winding roads towards the rarefied air of Big Bear. Generations of legendary boxing champions had based their training camps in the small town that sits 6,752ft above sea level, but I was dropped off at what was unmistakably an MMA camp.

Rampage's manager and trainer at the time was a Mexican-American named Juanito Ibarra. Like his adoptive home town, he'd migrated from boxing (his best-known client was Oscar de la Hoya) to MMA; he was running a fantastic camp in the wooded hills of San Bernardino County. That camp in the summer of 2007 was world class: the coaching was as good as I'd received during *TUF*, but the training and sparring partners were out of this world.

In addition to the UFC light heavyweight champion, UFC heavyweight contenders Cheick Kongo and Brandon Vera were there along with welterweight Zach Light and five others who had fights coming up in the next few months.

It was a stacked camp – everyone was a professional fighter – and Juanito ran it with the precision of a Swiss watch.

The term 'camp', by the way, never felt more appropriate than when I was in Big Bear. Most of us were staying in log-fire luxury cabins dotted around the centre of town. We took our meals at Juanito's place (where Rampage was staying), which was located across the street from the gym.

The gym was situated in one of the few buildings I set foot in during my stay that wasn't made entirely of wood. It was a two-storey structure and had a long matted section and a cage on the ground floor. Then, up a flight of stairs, was a naturally lit space with heavy bags creaking from wood beams. Rounding out the facilities on the same side of the road (it felt like there was only one) as Juanito's house was a surprisingly well-equipped weights gym that Kongo became fond of.

My first spar with Rampage Jackson, the UFC world champion of the same light heavyweight division I competed in, came on the third day of camp.

'When we spar,' Rampage said with his mouthpiece already in, 'Yo' kick my ass – all good. I kick yo' ass – all good. Okay?'

Only, Rampage wasn't really okay with getting hit in sparring. Whenever he was cracked with a good shot in the gym, you could visibly see his temper brewing behind his mouthpiece and eyes. More than one training partner of his was made to regret their momentary successes.

Like with my spars with Forrest Griffin six months earlier, I took a lot of confidence from how I measured up against the world's No.1 light heavyweight.

I also took full advantage of the chance to train at altitude for the first time (with all due respect to Castle Hill in Nottingham). Every morning the team went for a jog into the surrounding greenery of the San Bernardino National Forest. The idea was to loosen the muscles a little, get the blood pumping before the hard work began. Y'know, that sort of thing.

On the first day of these little jaunts, maybe 400 yards into it, I noticed Zach Light darting his eyes sideways at me. Then he put on a burst of speed and pulled a yard ahead. My eyes were darting now. And I pulled level. So he increased speed, slightly, once more. And I pulled level again. We both knew what would come next – we broke into a full-on sprint.

Every day thereafter was the same: Zach and I would have a race. We never spoke about it, but we were locked in a one-on-one three-mile race. He won the early meets, but by the end of the camp I was flying ahead of the group. This is a prime example of one of my character flaws – excessive competitiveness – manifesting itself in my fighting career.

Another focus of my work in Big Bear was wrestling. I knew from experience that Hamill was outstanding at takedowns and controlling opponents with his grappling. That's what everyone expected him to do in the fight. I was lucky enough to have a naturally good sense of balance, but this camp – grappling with a powerhouse like Rampage and heavyweights in Kongo and Vera – was my master's degree in takedown defence.

The night of *UFC 75* arrived and I was in the best shape of my career. I was markedly more experienced now. One of the biggest lessons I'd taken from my first year as a UFC fighter, so I thought, was not to allow my emotions to dictate the way I fought like I had at *UFC 70*.

So, as I made my way out of the tunnel into the O_2 Arena, I pushed my breath out in long exhales. Wave after wave of cheers from the 16,235 fans crashed around the former Millennium Dome but I kept my feet on the ground and refused to be swept away. I smiled and acknowledged that I appreciated the fans' support, but I kept it at arm's length. I declined to be pulled into the kind of shared emotional frenzy that got me into trouble in Manchester.

I calmly took my shoes off at the prep-point next to the Octagon. I took my T-shirt off and handed it to my cornermen. I gave the cutman plenty of time to apply grease to my skin. I took the stairs one at a time. I jogged lightly in circles across the canvas. I saw my mum at ringside and give her a smile, and I had a thumbs-up for Dana.

On the other side of the Octagon, my opponent was whipping himself into a frenzy. This was the fight he'd waited over a year for.

Hamill charged across the Octagon like a madman. He was fired up – but instead of going for takedowns like we expected, he was throwing bombs. With the 20/20 of hindsight, I'd overcompensated for Manchester and done myself a disservice by starting the fight so calm. I was scrambling, a pilot sprinting towards his plane during a surprise air raid. Hamill kept heaving forward with power shots.

At one point this ape of a bloke had me in the sort of headlock you'd put your younger brother in – only he was smashing me in the face with his other fist. I distinctly remember seeing blood curve around my nose and drip to the canvas and thinking, *Well, this isn't going to fucking plan, is it?*

He scored two takedowns and, while I nullified his ground and pound, I'd lost a round for the first time in my pro career.

The second round was a war of attrition and my California crash-course in wrestling and altitude training proved their worth. I'd drilled throwing punches from my back relentlessly and, when the fight went to the ground, I out-landed Hamill from inside my guard. As the round wore on, I countered Matt's lunging strikes on the feet with jabs and combinations more and more.

The third and final round was my strongest. I dug deep, set the pace and landed several satisfying power punches. The fight ended with me slamming home a solid head kick and stuffing a takedown attempt.

My first points decision of my pro MMA career was a split-decision victory. The two American judges awarded me the fight while the British judge had Hamill the winner. It was a very close fight.

What I should have said to Joe Rogan afterwards was, 'Wow, all respect to Matt. That was a hard fight. He surprised me in the opening round – I had to fight my heart out to get the win.'

But that doesn't even resemble what I broadcasted from the middle of the Octagon. I gave Matt no credit. I was obnoxious. I look back on my conduct and cringe. I deeply regret the way I behaved that night.

After I retired, 11 years after *UFC 75*, I was put on the spot by a live interviewer.

'Who gave you the toughest fight of your UFC career?' he asked.

He probably expected a big name like Anderson Silva, GSP or Dan Henderson.

Instead, he got the honest answer that I didn't give all those years before.

'Matt Hamill,' I said. 'Matt Hamill gave me the toughest fight of my career.'

Over five million Americans had watched the fight on US television – and they wanted the rematch. A month after UFC 75, the UFC called and asked me if I could be ready to face Hamill again at the *UFC 78* pay-per-view event scheduled for New Jersey. I had six weeks to train, but readily accepted the chance to underline my win, but Matt had suffered an injury and couldn't be ready until the New Year.

Just as I thought my 2007 campaign was over, the UFC came back and said they still wanted me for *UFC 78* – and in an even bigger fight.

Rashad Evans was 10–0–1 and had begun his UFC run by winning the heavyweight *Ultimate Fighter* tournament during season two of the reality show. He immediately dropped down to light heavyweight and began marching towards a title shot. The draw on his record had come in a fight many felt he'd won versus Tito Ortiz.

'This is going to be the first time two *Ultimate Fighter* winners have fought each other,' Joe Silva said, before adding the bombshell: 'This is going to be the main event of *UFC 78*.'

Less than two years since I'd travelled to London to audition for *The Ultimate Fighter* and only four years since giving up working in the upholstery factory, I would be headlining a pay-per-view event in the USA.

'They're throwing you to the wolves, Mike,' warned Tony Quigley. 'The UFC are setting you up to lose this one.'

Tony was from the world of boxing with its backroom schemes of protecting fighters by matching them with has-beens and never-weres until they'd built 32–0 (with 31 knockouts) records and were on the cusp of a shot at the half-dozen or so 'world' titles.

That wasn't how it worked in the UFC. In the UFC, there's only one champion per division, for a start. And I wasn't getting thrown anywhere, I'd fought my way from the reality series to the opening fight of the *UFC 66* pay-per-view, to the middle of the main card for *UFC 70* and co-main spot at *UFC 75*. The next step up was headlining, and you don't headline major UFC events without fighting elite contenders.

Tony thought he was looking out for my best interests, but I could have done without him expressing those sorts of sentiments. I'd never turned down a fight in my life, and I sure as hell wasn't turning down the chance to main-event a major show in America.

'Tony,' I said, 'I'm not in the UFC so I can cut the line at Las Vegas nightclubs to impress my mates. I'm there to go all the way. I'm going to win the world title – and you don't hand-pick opponents all the way to the belt in the UFC.'

Rampage – who'd defended his title in London – wasn't scheduled to fight again until the following summer and with less than two months to get ready for Rashad, I trained in Liverpool.

The quality of that preparation vis-à-vis what I'd experienced in Big Bear was stark. My main (and on a lot of days, only) sparring partner for Rashad – an explosive athlete and wrestling virtuoso – was Gary Kelly, a Liverpool lightweight training for his pro debut.

Gary was a scrapper; he could give me a workout but he wasn't any sort of wrestler at all. And he was a *lightweight* – Rashad had stamped his ticket to the UFC by winning *The Ultimate Fighter* heavyweight tournament. Fortunately, I'd trained wrestling like crazy for the Hamill fight. That, I hoped, would be enough against Suga Rashad.

Rashad and I had spent several days together in London earlier in 2007, signing autographs at a martial arts and sports convention in London along with Josh Koscheck and Anderson Silva. We were both light heavyweights at similar stages of our careers. We didn't need to mention it, but the thought we'd be fighting each other soon occurred to both of us.

Nevertheless, we got on great during those three days. And, today, Rashad is one of my absolute favourite people to share a commentary desk with. Love that guy now …

… but not so much in mid-November 2007.

The abbreviated build-up to our fight was punctuated with the pair of us sniping at the other in interviews. By the time I was in New Jersey, we'd worked ourselves into a definite dislike of each other. We exchanged glares during the press conference and whenever we saw each other at the hotel.

One of the times I spotted him was the morning of the weigh-ins. He was glistening in a rubber suit, the arms and legs taped shut, and on his way to a sauna to spurt out the last few pounds before he stepped on the scale.

I paused for a second. My opponent, a couple of inches shorter than me, was dressed as a cosmonaut and on his way to boil in a Turkish suite. Meanwhile – at the absolute insistence of the Liverpool gym folk – I was about to leave the hotel in search of a Chinese-meal lunch.

Three and a half hours after I chose the 'healthiest' dish at the Peking Pavilion, I stepped on the scale, set up on the New Jersey Devils' practice ice-rink at the Prudential Center arena.

Frigid surroundings or not, Rashad's temper was red hot. He refused to shake my hand after we both weighed within the 205lb limit and then we had to be separated backstage.

When I walked out to the Octagon on fight night, Mike Goldberg read out that I'd said Rashad's style was so negative that I'd seen more aggression from Rebecca when she hit the January sales.

Joe Rogan cracked up laughing, adding, 'He's a funny guy – he says lots of funny things like that.'

The US fans weren't so sure. At *UFC 66* less than 11 months before, I'd been cheered against an American on American soil. But the fallout from *UFC 75* had cast me as a pantomime heel, and the Americans booed the British baddie.

Unquestionably, Rashad was another distinct step up in competition. He was effortlessly athletic and his movements a series of controlled detonations. My previous two opponents were big and strong, but Rashad was different. He was explosively powerful. Instead of boaring in, he disguised his takedown attempts with strikes and feints (which are the key to MMA wrestling).

Rashad had advantages in wrestling. I had advantages in striking. He'd take me down; I'd get up. I'd rake him with a short uppercut or cross; he'd answer by pressing me against the cage. At one point he scooped me up and slammed me down; I gave him a receipt later in the form of a two-punch combo to the face.

As the fight went on, I began to read Rashad's takedown set-up and redistribute my weight to stifle his wrestling. Then, near the end of the second, I drew Rashad's attention with a knee to the guts and dived down for a takedown of my own. I lifted my opponent up and dumped him on the canvas as the horn to end the round sounded. It felt *really* good to give him a dose of his own medicine.

The first round was Rashad's. I had taken the second. Everything would come down to the final five minutes.

My opponent came swaggering out of his corner for the last. I went out to meet him, composed and confident. We fired single bullets at each other for a minute, then Rashad pressed for a takedown that, eventually, he won. Twenty seconds later we scrambled, and I took him down. The fight returned to standing and I landed a solid left hook. Then Rashad did. Half the round had gone and we were deadlocked.

'Who wins this fight may be determined in the next two and a half minutes,' Goldberg said.

My future friend chased a right cross across the canvas and took me down. We got up and he landed a one-two. He went for another takedown. I sprawled and landed a punch to his jaw. I put another knee in his ribs. Neither of us could hold on to the initiative for long.

I'll win this in the last ten seconds, I thought. *When I hear the 'clapper' announce we're in the last ten seconds of the fight, I'll throw everything at him – give the fans what they want, draw a cheer and impress the judges.*

Clap-clap-clap! There it was—

Rashad took me down again.

Fuck, no!

That last, final takedown was enough to win Rashad the decision 29–28, 29–28, with one judge disagreeing and giving it to me 28–29. Even when I watched the fight back on tape, my honest impression is that Rashad nicked it in the final moments and deserved to win.

'Will you shake my hand now?' I said to Rashad in the middle of the Octagon.

He smiled and took my hand. We hugged and congratulated each other. The respect we earned from each other that night would, in time, develop into a real friendship.

On the way to the post-fight press conference, Joe Silva shared an encouraging word: 'Your wrestling was phenomenal.'

Prompted by Gareth Davies and Kevin Francis from the UK newspapers, who were angling for a quote for 'Brit Bisp Will Be Back!' type stories, Dana said: 'I don't think Michael lost anything tonight. He proved he is for real.'

Under some circumstances, those could have been nice, smoothing sentiments. They weren't that night. Not at all. As the reality of my first professional loss sank in, I began to take an honest inventory of what I could have done differently.

First, I'd given Rashad far, far too much respect in the fight. While everything I said above about Rashad's ability is 100 per cent accurate, I flew the length of the Atlantic back home knowing that

I could have done more in the Octagon. I would never wait until the final seconds of a fight to push the pace again. From then on, if I had energy to attack – I attacked.

And second, there was no more hiding from the fact that I could do more – much more – outside the Octagon, too.

'I need to make changes,' I told Rebecca first, and then the Liverpool gym. 'I'm not making the sacrifices I could make to get the best out of my ability and the opportunities I'm earning.'

Okay, they said. But – was I sure I wanted to drop from light heavyweight to the middleweight division?

'That's a 20lb drop,' they said.

Yes, I was sure. I'd avoided thinking too much about it because I'd been winning all my fights, but the evidence had been there all along. True light heavyweights were the size of Forrest Griffin and Rampage. They had to cut weight to make 205lb – they were 205lb for a handful of minutes a year. I was 205lb all year. They wore rubber suits to saunas and rubbed thermogenic liniments on their skin to make them lose water-weight faster. They didn't wolf down Whoppers the day before weigh-ins or go for a Chinese for lunch hours before stepping on the scale.

The call went out to Joe Silva.

My first fight of 2008 would be in the UFC's middleweight division.

CHAPTER TEN

ONE EIGHT FIVE

Ever since I first landed in America to do the medicals and final interview for *TUF 3*, I'd gotten puzzled comments from MMA people regarding my choice of weight division. In MMA, the light heavyweight championship limit is 205lb (14st 9lb) and to fight in the middleweight division you cannot weigh more than 185lb (13st 3lb). And everybody thought I should have been competing as a middleweight.

Now the '0' in my record was gone forever and I forced myself to face the reality that I hadn't been making the sacrifices I could have made. I owed it to myself, my family and supporters to work for every last possible advantage in the Octagon and I'd not been doing that. I never fought as a light heavyweight again.

One of the many advantages of America's obsession with high school and college wrestling is every year thousands more young athletes are indoctrinated into the dark arts of the weight cut. 'Cutting weight' is a process where an athlete rapidly loses enough fluid and salts to temporarily lower their mass for an official weight check, only to equally rapidly replace that fluid and return to their previous poundage and strength. The result is an athlete who was a 185lb middleweight on Friday's official weigh-check weighing 200lb or more come fight time.

Cutting weight can be a horrible and sometimes dangerous process, I knew. Athletes in several sports, including MMA, have become seriously ill and have even died when cutting too much weight or not going about it properly. No one on my team had the experience to help me yoyo down to 185lb for the weigh-in and safely back to around 200lb for the fight 24 hours later.

So I elected to diet and exercise my way down to 185lb.

Twenty pounds is a lot of person, though, believe you me. It is twice as much weight as the average person's head – skull, brain, the lot – for example. Put another way, if you took nine and a half litres of water out of Michael Bisping the light heavyweight, you'd be looking at a Michael Bisping who would just about be small enough to compete as a middleweight.

To complete the move to 185lb, I'd need to lose a full 10 per cent of my body weight. Because I'd not weighed 185lb since I was a teenager, Joe Silva had suggested pushing my next fight to the springtime. 'Give your body time to adjust, try out a weight cut. Get this right,' the matchmaker said.

Silva's concern wasn't purely altruistic. While every fighter on the UFC roster was entitled to pick whichever division they wanted to compete in, Silva had a responsibility to the company to ensure fights were safe as well as competitive.

So, in January 2008, I set about transforming myself into a middleweight. Only, I was totally naive when it came to how to go about it. Instead of cutting the weight, like almost every other fighter on the roster, I dieted and exercised my arse off. Rather than bungee-jumping in down to 13st 3lb for a few moments, I spent months slowly lowering my mass from around 15 stone towards the middleweight limit.

First, obviously, anything remotely resembling fast food was eradicated from my diet. Then processed foods and anything containing sodium, refined sugar and carbohydrates was cut out.

And I'd run, my God did I run. I'd run four miles – at a pace – in the morning on an empty stomach.

It wasn't as hard as you might be imagining. At light heavyweight, my breakfast staple of choice was chicken sausage, eggs and mushrooms. Omelettes, boiled eggs and salads with lumps of chicken were also my go-to meals for later in the day. Without that kind of calorie intake and with the additional running, plus two training sessions and sparring or weights in the evening, the weight came off me and a call was placed to Joe Silva to arrange my first fight as a middleweight.

'There's a lot of guys at one-eighty-five who want to fight you,' Silva said over the phone from his basement office in his Virginia home.

He was excited about his middleweight division, which had also just added Dan Henderson, bonkers BJJer Rousimar Palhares, submission specialist Demian Maia and half a dozen fresh newcomers from the latest *TUF* season.

The way MMA sports writing works a lot of the time is that a fighter (in this case me) will make an announcement (in this case my middleweight move) and the media will then call people who may be able to offer an interesting response to that announcement (in this case middleweight fighters who wanted to fight me). So, I was already well aware of my popularity among my new peers. For example, fan-favourite brawler Chris Leben went out of his way to inform the MMA media he fancied his chances. Alan Belcher, a ginger kickboxer from Mississippi who I knew mainly as the owner of the world's worst arm tattoo, was another vocal campaigner to welcome me to the division.

In the end, my middleweight debut was scheduled for 19 April 2008, at *UFC 83* in Montreal, Canada. My first middleweight opponent was to be 'Chainsaw' Charles McCarthy, a submission specialist from Florida who'd made his way to the UFC roster via the fourth season of *TUF*. McCarthy was dangerous on the ground – all ten of his pro wins were via submission – and my game-plan obviously included keeping the fight standing.

On the morning of the weigh-in in Montreal, I bumped into Eddie Bravo in the host hotel.

'How's your weight-cut?' the dark-haired BJJ icon and flat-earth aficionado asked in that distinctively raspy So-Cal accent of his.

'I've actually not cut anything,' I answered. 'I've done it all by dieting. I've got about a pound to get rid of now, and then I'm good.'

Bravo's eyebrows levitated as I explained that the last pound would vanish over the course of a brisk walk to get some post-weigh-in protein drinks from a GNC health store down the road. 'I'm wearing a rubber sweat suit under this hoodie and jogging bottoms, just to make sure,' I added.

'Wow,' Bravo said. 'That's it? If you cut weight you could make welterweight, bro. You're walking around at eighty-six? You could cut the fifteen down to one-seventy, no problem. I know guys who fight at welterweight and they walk around at ninety-five all the way to two-ten.'

As I paid for my protein shakes at that store up the road, I couldn't help but think I was still getting this aspect of the game wrong. I mean, I was no welterweight, I knew that for a fact. I'm 6ft 1in tall; if I went down to the 170lb division I'd be so skinny I'd be able to grate cheese with my ribs.

But ... Bravo knew his shit. He's been around wrestling, grappling and MMA for years. If American-based welterweights were cutting down from around 200lb, it obviously followed the middleweights were cutting down from 215lb or 220lb. In terms of making the most of my drop to middleweight, I was doing the equivalent of using first-aid kit bandages as handwraps.

The *UFC 83* weigh-in was memorable for two reasons.

First, the atmosphere in the Bell Centre in downtown Montreal was like being inside a lightning storm. The fans there had waited for years to finally get a UFC event in Canada and that pent-up excitement saw all 21,390 tickets sold out in minutes, breaking the UFC attendance record.

Adding to the anticipation was the main event. Georges St-Pierre – who grew up and still lived in Montreal – re-matched with brash Long Island champ Matt Serra for the UFC welterweight title. The fight had every ingredient a promoter could wish for: a hometown hero challenging for the belt against a cocky champion who delighted in playing the bad guy.

Serra had stopped GSP with strikes a year before, ripping the Canadian's belt away in what is to this day the biggest upset in UFC history. Now, as a people, Canadians are typically a laid-back, friendly bunch, but months of Serra's insults ('frog-eating Frenchies', 'red-wine drinkers') had them foaming at the mouth to see their fighter shut the American up.

Meanwhile, the polite and professional St-Pierre was cheered and high-fived everywhere he went.

Funny, I couldn't help but think. *I'm GSP when I fight in the UK and Matt Serra when I fight in America.*

The second reason this weigh-in sticks out in my memory is that I accepted a second fight before even weighing in for the one I was in town for.

Marshall was hovering around while I went through my pre-weigh-in medical checks. When I retook my seat on the Bell Centre riser, he and Joe Silva approached me.

'We need you on the London show,' Marshall said, referring to *UFC 85*, scheduled for seven weeks later. 'We did all this PR for Chuck Liddell, but he's out hurt. Every fight Joe lines up for the event falls apart due to injuries. It's like the event is cursed. You know how big that O_2 venue is – we could really use you to help fill it.'

UFC marketing had dubbed the *UFC 85* event as *Bedlam* without realising just how apt the name would be. The term bedlam comes from the nickname of London's infamous lunatic asylum and its centuries of urban legends which have literally inspired horror movies. Apparently, this 'Bedlam' had already driven the UFC's matchmaker insane.

'We could really use you on that card, Mike,' Marshall said again. 'Would you think about it?'

I gave them a puzzled look.

'There's not much to think about,' I answered. 'Of course I'll fight, assuming tomorrow goes well.'

And so, there and then, I agreed to a 7 June fight against popular brawler Chris Leben.

'You've got to come through tomorrow night okay,' Silva added, like he was trying to jinx me.

By the time I stepped through the curtains to weigh in, I'd managed to push London and Leben out of my thoughts. I was 100 per cent focused on the battle at hand. The noise from the crowd would have jarred me back to the present anyway – the weigh-in attendance was the largest I'd seen yet. It was like a huge heaving mass of faces and cheers. After I hit 185.5lb on the scale (most athletic commissions give a one-pound allowance for non-title fights), McCarthy and I faced off on the stage.

'I'm going to break your arm,' the BJJ fighter informed me over the cheers. 'You won't have the chance to tap! I'll break it!'

McCarthy had a high opinion of himself and the brown belt he'd just earned from the American Top Team gym in Florida. He didn't hold yours truly in such high regard, though. During fight week, he referred to me as a 'stepping stone'.

Chainsaw carried that confidence all the way into the first round, bless him. I disabused him of it right away, setting up right hands, hooks and knees to his face off of my jab. I felt razor-sharp and a lot of commentators remarked I looked physically imposing as a middleweight.

McCarthy scored a good takedown, though, halfway through the round; he snagged my arm as I was scrambling to my feet, and wrenched for the armbar with all he had. I remained calm and, after a couple of long moments, worked my limb free using a textbook armbar defence.

Back to the feet with a minute to go, I forced my opponent against the cage. McCarthy buried his chin into his chest and welded his forearms in front of his face. I laid siege to those defences, firing broadsides of uppercuts and hooks before using a Thai clinch technique I'd learned while in Ramkhamhaeng. My Thai coaches had me grabbing a heavy bag as if I had an opponent in a clinch, and then skipping knees into it for round after round after round. That's what I did to McCarthy, I drove over 20 knee strikes into him, smashing through his defences until they landed flush on his face. He dropped like a stone and I continued to throw at him while he lay on the ground.

The round ended but my opponent couldn't get to his feet. Sensibly, the referee waved the fight off before round two could happen. McCarthy had said he was going to break my arm – instead it was his ulna forearm bone that had been fractured by my knees.

My middleweight campaign was up and running.

'We've never seen Michael Bisping look as good as he did tonight,' Goldberg said on the broadcast of my middleweight debut.

'I'm looking forward to seeing Bisping compete in this division again,' Rogan added.

He wouldn't have to wait long.

There wasn't a whole lot of downtime between *UFC 83* and *UFC 85*. The UFC had a lot of tickets to sell in London and while there was an increasing number of British fighters joining the UFC roster – Birmingham kickboxer Paul Taylor, Liverpool submission specialist Terry Etim and, to his delight, a slimmed-down Paul Kelly – most of the heavy lifting in terms of PR was still on my shoulders.

But, apparently, the Bedlam curse wasn't done with the *UFC 85* event quite yet. The news soon came down that Leben had an issue getting a passport at short notice and he was pulled from the event. (Basically, Chris decided moving to a Hawaiian beach house was sufficient excuse not to bother with a court-mandated anti-drunk-driving class in Oregon; an Oregon judge disagreed.)

It was a shame; I'd been looking forward to the match. Leben was a big name and coming off two Fight of the Night and Knockout of the Night performances in his last five outings. Beating 'The Crippler' would mean something to the fans and from the excited tones they spoke about him, it would clearly mean something to Joe Silva and Dana, too. Plus, Leben had been talking some crap about me in interviews and I preferred it when opponents made it a little personal.

Instead, Jason Day would be facing me from across the Octagon in London. Day was a polite Canadian who went about his work as unassumingly and professionally as a trade union worker. He had beaten Alan Belcher at *UFC 83* in the first round.

'Fair play to Jason for accepting the fight on even shorter notice than I have,' I told the media on the conference call to announce the fight. 'I want to thank him and look forward to a good fight in London.'

The short training camp and change of opponent didn't bother me in the slightest. I was young and I loved what I did for a living. It wasn't that I felt invincible, but I'd earned a rock-solid confidence in myself and my ability to read and adapt to what my opponent was doing. But the build-up to the contest was far from routine.

Two weeks out from the fight, my manager called and said one of his business partners was going to be in my corner at *UFC 85*. I was about to say, 'Oh, that's nice to hear,' but of course he meant *literally* in my corner.

Apparently not content with his Octagonside seat, this business partner wanted to displace one of the three people officially allowed in my corner and get himself even closer to the action. At his own invitation, he would be backstage in my dressing room, walk out to the Octagon with me (which, I suspected, was the whole appeal), stand on the Octagon apron during my fight and even enter the Octagon between rounds and after the fight.

The advice a fighter receives in the 60-second breaks between rounds can be vital. Even mundane tasks like handing over water bottles and rinsing out a mouthpiece takes on mission-critical importance in the few spare seconds between a fighter sitting and rising back up from his stool.

'Yeah, sorry,' I told my manager, 'but he's not a trainer. He's not a fighter. He can't give me any advice on any facet of the sport if things aren't going my way. The answer is no, sorry.'

'I insist . . .' he said slowly.

'You don't get to insist on this.' I stood my ground. 'Sorry, it's my corner.'

'Who do you think you are?' he said, with an edge I'd not heard in his voice before.

I couldn't believe what I'd just heard.

'I'm pretty sure I'm the guy who'll be getting punched, kicked, kneed and elbowed in there.'

'He's going to be very upset . . .'

'Listen, I'm not trying to upset anyone,' I explained, trying to keep an even tone. 'But every fight is the biggest fight of my career at this point. He's got no business trying to force his way into my fight-night team.'

There was a silence.

Then: 'We'll have a fucking conversation about this after the fight,' and he ended the call.

That was the last I heard from my management/camp until fight day. Every other fighter in that Docklands hotel had a full team around them all week, helping them cut weight, liaising with the UFC over their promotional schedule and basically providing support.

My support consisted of Kazeka Muniz, my moody companion from the lonely Christmas of 2006, who'd been sent to float around and, no doubt, report back my every word and movement to Liverpool. And I had my friend from Clitheroe – Jacko – for company. For keeping sharp, I had the heavy bag in the hotel workout room and the pavement outside.

After making weight, Jacko and me went out for the post-weigh-in meal with Midlands fighter Paul Taylor and his team.

Finally, on fight day, and after I'd paid for his petrol, Tony appeared with an hour to go before I left for the O$_2$ Arena.

In a quiet word away from the others, Tony informed me the gym owners 'had been going ballistic all week' about my perceived snub. He wouldn't elaborate further.

Even though we'd both won in Montreal, I didn't meet Jason Day until we found ourselves in the UFC office at the same time on the Tuesday before our fight. I stood up from signing posters for the UFC and shook my opponent's hand.

Fucking hell! I thought. *He's considerably bigger than me.* What happened to dropping down to middleweight and fighting smaller guys?

That was the first time I realised that I'd still be fighting bigger guys, even at 185lb. It was kinda shocking.

The Jason Day fight itself couldn't have gone any better. The form that I showed day in, day out in the gym was – for one of the few times in my career – on full display in the Octagon.

The 15,327 British fans gave me a thunderous reception when I walked out. The support from them was unwavering and gave me an extra boost to put on what Joe Rogan told the viewers was my best UFC performance so far: a 3-minute, 42-second TKO via two well-placed takedowns and relentless ground and pound.

'Huge, huge performance by Michael Bisping,' Rogan said. 'Bisping was all over Jason Day, landing big punches early on, taking side control and dropping bombs, elbows and everything. Michael Bisping just overwhelmed Day. Out of all the performances in the UFC, that was his most impressive to date.'

In my post-fight interview with Joe in the Octagon, I began by thanking the British fans. 'The support I get from you guys – I could cry. I do not take it for granted. Every one of you – thank you from the bottom of my heart.

'Regarding my performance, I've said that I've not performed to the best of my ability in the UFC. I think I've started to do that. Yeah, I'm happy.'

'You've just served a big notice to the middleweight division,' said Joe, wrapping things up.

There were a lot of people on the dais at the *UFC 85* post-fight press conference. Besides me, Thiago Alves was there to talk about his main-event win over Matt Hughes, Hughes was there to take the loss like a man, Mick Swick was asked for words regarding his points win over fellow welterweight Marcus Davis, Thales Leites and Nate Marquardt argued about their split decision and UFC newcomer Kevin Burns was given time to talk the press through his Submission of the Night win.

With so many fighters fielding questions, there were long minutes while I was just sat there listening. So I took a sneaky look at my phone, which had been vibrating like a sex toy convention with incoming texts.

I wished I hadn't checked. I'd been sent a series of text messages from my manager. The texts were abusive. I sat there, in front of thirty reporters and five cameras which were live-streaming to hundreds of thousands of fans around the world, and stared at what was written on the screen.

Then I was asked a question by one of the reporters.

I turned the phone off and put it in my jacket pocket.

Ninety minutes later the coach, loaded to capacity with bruised and bloodied fighters and sports bags overstuffed with gloves and target pads, pulled up outside the Ibis hotel in the Docklands area of London. It was just before 1am, three hours after Alves's flying knee had brought *UFC 85* to an official close. The *UFC 85* host hotel bar was already five-deep.

It was time to jog upstairs for a quick shower and fresh clothes and then me and Rebecca – who I met up with backstage – were going to see about a drink and a bite to eat.

Paul Kelly was in the hotel lobby; when he saw me waiting for the elevator, he came over and confirmed that our mutual 'friends' from Liverpool were on the warpath. I told him about the texts I'd gotten while I was at the press conference. It was then that Paul clued me in about the type of people who we'd involved ourselves with.

When I got to my room, the landline was already ringing. Rebecca answered the phone and told me it was the business partner of the Liverpool gym. The same one I'd refused to allow work my corner.

I said hello.

'Can I speak to the superstar, please?' He repeated this three times in a ridiculously high-pitched voice before launching into a screaming rant.

I'd have loved to have ended my association with them and there. But that wasn't an option at that time.

So, while I couldn't bring myself to give the apology they demanded, I made peace by saying that, after thinking about it, maybe I'd not considered their request like I could have done and, fair enough, maybe I had a bad attitude about it. It was, probably, y'know, due to the stress of the fight. That kinda stuff.

Nothing was the same again, no matter how it appeared when cameras were rolling in the gym. Tony Quigley left the team for his own reasons around this time, leaving me feeling even more isolated. My mate Jacko was studying film production, and I hired him as my social media manager to keep me company as much as his skills as content creator.

CHAPTER ELEVEN

I'M GOING TO BE A CONTENDER

It was more of an emotional fear than something I thought was a genuine possibility, but I'd sometime worry that any career that had skyrocketed as quickly as mine could crash just as fast. In interviews I did at the time, I found myself bringing up how I used to wander from job to job and add comments like 'I've left all that behind me for now,' or 'I've shown my family a better life and it's up to me to make sure that continues.'

It always terrified me, the idea of going back to living pay cheque to pay cheque. To be constantly overdrawn, unable to buy the kids new clothes – the thought of finding myself back in that situation fuelled me in training. There wasn't anything in particular I was worried that could happen, it wasn't like I was dealing with a career-threatening injury (that would come later), or that I'd lost two fights in a row and feared getting cut from the UFC roster. It was the indistinct dread any decent family man feels when he finds himself with something to lose.

This fear helped push me in training all the way to having a resting heart rate of 36 beats a minute.

My next fight was scheduled for 18 October 2008. Having expressed sufficient contrition for not previously giving a fuck, Leben was cleared to leave the US and our fight was rebooked as the main event of *UFC 89*. Headlining a UFC card in the United States had been a huge feather in my cap – but topping the bill in my own country was very special.

The assignment at Birmingham's National Indoor Arena came with extra expectations, of course. As one half of the headline attraction, the box office of the event would be a reflection on me and my fight. I'd benefited from being on cards headlined by Rampage, Chuck Liddell and Tito Ortiz, and wanted to play it forward to fighters up and down the *UFC 89* card, including Paul Kelly and my old Nottingham training partner Dan Hardy, who was making his own UFC debut.

Plus, this was around the time the UFC had – finally – exhausted every macho-sounding subtitle in the English language: *UFC 42: Sudden Impact, UFC 48: Payback, UFC 55: Fury* etc. To be honest, for some of the historical UFC events, the marketing people seemed to have gone down to the local Blockbuster Video store and picked titles to copy at random. I mean, *UFC 19: Young Guns* was bad enough, but who the hell thought *UFC 26: Field of Dreams* was the one to go with?

And so *UFC 89* would be marketed as simply *Bisping vs Leben*. And of course, I wanted an event with my family's surname in the title to be a success.

'Tickets are going great, almost sold out,' Marshall assured me during one of the PR days the UFC arranged with me.

He felt horrible about it afterwards, but Marshall added to the pressure when he confirmed rumours the next season of *The Ultimate Fighter* could be based around a Team UK vs Team USA concept. Dan Henderson and Rich Franklin were under consideration as the American coaches, but I needed to beat Leben in order for the concept to make sense.

Coaching *TUF* was a huge opportunity for me. Being on the show as a contestant had changed my life. I really wanted to return in the mentor role; it would be months of great exposure on television on both sides of the Atlantic and a chance to help other British fighters get to the UFC.

The pressure to beat Leben increased again when the UFC advertised open auditions for British fighters – lightweights (155lb) and welterweights. Everyone on the forums and websites put two and two together: a British team would need a British coach. And so began the bombardment of questions regarding my involvement.

'I know about as much as you do,' I answered. 'I'd love to do it, if the UFC ask me, but I have Chris Leben to focus on right now.'

The other question I began to get over and over was, 'When are you going to fight for the title?' Many of the media people putting me on the spot were used to covering boxing, where one or two wins over American opposition was considered enough to get a shot at a belt. I had to explain to them, while trying not to sound like I didn't have confidence in myself, that, unlike in boxing, the UFC had only one middleweight championship, not four or five, and I still had work to do before I got my shot.

Speaking at the time, I said, 'One of the toughest parts of my career is other people's expectations. I already put a ton of pressure on myself – this is how I provide for my family, after all – but on top of that there's people pressuring me to call out the champion, Anderson Silva.

'I just want to earn the right to fight for the belt. I'm not here to make up the numbers, I'm here to become the champion of the world. Of course, I want to fight for the belt more than anything; I want to fight the best of the best. But I don't want to sound arrogant and call anyone out. I want it to be obvious I am next in line for the belt and whenever the UFC gives me the chance, I'll be ready to win that belt. So I'm not watching Anderson Silva that closely right now – all my attention has to be on Chris Leben.'

In fact, I was watching Anderson very closely. Live at 6am UK time or not, I never missed one of the Spider's fights live. The greatest fighter in the world was the champ of my division. He'd come from Cage Rage, like me, and we'd reached UFC level at the same time. I was doing well, but Anderson was doing phenomenally well, winning the world title in his second UFC fight and already having defended it four times. He wasn't just the best in the middleweight division, he was the best fighting in the sport, full stop.

With no real option, I compartmentalised the thuggish antics of my management and got on with my job of training for a UFC fight. Quigley had been replaced by respected boxing coach Mark Kinney, who I happily credit with helping me tighten my striking and footwork during the time I worked with him.

The Leben fight came soon enough. I spent the Monday of fight week doing PR in Manchester and Birmingham while Leben, who'd smartly flown from the US early to give his body every chance to shake any jetlag, did interviews in London.

We both checked into the host hotel on the Tuesday, where more media commitments awaited us as headliners. Kevin Iole, in Birmingham to cover another UFC for *Yahoo! Sports*, began his one-on-one interview with me with: 'Have you seen Chris Leben yet? He's shown up looking quite the physical specimen.'

When I did lay eyes on Leben, I knew what Iole meant. After hearing Leben talk about me having a speed advantage over him, I'd expected him to come in leaner, and with an expanded gas tank.

Instead, he'd shown up with the upper body of a rhinoceros. I got a real good look at him when we found ourselves riding the same tiny elevator in the hotel. The muscles along his neck, shoulders, biceps and chest had been built out so far his sponsored T-shirt creaked like the deck of a galleon.

Leben was a fan favourite for two reasons: his 'don't give a fuck' approach to life and his fighting style. Actually, those reasons were probably one and the same. He'd only been stopped once – by some bloke called Anderson Silva – and had since re-established himself with two Knockout of the Night performances. His intentions at *UFC 89* weren't exactly a secret.

'My style is a little loopy, a little wild, but – guess what? – that style knocked people out,' he said at the pre-fight press conference. 'I put guys to sleep. Bisping hasn't fought a striker of my calibre. There's no one out there I can't knock out and until the referee raises your hand – you're not done fighting me. When I take him into the deep water of the fight, he'll lose.'

Despite the swollen muscles under his tattooed skin, Leben's strength wasn't massively out of the ordinary, not to a guy who'd grappled with light heavies like Matt Hamill the year before. And while I gave Leben full respect and definitely felt his southpaw left hands and hooks when they landed, Rashad's power had given me more to worry about. (In fact, at *UFC 88* the month before, Rashad had blitzed Chuck Liddell – sparked the legendary 'Ice Man' out cold – to earn a UFC light heavyweight title shot that he'd also win via knockout.)

Leben fought a great fight, though. He started off by throwing a lot of leg kicks, trying to moderate my speed and footwork advantages, and marched forward throwing his short, thick arms like they were wooden baseball bats. I landed with right hands, jabs and hooks as Leben shelved his leg-kick strategy.

On commentary, Rogan accurately relayed my game-plan to the viewers around the world: 'Bisping is using Leben's own aggression against him. He's moving back and countering, relying on the fact that Leben is always going to come forward.'

My punches were straighter and faster, plus I had a five-inch reach advantage over the Crippler. The first round ended with me knocking the American back on his heels with power punches; he went back to his corner bleeding from his nose and eyes.

At the start of the second round, Leben seemed to have tired himself out a little throwing those kicks. His nostrils, flooded with blood, would be little help in getting oxygen to his lungs for the rest of the fight. He got a little breather as the ref called time out when he kicked me low, but after I'd recovered the pattern of the fight was established: Leben doggedly aggressive, swinging away with big punches to the face and kicks to my legs, and me timing his attacks and countering with punches and knees.

My strikes were slicing Leben's face up pretty badly. I was winning every minute of every round but he drew blood, too, after a right hook exploded my left earlobe. That would sting like crazy when the adrenaline of the fight wore off.

By the time he came out for the third, Leben's right eye was now almost completely closed. I made sure I touched gloves with him; this guy was a warrior and giving it his all.

In the third round, I landed 30 power strikes, more than double the amount Leben found a target for, despite his best efforts. The

Crippler knew he'd been beaten; he raised his hands in the air in the last few seconds to goad me into hitting him – and I responded by kicking him in the face. I'd closed the show with my most dominant round and had won all three comfortably. Two of the three judges agreed, awarding me the decision by scores of 30–27, while the third official gave Leben one round for a 29–28 scorecard.

Chris and I had a good chat in the cage and a lot of mutual respect was expressed. Callum came into the Octagon again. He was a lot bigger than he'd been at *UFC 70* and much more aware of the realities of what his dad did for a living.

'Chris is tough as hell,' I told Joe Rogan in the interview. 'I knew he could take a punch. The fight went down how I felt it would, I needed to use footwork. I was countering, landing shots and got the decision.'

Leben was magnanimous in defeat. He conceded I landed a lot more shots and said he was content enough with giving the fans an exciting fight. 'This right here is my favourite fight,' he said.

He was a likable bloke. I suspected we were similar people; two guys who got their sense of pride and self-respect from competing. He also had a sense of humour. When he'd stepped into that elevator with me we'd cracked up laughing ('Well, *this* is awkward!').

Then the news broke that Leben owed his new physique to stanozolol, an anabolic steroid banned in sports since the 1970s. I wasn't angry, exactly, because I'd won. If anything, it made my win even more impressive, but I couldn't help but feel disappointed. The fight had an asterisk now and Chris had been fined a third of his purse and lost his livelihood for nine months.

He at least admitted he took the stuff on purpose, though. That wouldn't be my last encounter with an artificially enhanced opponent and – unlike Leben – most didn't have the stones to admit they cheated.

The night of *UFC 89* was a lot more fun than after *UFC 85*. I had a bunch of mates who'd come down the M6 and we had a great night out. Referee Marc Goddard, who'd given me that grappling session in Birmingham years before, knew everyone in every club in Birmingham and was ensuring every fighter was having a good time. Dan Henderson, potentially my next opponent, was in town for the fight and was sat at a table next to us. We had a brief chat and my sister and a couple of mates took photos with him as we partied the night away.

The following day I caught the train to London. I was enjoying a hearty dinner while chatting away to a blue-rinsed old lady who'd found herself sitting opposite me in First Class. Rumour has it that I love talking, and I admit I'll hold a conversation with anyone given half the chance.

While I was chatting away to the old girl I began scratching my left ear ... and with a creeping sense of embarrassment I remembered that the previous night I'd had stitches in my left earlobe – and had just pulled them out in a squishy glob of jellied blood.

The old lady's dismay cannot be exaggerated.

'Sorry!' I told the grandmother, 'this isn't what it looks like. I'm not a thug or anything. I'm a UFC fighter.'

I may as well have told her I was a UFO pilot.

'A mixed martial artist ...' I tried.

Still no recognition.

'A professional fighter … an athlete … kinda like a boxer? You hear of it?'

She clearly hadn't.

'I'm a … cage fighter.'

'Oh,' she said, with palpable disappointment in what I was doing with my life.

If the UFC marketing machine hadn't quite reached the sexagenarian demographic Generation X and the millennials had heard the siren call of the fastest-growing sport in the world loud and clear. If I had any remaining doubts just how quickly MMA was growing in the UK, they were set to rest at the *TUF 9* open auditions on Monday, 20 October 2008.

Over 140 young hopefuls showed up to try out at Earl's Court. They walked through the doors full of confidence and dreams and nerves, just like I had three years earlier. Dana and Craig Piligian were there, like they were in 2005, but instead of Forrest Griffin I was now the guy in the room the young fighters wanted to emulate. It was a weird moment, stepping into the role of giving 'big brother' advice for the first time.

'Take this seriously, this is everything you've worked for,' I told the room when Dana asked me to say a few words. 'If you make it to Vegas, show up in shape – be ready to go on day one. In the season I won, a couple of guys showed up expecting to use the show to get in shape. Don't do that to yourselves – train your arses off and we'll have two more *TUF* champions from this part of the world.

'I was you three years ago, and *The Ultimate Fighter* changed my life in ways I couldn't even believe. Show us what you got. Make Dana pick you!'

This time round, the producers were looking for eight British fighters, not just two, and the interviews all took place on the same day. The auditions began at 10am, and the last fighter interview with Piligian took place after 7pm.

The rumoured coach of Team USA was either Dan Henderson or Rich Franklin, and when the pair were matched in the main event of *UFC 93* in Dublin, Ireland, it was obvious what Dana was planning.

'The winner of this fight will be the coach of Team USA,' Dana confirmed at a pre-fight press event in the Irish capital. 'Whoever wins will fly to Vegas next week and begin coaching against Team UK's captain Michael Bisping.'

I didn't have a preference who I wanted to win between Franklin and Henderson. They were both world-class fighters; Franklin was a former UFC middleweight champion who hadn't lost a fight to anyone not named Anderson Silva in six years and Henderson was a two-division champion from PRIDE who'd beaten everyone from Minotauro Nogueira to Renzo Gracie and Vitor Belfort to Wanderlei Silva. And of course, I'd been there when he gave Rampage a war for the light heavyweight belt at *UFC 75*.

Maybe Franklin would have been more fun to do *The Ultimate Fighter* with, though. You don't automatically think of ex-algebra teachers as wildly charismatic, but 'Ace' had a personality and, well, 'Hendo' never had a conversation he didn't want to cut short.

Whoever won the 17 January 2009 fight at the O_2 in Dublin would be the toughest opponent of my career, no question. In the end, Henderson won an exciting fight by split decision. He was now the guy I had to beat, the gatekeeper to my shot at the UFC world title. Filming had already begun for the ninth season of *TUF* and Henderson, myself and Team UK flew the Atlantic to join the already selected Team USA in Las Vegas.

My foot was in water.

Running fast over my toes. And down my shoulders and my neck.

My forehead was laying against something cold. I was standing up. There was a white noise crammed into my ears. I heard voices miles away.

I was standing in a shower, resting my head against a cool white wall. Probably to help with the headache I'd just noticed.

It felt like I was about to wake from a dream. But I didn't, so I knocked the shower off. The white noise melted away and the talking sounded closer. I turned around in the steam. I was in a small bathroom with a box shower in a corner.

I put a towel around myself. I was a little dizzy. I was carrying two headaches, one at the back of my skull and one dangling above my left ear. The white noise changed pitch into a long ringing. My jaw felt funny as well. I walked through the archway of a door and there was a larger, too much brighter room with six men in it. I knew them. There were bags crammed with stuff on the floor. One of the men gave me a friendly nod as the rest kept talking in muted voices.

My mate – Jacko – was sat on a bench nearest to me. There were people wearing ID cards going in and out of the room. Something had happened. I didn't know what.

Acting as normal as possible, I quietly gestured for Jacko to come closer.

'Hey – what's going on?' I whispered.

Jacko had a sympathetic look on his face. 'It's alright mate,' he said. 'Go get dried and we'll go.'

'Yeah, yeah, alright,' I said, and turned back into the bathroom. I dried myself and put some clothes on but then I went back to Jacko, confused all over again.

'Hey,' I whispered again. 'Where are we going? What's going on?'

'You've just fought.' He looked concerned. 'They are waiting to talk to you to check you out … you remember, yeah?'

'Oh yeah … course. Gimme a minute.'

I put the rest of my clothes on slowly, buying time. Not enough.

'Tell me again – what are we doing?' I asked Jacko.

'You've got to go the hospital, mate.'

'What are you saying?'

He turned to the rest of the guys in the room, attracting their attention.

'Do ya remember what happened, Mike?' asked one of them.

'Yeah, yeah,' I lied again. 'But … what are we all doing now?'

'You got knocked out,' he replied. 'You'll be okay but they are going to take you for a check-up.'

'Okay,' I said. 'Let me get my shoes on.'

Jacko followed me into the shower room. I began lacing up my shoes.

'What they on about?' I asked him. 'Knocked out? I'm not fighting for another two months. Why was I knocked out?'

'You just fought – you lost by knockout,' Jacko said. 'They are going to take you to get checked out as soon as you are dressed.'

What on earth were they all talking about? I was fighting in Las Vegas in two months' time. In July, at *UFC 100*. But I couldn't remember why I was in the shower, or in this room.

'Why have I had a fight?' I asked, almost angry. 'Did I take a short-notice fight or something? I'm fighting in July, why did I fight just now?'

'It's July now, mate,' I was told. 'We are at *UFC 100* now. You lost the fight to Dan Henderson.'

Not being able to recall a few hours is one thing, but losing two months? Crazy. Didn't make sense. I kept trying to remember what had happened earlier that day, or the day before or earlier in the week. It was like typing in a password that you know is correct, only to get an error message over and over no matter how slowly you pushed the keys.

Jacko could see I was struggling. 'Let's go, mate. They are taking you to get looked at in the hospital.'

It took the lot of them to convince me to climb into the ambulance. I'd learn later that this was the third time in twenty minutes that my team had pleaded with me to accept what my brain would never remember. They'd explained what had happened to me in the Octagon and before I'd gotten into the shower.

'You okay, Mikey?' Mark Kinney asked.

'Yeah, yeah,' I said, waving everyone's intense attention away as the ambulance door shut. 'Yeah, I'm fine. Don't worry.'

I doubt I sounded convincing.

The euphemism the UFC use for fighters getting taken away in an ambulance is 'transported'. On 11 July 2009, around 10:15pm Pacific Time, I was transported from the Mandalay Bay Events Center to Sunrise Hospital on South Maryland Parkway, Las Vegas.

Jacko was with me, and Frank Mir, who'd lost his claim to the UFC heavyweight title in a brutal beatdown from Brock Lesnar in the *UFC 100* main event, was my rideshare buddy.

While my face was unmarked – you'd never have guessed I'd been on the losing end of a fist-fight – Mir's jaw, cheeks and eyes were swollen purple and blacks. Yet the seventeen-and-a-half-stoner's sense of humour remained undamaged.

'So ... how's your evening going?' he asked as the ambulance pulled out of the Mandalay Bay back entrance.

Then the ambulance turned off the Strip and into the more residential parts of the city and something turned a corner inside my head, too.

'Awww ... mother-fucker!' I suddenly said.

'What's up?' Jacko asked.

'Well, y'know when I said I was alright? That I could remember the fight?'

'Yeah?'

'I was lying. I couldn't remember a thing. I was just saying that so you'd all stop asking me if I was okay. But now I can remember the whole fucking thing. Fuck!'

Coaching Team UK during season nine of *The Ultimate Fighter* had been a privilege. Fuelled by patriotic pride, we wiped the floor with Henderson's US team. Not only did Ross Pearson and Andre Winner from our team fight each other in the all-British lightweight finale (Ross won a great fight) but James Wilks won the welterweight finale. It felt great to see Team UK win both tournaments and have three of the four finalists; and it was very satisfying to help a group of fighters – British fighters – in the way Tito Ortiz, Saul Soliz and Dean Lister had helped me.

I was emotionally invested and that passion led me to get a bit carried away in front of the cameras. After one particular incident when I got a little too wound up, I approached Dana in the car park and asked if maybe some of my edgier moments could hit the cutting-room floor.

'Bisping,' the UFC boss said while getting into his sports car, 'if you don't want to look like a dick on TV, guess what? Don't act like a fucking dick on TV.'

Obviously, I got no favours, and I shouldn't have been surprised. While it was shown on Sky in the UK and elsewhere around the world, the reality show was produced for an American audience, and Americans love their British bad guys. Plus, Henderson's coma-like charisma left the producers with no choice but to fill running time with me doing almost all the talking. If they had given Dan equal screen time, audiences would have been as bored as a gang of midgets in a theme park.

For two sessions a day, six days a week, for six weeks, I was a very hands-on coach. But, unfortunately, I also enjoyed getting my hands on a pint and the best food Vegas had to offer. I'd spent a year and a half dieting to keep my body way south of my natural walking-around weight and, with a nine-month break between the Leben fight and *UFC 100*, I was glad to dodge chicken salads for a while.

Unfortunately, I let my weight creep up to a mortifying 239lb (16st 9lb). I shake my head to recall it, to be honest. One of my biggest regrets is that I didn't maintain the lifestyle of an athlete all year round during my career; I actually eat better and exercise more consistently now I'm a retired 40-something than I did during my UFC run. That's pretty ridiculous to think about, isn't it?

Don't get me wrong, once it was time for me to train, I could flip a switch. Once filming for *TUF 9* wrapped in early April, I got back on my diet, hit the road for five miles plus a day and attacked the gym like a psychopath. In other words, I went from enjoying myself too much to training too hard.

My training for *UFC 100* saw the team join a massive camp based in Big Bear, California, once again run by Juanito Ibarra. I'd been training like a madman for months when, on 2 June, the UFC publicly confirmed that whoever won the showdown between me and Henderson would be declared the official No.1 contender.

This was the big one. This was it. A chance to earn a UFC title shot and match my skills against my generation's Sugar Ray Robinson. It was everything I'd been working towards. The raised stakes made me train even harder. Whatever Henderson was doing – running, sparring, lifting, rolling – I needed to do twice as much!

You can only do as well as you know, and I didn't know any better in the summer of 2009. So I pushed myself over the border between working hard and overworking. With three weeks to go until I faced Henderson, my body was shipwrecked.

My knees, hips and back became so sore every training session had to begin with half an hour of slowly running in circles on the padded mats. I'd begin, with gritted teeth, at walking pace and slowly encourage warm blood to travel to pained joints that just wanted to be left alone for a few days. Then I'd push myself through a four-mile run, sparring, drilling and rolling all day. I was hammering at it so hard I was taxing my immune system; the little nicks and scrapes of everyday training loitered on my elbows, knees and lips. I remember one particularly painful cut in the tight skin on the top of my left foot that just wouldn't heal up.

In the years that followed, I'd come to understand that it takes confidence to take a day off when preparing for a fight. As the weeks and days counted down to *UFC 100*, I didn't have that confidence. That was my fault, too. I'd spent over half a year with Dan Henderson living next door to my thoughts. I'd watched his fights over and over, witnessing him beat up legends like Wanderlei Silva and Renzo Gracie and even UFC *heavyweight* champion Minotauro Nogueira.

The worst Henderson could do to me was played on a loop, over and over, when I should have been focused on what I was going to do to *him*.

When I checked into the site of *UFC 100*, the golden Mandalay Bay hotel, in early July I was over-trained, over-tired and over-anxious.

The sport came of age at *UFC 100* and I am gratified to have been part of that milestone event in the sport's history. The high-water mark of *UFC 66* was beaten and then some. There were hundreds of media in attendance from around the world, ESPN and other TV cameras were everywhere. The UFC put on a three-day fan expo which reportedly drew over 50,000 attendees each day.

The pay-per-view event itself was stacked beyond belief. The double main event was WWF wrestler turned UFC kingpin Brock Lesnar clashing with enemy Frank Mir for the UFC heavyweight title, and Georges St-Pierre's latest UFC welterweight title defence against top contender Thiago Alves. Japanese judo champion Yoshihiro Akiyama – the UFC's big new signing – made his much-anticipated UFC debut on the card, plus UFC Hall of Famer Mark Coleman continued his unlikely comeback and a massively exciting 22-year-old talent named Jon Jones was given 15 minutes in the spotlight.

I'd gotten used to even the biggest Las Vegas hotels becoming MMA mini-cities, but *UFC 100* transformed all of Vegas to a fight town. A huge crimson carpet had been laid in the exterior lobby of the Mandalay Bay Resort, emblazoned with the centennial numbers and 'UFC' and everywhere you looked – from the restaurants to taxi ranks to the lines in Starbucks – people were wearing MMA clothing and talking about the fights.

It was like being at Woodstock, if instead of music and free love Woodstock was about fighting and overpriced skull T-shirts. This was the sport's coming-of-age party and MMA took its place among the major sports in America.

And I couldn't wait for it to be over.

Two nights before *UFC 100*, I went to the Noodle Shop in the Mandalay Bay with Jacko. It was early in the evening so we were the only ones sat in the hotel's resident Chinese restaurant. I had a three-course meal. When I weighed myself in my room two hours later, I was only 187lb. I felt skinny.

My memory of the first Dan Henderson fight comes from watching it on tape years later. I can't give you any insight into what happened other than what you can see for yourself. We had a close first but in the second round I was knocked out.

Henderson's weapon of choice was a right-handed punch thrown in an arch, raising up before crashing down like an artillery shell. At 3 minutes 17 seconds of the second round he landed one directly to the left side of my jaw. I was out before my head bounced off the canvas.

I go back and forth on how I feel about the second shot Henderson chose to throw while I was laid out and defenceless. Either way, I'd been knocked out in the most devastating fashion. A decade-plus later, *Henderson KO 2 Bisping* remains one of the top three knockouts in the sport's history.

'I remember the whole thing now, Jacko,' I repeated in the ambulance on the way to hospital.

'Sorry, mate,' he said.

'We're all fucking sorry in this vehicle,' Mir added.

We all shared a laugh or two, gallows humour for two guys who'd already been to the gallows. The hospital ran their tests. I was fine. 'You're good to go,' they said.

And I did go ... out for a drink. I felt I had to. When I got back to my hotel room a dozen family and friends were waiting for me, they all cheered and clapped me as I walked in the room. I was hugged and had my shoulders slapped. These people had travelled to the other side of the world to support me and for some of them this was their one holiday of the year. Even though I wanted to crawl into bed and shut off the lights, I owed it to them to suck it up, put on a brave face and spend some time with them.

'Alright, let's go drown my sorrows!' I announced to cheers.

In hundreds of MMA, kickboxing, KSBO, BJJ and every other type of fight I'd been in, I'd hardly ever lost and had never once been defeated conclusively.

Even the impact of the Rashad loss had been cushioned. After all, I'd told myself, it was a split decision in a weight division I clearly wasn't best suited to. Plus, there were positives (my wrestling, the second round) and clear corrective action (moving to middleweight) to focus on and get busy doing.

The Henderson result was something else entirely. I hadn't just been beaten; I'd been KO'd at the biggest show in UFC history. There was no commuting this defeat; I'd trained harder and for longer than for any fight in my life and still didn't get the win. There were no positives to take away or easy answers to implement.

UFC 100 never ended. The image of Henderson, arched in mid-air, swinging the base of his fist downwards towards my unprotected chin, was everywhere. On T-shirts, banners, posters and every UFC broadcast. A plastic figurine (aka a toy for under-sexed grown-ups) was released of Henderson swooping down with that hammer fist.

The final seconds of the fight were omnipresent on every website, forum and embedded in every nasty tweet I was sent.

It felt like half the world was celebrating the worst moment of my life and so I hid behind self-deprecating humour.

'Who'd circle into his opponent's best punch?' I asked rhetorically in interviews.

I was smiling as I spoke, but inside I was *crushed*.

CHAPTER TWELVE

AIN'T GOING NOWHERE

Growing up, I felt like I was good at one thing – fighting. All the way to my early twenties, my sense of self and, really, self-worth was based on being a good fighter. Now it felt like half the world was insisting I wasn't a good fighter. The online abuse was insane. My entire career was getting torn apart. It bothered me more than I let on to anyone.

It's a lonely place to put yourself, hiding what you are really going through. I even kept Rebecca in the dark.

Right after *UFC 100*, Rebecca, the kids and me joined her parents in Malaysia for a long holiday. Kate and Graham had moved there earlier in the year and they were dying to show their grandkids their pool and nearby beaches. Lying around in the moist heat in the morning and playing in the cool saltwater of the South China Sea with my kids in the afternoon was exactly what I needed. I remember lying down on a towel on the sand, watching Callum and Ellie build sandcastles. *This is why I work so hard,* I thought; *this is what Rebecca and me get in return for me going away for weeks and even months on end.*

It was a great holiday. But *UFC 100* sat in my guts like a rusty beer can the whole time.

Early on the second Sunday morning we were in Malaysia, *UFC 101* was broadcasting live from Philadelphia, 13 time zones away.

The top attraction was Anderson Silva, in search of someone to give him competition, stepping temporarily up to light heavyweight to take on former 205lb champion Forrest Griffin.

We sat down as a family to watch in my in-laws' living room while eating a fruit breakfast. The kids were kept happy for a couple of hours with the promise of another day at the beach.

As everyone who was a UFC fan by 2009 knows, Anderson blew Forrest away. Despite Forrest's size, courage and world-championship-winning abilities, Silva knocked him down three times in a three-minute blitz.

My mother-in-law couldn't contain her astonishment.

'What's his secret?' Kate asked me. 'He's so good! Why is he so much better than everyone else?'

My comeback fight was scheduled for *UFC 105* in Manchester in November. I asked for Wanderlei Silva, the Brazilian whose five-year reign of terror as PRIDE FC champion had already made him a legend in the sport, but he was out for the rest of 2009. Instead, I was matched against another PRIDE stand-out, Denis Kang.

The 'Super Korean' had been the runner-up in PRIDE's 2006 Grand Prix, fighting in the finale despite tearing a bicep in the semi-final earlier than night. Kang was the kind of assignment every fighter faces without an abundance of enthusiasm: a dangerous opponent whose name isn't well known outside the hardcore fan base.

Kang was installed as the odds-on favourite to win the fight on 14 November, while I was listed by American sports books as a +175 (7/4) underdog. What that meant was the bookies gave Kang a 64 per cent chance of winning the fight and me a 36 per cent.

'I'm going to go out there and win big,' I told the fans and media at a ticket on-sale event at the Manchester Arena. 'I'm looking to finish in the first round, be very aggressive like I was early on in my career.'

My training for the fight began in late summer. I don't remember feeling any difference in returning to the gym after the Henderson result than any other first week back. My confidence wasn't shaken or anything, I wasn't gun-shy in sparring and there were no doubts or hesitations I needed to address.

Apparently the team around me felt differently. We had several established boxers in the gym with us for a week, and I took the opportunity to spar with them. In one session, one of the pugilists dropped me a couple of times. I could feel an anxiety tighten around the room. Heavy bags went unpunched for a few seconds and Zach Light, who was now coaching at the gym, put both his hands on the ring apron and trained his eyes on me.

Then I touched down a third time and Zach leapt into the boxing ring to wave the sparring off.

'No more today,' he said as he stepped in front of me.

My sparring partner looked at me for confirmation.

'Nah, I'm good to go,' I said, rolling my shoulders and getting back into stance.

'No!' Zach insisted. He stepped back in front of me. 'It's over. You are done for today.'

It was frustrating. I really was perfectly fine but everyone in the gym was sliding me glances. I can understand it. From the outside looking in it can't have looked good. Most of the people in the gym were there in the Mandalay Bay Arena dressing room when I literally couldn't remember where – or when – I was. Now I was getting dropped in sparring. I got it, Zach felt he needed to look after me.

One Sunday evening in August, I was in bed at home enjoying *Rocky III*. The kids had commandeered the TV downstairs. I love the Rocky movies; even the ones that are heavy on 80s excess have devastatingly accurate character beats for fighters.

I got to the part where Balboa was knocked out by Clubber Lang and had to hide his anguish from Mickey. Sly Stallone's character was beaten and heartbroken but still trying to pretend everything was okay. I teared up. Then I broke down. It had taken two and a half months for me to not choke these feelings back down.

That's when Rebecca came up to check on me.

'What's the matter?' she said, slipping through the door.

I had one hand pressed against my eyes, holding the tears inside, and waved for Rebecca to shut the door with the other. I didn't want the kids to hear.

'It's okay,' Rebecca said, holding me. 'I had no idea, I'm sorry.'

'I'm sorry,' I said. 'I didn't let on ...'

That was a big first step.

Slowly, piece by piece, I began to reconstruct myself.

Losing like I had sucked. Missing out on the title fight sucked. The abuse I was taking was awful and it sucked. It all sucked but ... I wasn't finished. I'd made some money by that point, enough to propel myself into a different career. If I truly thought that was as far as I was going in the UFC I would have walked away.

But I wasn't done. Fuck, no, I wasn't done by a long way. The naysayers were wrong. I was one of the best in the world. I would fight my way to the world title.

'You'll get there,' Rebecca said.

'We. *We'll* get there,' I reminded her. 'I wouldn't have even had one pro fight without you.'

We also decided to have another child.

A couple of weeks later I was on my way out the door to have a quiet drink with my friend Blenky when Rebecca shouted for me to come upstairs for a minute.

'I've news,' she said. 'We're pregnant.'

I was looking forward to at least a couple of months of trying every night but baby number three was already on the way. Michael 'The Count' Bisping, 67 per cent accuracy in the Octagon, 100 per cent accuracy in the bedroom! Ha!

We hugged and laughed and then I shouted Blenky, who was waiting for me in the kitchen.

'Blenky!' I yelled. 'Me and Becks are having another baby. This isn't a quiet drink any more, mate – you and me are going to go get shit-faced!'

There were factors that, while they had nothing directly to do with me running into Henderson's atomic right hand, had still contributed to the loss. I couldn't afford to ignore them any longer. My body had been a ruin in the weeks leading up to *UFC 100* and, while I would struggle not to over-train for the rest of my career, I now accepted that there was such a phenomenon.

The way I'd been making weight – dieting and running the pounds away weeks and weeks before the fight – was thrown out of the window, too. The Liverpool gym coaches had no experience with or inclination to learn how to properly cut weight, but after three years in the UFC I had dozens of contacts who did.

UFC 105 was the first time in my career I did my weight correctly. I reported to the UFC hotel HQ on the Monday weighing a stone (14lb) above my weigh-in weight. I loaded myself with gallons of water, literally flushing out toxins and sodium from my body, for three days. That dropped my weight by 4lb. In the 24 hours before the weigh-in I used salt-baths and a sauna to drag out every drop of moisture from my body. Then at 4:20pm on the Friday, in front of 4,000 fans at the weigh-in, I scaled 185lb exactly. By 10pm that night I was back up to 195lb and by fight time I was a little more than that.

It's important to realise that social media isn't real life; and that MMA bloggers' opinions only matter as much as you think they do. I got that message *deafeningly* loud and *crystal* clear from the 16,693 fans packing out the Manchester Arena.

The ear-splitting cheers those people gave me at *UFC 105* meant *everything* to me. They didn't hold back their emotions or hedge their bets until I had the fight won. They put their heart and souls on the line and declared – as loudly as their voice boxes could – that they were with me. All the way!

It wasn't just the decibels ringing in my ears or the rumble under my feet, it was the outstretched hands, the fists pumping in the air and the expressions on their faces. Not one of them had written me off. They still believed in me. The energy surge was intoxicating. I pointed down the TV camera tracking me to the Octagon and screamed at my critics: 'YOU HEAR THAT, YOU FUCKERS?!?'

On commentary, Joe Rogan mistook my gestures for anger – 'Man, Bisping is pumped up! Look at him! He looks psychotic!' – but it wasn't anger. It was determination. Weapons-grade determination. I would not let these people down.

The first round against Kang did not go to plan, though. He caught me with a right hand and I spent the next four minutes grappling to defend against his attacks. When the horn sounded to end the round I turned to all four sides of the arena and mouthed, 'I'm sorry, I'm sorry.' I'd promised them that I'd be aggressive and go all out for the first-round finish, and I'd spent most of the first round on my back.

Everything clicked together in the second round. I landed combinations, changed levels, took him down and unleashed an arsenal of punches, elbows and knees. Every success was cheered. I felt like myself once more. Kang got up briefly. I took him down again. I continued to hack away. Then I let him up and landed more strikes from a standing position until he fell.

Referee Dan Miragliotta waved it off at 4:24 of the second round.

The fans went mental and I was so overcome with emotion that I had to sit down on the canvas for a few seconds to compose myself.

'That answered every single question,' Rogan had to yell into his mic over the noise in the arena. 'Every single one of them. Bisping's back was against the wall, he took on a very tough guy, and – in my opinion – had the performance of his career. He was put in a bad position, he got dropped, he defended on the ground and when it was time to finish – he finished. He beat up Denis Kang and finished him.'

As Rogan took his headset off to walk up the stairs and interview me, Callum sprinted across the Octagon. I saw him coming and knelt down to hold him tight.

'I love you,' I told him.

'I love you!' he said.

Joe touched me on the arm to signal the start of the interview. The fans were still cheering.

'You've no idea how I felt after the last fight,' I said into the microphone. 'This is my life, I dedicate everything to this and it really hurts me when people don't give me the respect I think I deserve. I've never, ever, turned down an opponent in my life. I'll fight anyone. I want to go right to the top. I know I've got a long way to go. Bear with me. I'm trying, guys.'

After rebounding from *UFC 100*, something changed in me. I stopped worrying about my MMA career abruptly ending and me going back to my former directionless life. There were no more unforced and almost superstitious references to leaving my old life behind 'for now'.

Our family had moved just outside of Clitheroe to a newer, bigger house. We'd given my mum the place on Nelson Street. We weren't rich, but the debts were long gone, the house was paid for and there was money in the bank.

One midweek lunchtime I was slowly driving a brand-new silver Audi S5 through the narrow roads of Clitheroe town centre. I was going to pop into my dad's for a cup of tea. I passed the Key Street pub on the left and the car park where my life had once jumped the tracks and derailed on the right. The night of the arrest seemed ages ago, in a lifetime lived by a completely different guy.

That was the moment when I realised I'd come too far to ever be pulled back. I'd done it – I'd made something of myself.

'YES!'

I thumped my fist into the car roof and drove on.

The fight with Wanderlei Silva materialised as the co-main event of the promotion's first ever event in Australia. *UFC 110* was booked for the Acer Arena, Sydney, on Sunday, 21 February 2010. To keep the US pay-per-view slot of 7pm on Saturday night, *UFC 110* would start at breakfast, local time, and I'd be fighting in the early afternoon.

I flew out with Jacko two weeks before the fight. We stayed with Tama Te Huna, a former fighter turned gym owner whose younger brother James was making his UFC debut on the card. One of the best things about the MMA world is the sense of community. It's a crazy thing we do for a living, and there's often an immediate camaraderie between those of us who do.

The warm weather had a great effect on my body; old injuries didn't nag nearly as much and sweat flowed evenly from my pores. I felt I was getting healthier as well as stronger and fitter.

The first order of business was getting my body used to providing maximum output at the time I'd be fighting. To drag the hands of my body-clock to AEDT time, I would go for sprints in the surrounding woods and hills early in the morning. Then I'd eat a light breakfast and rest for a bit before heading to Tama's Elite gym for pad and bag work and light sparring.

The MMA scene in Australia was still developing, but the Elite gym was always packed. They weren't all pro-level in terms of skills, but they were in shape and the facilities they had access to were great. It was impossible not to consider moving down under permanently; Rebecca and the kids all had Aussie passports, after all.

While I was considering my future, there was a sucker punch from my past.

It was around this time that Paul Davies, who I'd not even had as much as an email from in five years, got back in touch. Ultimately, he would serve me with a lawsuit. Remember that document I'd signed just before he emigrated? Davis was claiming management fees for while I'd been in the UFC. I was shocked and hurt, to say the least. I'd looked up to this man my entire life. He'd offered me a path forward when my life had reached a complete dead end.

If he'd have made a phone call or sent me a message I'd have been happy to pick up the conversation exactly where we'd left off half a decade before, when we were sat at his kitchen table in Nottingham.

I put the legal letter out of my mind for the moment but, months later, I settled out of court with Paul for an amount I would have been happy to have given to him if he'd have gone about it any other way.

Naively, I thought a British guy who had kids with Australian passports and had a long-time partner who was an Aussie would be welcomed in Sydney as an adoptive son. I also thought the English vs Aussie sporting rivalry was just a bit of fun, and mainly confined to cricket.

Nope. The Aussies booed the hell out of me at the Acer Arena. Yeah, I was fighting a living legend in Wanderlei Silva, but the abuse they yelled made me wonder if *Mad Max 3* was a documentary.

'I HOPE HE FUCKING KILLS YOU!' screamed one bloke, his upper body locked rigid in fury.

'FUCK YOU, YOU POM!' another managed to say despite the white foam in his mouth.

'GIVE US BACK KYLIE, YOU ENGLISH PIG-DOG!' howled another.

(Alright, I may have made that last one up.)

As much as they booed me, they cheered for Wanderlei even more. They roared like mad when he landed anything on me – and sometimes even when he didn't – while my best work was met with glum indifference. That may have affected the judges' decision, who knows, because other than two big moments when he got me in a deep guillotine choke and a brief knockdown in the last few seconds of the fight, I felt like I controlled the action.

I'd been knocked back down the rankings with another decision loss. It was disappointing – losses always are – but it wasn't massively discouraging. I truly felt I'd won the fight and asked the UFC for another match-up soon.

The UFC came back with an assignment and a date – Dan Miller in Las Vegas, *UFC 114*, 29 May 2010 – faster than I expected. One the one hand, Rampage was fighting on the card (vs Rashad Evans in a much-anticipated grudge match) so I'd have him to train with in Liverpool, but on the other, my third child was due in the middle of May.

There was no way I was going to leave Rebecca and miss the birth of our child, so Rampage and the rest of the team departed for the US two weeks before the fight without me. Days went by with no sign of a contraction. When we got to within a week of when I would be fighting Miller, I turned to Rebecca and cheerfully said, 'No pressure or anything, but you've got to have this baby today.'

We googled a million old wives' tales as to how to trigger labour and our house smelled like an Indian restaurant with all the spicy food Rebecca ate. Then, on the Monday of fight week, the little guy who'd go on to troll his old man to the amusement of an international audience, finally signalled he was ready to make an appearance.

Rebecca took no pain medication and gave birth like it was something she did most Monday evenings. Our baby boy – who we'd eventually name Lucas – was super-healthy and we took him home early Tuesday morning. I woke up after a few hours' rest to the sizzle and smell of chicken sausages and eggs. Upon staggering downstairs, I found a steaming pot of coffee freshly brewed. Rebecca had gotten up with the baby and had made me breakfast.

'Your flight's in five hours,' she said as she sat down at the kitchen table with our newborn in her arms. As blown away by this woman as I routinely am, this was one of the occasions where I just looked at her in awe. I just shook my head.

'What's the matter?' she asked.

'Nothing,' I smiled. 'I'm just thinking it might be better for me to stay here and you go fight Miller on Saturday.'

On the night, I managed to get the job done. Miller was every bit as tough as his reputation and had a great engine, but I won a unanimous decision. That set up a fight with contender Yoshihiro Akiyama in a main event in the autumn.

UFC 120, 16 October 2010, was UK MMA's coming-out party. The UFC put on a two-day Expo at Earl's Court; over 30 UFC fighters and personalities did Q&As, seminars and autograph sessions for over 20,000 fans. The *UFC 120* card itself at the O_2 Arena was stacked with British talent and set a European attendance record of 17,133. Me and Dan Hardy, who was the co-main event attraction, did more media than either of us had ever done in the UK. The whole country, it seemed, was buzzing about its emergence as an MMA power.

Then the fights started.

The fight card was a disaster from a British standpoint. One by one the UK fighters were defeated. London heavyweight James McSweeney was knocked out in the opening fight and Curt

Warburton from the gym I trained at lost his UFC debut. Then *TUF 9* champ James Wilks was defeated.

There were three fights to go before I made my walk to the Octagon. My phone rang. The display read 'HOME' and I answered.

'Hi, I'm sorry, can you talk?' Rebecca's mum, Kate, asked.

'Yeah, of course. I'm not on for another three fights.'

'I know – we're watching the fights in the front room,' she said. 'Callum's really upset and worried. Can you have a word with him?'

'Yeah, put him on.'

The potential consequences of what Dad did for work had become more rooted in reality for Callum over the previous 12 months. He'd watch the fights but if I got hit or taken down, he'd bolt out of the room upset. When I fought in the US, he'd be unable to sleep until he was told – around 5am – that Dad was okay. And obviously, hiding the fact I was fighting on a particular date was impossible.

'Hello, Callum,' I said in my Dad voice, 'you alright? You're not nervous, are you?'

'Maybe a little bit,' he said quietly.

'Aww, there's no need to be. I'm not going to get hurt, am I? What do I always say, it doesn't matter if you win or lose, as long as you go out there and try your best. Isn't that right, Cal?'

'Yeah ...'

'Listen, I can't promise you that I'll win, Cal. I can't do that for you, mate, I'm sorry. But I can promise that I'm going to try my very best. Is that okay?'

'Yeah.'

'You go back and sit with Grandma and Gramps. I'm going to try my best, okay? Promise. And no matter if I win or lose, I'll give you a call right after the fight, okay?'

'Yeah! You home tomorrow?'

'Yeah, me and Mum will be home tomorrow afternoon.'

'Okay. Love you, Dad.'

'Love you too, Cal.'

Back in the Octagon, the night was going from bad to worse from a British perspective. Previously unbeaten wonderkid John Hathaway, coming off an impressive win over Diego Sanchez, was routed by Las Vegas welterweight Mike Pyle. Then came the co-main event, when the 17,133 fans, who'd been chanting 'Hardy! Hardy! Hardy!' so loudly I could hear it through the walls, were silenced when Dan was knocked cold in the first round by Carlos Condit.

Dan and I were sharing the same dressing room. We'd warmed up together on the thick red training mats. We'd tapped gloves just before he made his ring walk and I'd joined everyone else in clapping him out of the room. 'Let's go, Dan!' I shouted. He returned 20 minutes later with the same evacuated look in his eyes that, I knew, I'd had at *UFC 100*. My heart broke for him.

'I've been there, mate, it fucking sucks,' I said, trying to say something. 'I'm sorry, mate. You'll be back. Just listen to the people around you and go get yourself checked out.'

Dan nodded affirmatively but, given how I'd been after the Henderson KO, I wasn't at all sure he knew what was happening. Between the phone call with Cal and seeing Dan like that, I could have used a few minutes to gather my thoughts.

But Burt Watson was at the door:

'LET'S ROLL, BISPING! LET'S ROLL! WE ROOOOOLLING! YEAH!'

The noise was as overwhelming as ever from the UK fans, but this time felt a little different. This time, they needed something from me. After watching half the British roster getting beaten one after the other, they needed me to win.

Akiyama was coming off two Fight of the Night performances and hadn't come to London to mess about. Barely 11 seconds into the fight, he landed a thunderbolt of a right cross to my temple. There was a flash behind my eyes and a ringing inside my ears. It was the same shot he'd used to KO Denis Kang with. I retreated for a couple of seconds, checked my equilibrium was good, and then set about winning the fight.

I'd landed some meaty punches and a hurtful kick to his ribs when an errant fingernail raked my right eyeball. So much wet gushed out I kept patting away at it with my glove to check it wasn't bleeding. While I waited for the eye to clear up, I made adjustments in my stance and footwork to use the peripheral vision of my other eye.

We had a great striking battle. This was high-level MMA. Language barriers vanished in the Octagon. The way we exchanged nods of appreciation when the other executed a great combination, smiled at each other when a huge kick or spinning back fist missed by less than an inch and nodded apologies after inadvertent fouls told us all we needed to know about the other's character.

Akiyama surged forward at the end of the first round, I countered with a left that was blocked, and a right that I knew he would slip – directly into a left shin to the face. I needed to think two and even three steps ahead with Akiyama.

The man known to Japanese women as 'Sexyama' threw a left hook at the beginning of the second, but I knew he was really looking for that right again. I was landing more and more combinations, hitting the shorter man with uppercuts and setting the pace I wanted to keep the fight at. We continued to exchange punches and kicks. I don't know what the yen was worth against the British pound but on that night I gave Akiyama 2.25 strikes for every one he gave me.

The fight stats show that I threw 268 strikes – and all but one of them were power punches or kicks. I came close to finishing the show in the third, but I mistimed a leg kick and caught Akiyama in his cup. He rightly took time to recover from the low blow – but he also recovered some of his strength and my chance for a stoppage had come and gone.

After 15 minutes, the judges confirmed I'd won all three rounds. The British fans went home happy.

Akiyama-san came to my dressing room after the fight with his cornermen and his translator, a tiny Japanese man in his mid-seventies who could have been the inspiration for the Mr Miyagi character in *The Karate Kid*. Through his translator, Akiyama told me it had been an honour and pleasure fighting another martial artist.

'It was a pleasure,' I said, and I bowed.

Then I called Cal up. He already knew I'd won and, bless him, asked if Akiyama was okay.

At the post-fight press conference, I said I wanted to fight again quickly.

'I think I'm one or two more fights away from a title shot,' I told the press. 'I'm getting better and better each fight. I'm putting it together now I have this experience. Mr Akiyama gave me a great fight and I'd like a top-five opponent next.'

Three weeks after *UFC 120*, I was sitting on my couch at home watching TV when my manager called my mobile.

'Alright, Mike, the UFC have got ya an opponent for *UFC 127* in Australia like ya wanted,' he said.

I muted the TV and sat up. I was excited. Despite the boos, I'd loved fighting in Sydney at *UFC 110*. Rebecca and me were seriously thinking of relocating our family there. So when we'd heard the Octagon would be going back to the same Acer Arena in February 2011, I let the UFC know I wanted to be part of it.

'That's great,' I said. 'So, am I the main event for this one?'

'Co-main,' he said. 'I think they've got B.J. Penn to headline.'

Fair enough. My mate 'Baby Jay' was only two fights removed from his legendary run as UFC lightweight champion and the Hawaiian 'Prodigy' was a massive draw worldwide.

'Let's have it, then,' I said. 'Who am I fighting?'

My manager paused before answering, 'The UFC have got ya Jorge Rivera.'

'Got me? Jorge Rivera? As what? A sparring partner?'

'I know, Mike,' my manager continued. 'But that's all who's available. The guys above you in the rankings who aren't out injured are already booked for other shows. If you want to fight in Sydney – or any time before the spring – all the UFC have for you is Rivera.'

I sighed out a swear word. The New Jersey-based Puerto Rican was a 39-year-old undercard lifer winding up a 19–7 career. He was a good puncher with his right – he'd knocked out Kendall Grove with it recently – but he just wasn't the kind of name I was expecting for my 14th UFC opponent.

Even his name – pronounced 'Horr-Hey Rivera' – made me roll my eyes. It sounded like some sort of floating brothel.

'Alright, fuck it,' I said at last. 'Let's just get the win. I'll put on a great performance and make everyone take notice despite the opposition.'

I parked my car in the tiny, broken tarmacked car park across the road from the Liverpool gym just before 10am on 3 January 2011. The car boot opened and I grabbed the large blue bag which contained all my training gear. I slammed the boot shut. *UFC 127* was now eight weeks away.

It was bitter cold out. Not as cold as the record-breaking, ball-numbing December had been but frigid enough to make the grass between the car park and gym white and crunchy underfoot. Training bag swung over my shoulder, I hurried to the gym door which – as usual – was locked from the inside. All I could do was bang away at it with my fist, praying someone would answer before my ears froze off.

Eventually, Paul Kelly opened the door. As I stepped inside, I realised it was actually colder in the gym than it was outside with the frozen white grass. Paul saw the look on my face. 'Wait till you get on the fuckin' mats,' he said. 'It's like March of the fuckin' Penguins in 'ere.'

I'd recently begun training Muay Thai with a new coach – a master of the eight-limbed art named Daz Morris – several times a week and how I missed his centrally-heated Salford gym that morning.

Training at the Liverpool gym during the winter was like swimming in a freezing pool – you just had to commit to jumping in and getting your body temperature up. I pulled a T-shirt over my rash guard and joined my teammates doing shuttle runs from one side of the gym to the other. The whole squad bounced from wall to wall and you could see breath swirling out of our mouths and shooting out of our nostrils. In a few minutes, those of us working the hardest had sweat literally steaming off our skulls and necks.

With hindsight, I could have been a little burned out. I'd fought 4 times in 11 months already. Put another way: I'd spent 29 of the previous 48 weeks of my life doing exactly what I was about to do for the next 8 weeks.

But Rivera himself was about to provide all the motivation I needed.

A month out from *UFC 127*, Rivera's camp began putting out a series of YouTube videos designed to hype up the fight and annoy me. It was bizarre stuff; him and his team working their way through every British stereotype and jerking themselves through rehearsed dance routines and yelling penis jokes cribbed from *South Park*. The videos kept coming and continued to get more personal until there was a reference to my family. The following Monday, Callum, aged nine at the time, came home from school upset. The kids at school had been playing Rivera's videos.

Now I couldn't wait to fight him.

I made my way through Australian immigration on Sunday, 13 February. The fight was scheduled for the morning of Sunday 27th. We'd again arranged to acclimatise for a week at Tama Te Huna's Elite Fighter gym in the suburb of Penrith. For the second year in a row, the difference between spiky British winter and Sydney's summer climate took me by surprise.

Like at *UFC 110* the previous year, Tama's younger brother James was in action at the UFC event. Two other fighters from the Liverpool gym were also fighting at *UFC 127*, along with Ross Pearson from *TUF 9*. My mate Jacko was with me again, doing video blogs for my website and keeping my mood light. All in all, we had a huge English posse with us and Tama Te Huna graciously put us all up.

In the evenings, Dean Amasinger – a *TUF 9* alumnus who was now branching out into personal training and nutrition – would barbecue our meals as we all sat around a giant circular table under a low sun. Yep, I could really see myself living and training here.

When we all moved to the host hotel on the Sunday, the mood changed. At *UFC 110* we'd stayed at a Hilton in Darling Harbour, where the famous white opera house sits next to the water. This time we were closer to the middle of town at the Star City Resort, a modern hotel/casino doing a decent impersonation of mid-sized Las Vegas property.

I'd barely made it to the hotel lobby when several reporters ran up to me. They excitedly repeated quotes they'd gotten earlier from Rivera where he said if I were 'really a man' I would come find him there and then and not wait until we were in the Octagon.

That nonsense set the tone for Rivera's conduct all week. Every time we were within 100 metres of each other, Rivera or his tough-guy sidekick (a boxing coach turned wannabe UFC fighter) would sneer and shout at me like we were in rival street gangs. The wannabe was especially pathetic – the way he acted in public embarrassed everyone. I couldn't wait to put this fight behind me.

The only time I responded verbally was at the press conference, which took place at 2pm local time on Friday, 25 February, in a mini theatre area to the side of the casino floor.

Despite under-21s not being allowed in, there was still a fairly big crowd of fans present. *UFC 127*, after all, had sold out all 18,186 tickets ($3.5million worth) in just 22 minutes. And, bless 'em, several US- and UK-based journalists had once again persuaded their bean counters that a week in the Sydney sun was an absolute editorial necessity.

No doubt because of me and Rivera, the UFC kept opponents far apart. Red corner fighters – B.J. Penn and myself – were held in a dressing room behind stage left while Rivera and B.J.'s opponent Jon Fitch waited in a room behind stage right. Also joining us on the stage would be two Aussie fighters – Kyle Noke and George Sotiropoulos – who were fighting Dennis Siver and Chris Camozzi, respectively, on the 12-fight card.

While we were waiting, B.J. showed me an enormous swelling on the back of his head. He'd been bitten by some sort of spider on his first day in Australia and had a throbbing pink L-shaped pus-pocket to show for it. The doctors had told him it was fine and not to touch it, but he joked he was planning on bursting it with a knife before the weigh-in. 'This shit all squirts out? I'll make 170lb easy.'

Speaking of rancid pus, when the press conference began I tried to keep my emotions even but the few words I allowed myself to say were dipped in bile.

'I'm a professional fighter, not an idiot in a schoolyard,' I said. 'This is a press conference, by the way, Jorge. These people are journalists. This is what you do when you are on the main card – but after this fight you'll be back on the undercard, believe me.'

Rivera was mute with stage fright.

There were security guards at the ready for the photo-op face-off. Rivera was wearing a branded baseball cap which cast a shadow over his eyes but, stood barely two feet away, I detected a look of fear in them.

'I hope you're ready,' I told him, loud enough for only him and a clearly nervous Marshall to hear.

Rivera nodded slowly as the cameras flashed away. Marshall tapped me on the back and began to tell the pair of us to exit via opposite ends of the stage. But I wanted to give Rivera a clear message.

'Now you're gonna have to back that shit up!' I told him, loudly. It felt good not to choke my feelings back – so I said it again, even louder: 'Now you're gonna have to back that shit up!'

Rivera slunk away without a word.

The 5,000 fans at the weigh-in at the arena were into our fight, I'll give Rivera that. I hit just over 84 kilos (the 186lb maximum) and stepped off the scale. I quickly loaded my body with fluid and then stormed forward four steps to where Rivera was waiting.

Perhaps feeling he'd been punked the day before, the Puerto Rican threw his hands up and started cursing.

'Mother-fucker – bring it! Bring it! Mother-fucker!' he said.

'You're the mother-fucker, you prick,' I told him. 'You're fucking dead!'

Dana signalled us to break it off; I turned to the fans and gave them a cheeky smile.

Job done, I thought. *The next time I see that guy I'll be able to give him exactly what he's been asking for. I made it the whole week without lowering myself to Team Rivera's level. Well done, Mike!*

The fight was here. Referee Marc Goddard was giving me and Rivera final instructions in the Octagon.

'When I say stop, you stop,' he yelled over the crowd. 'Touch up and let's do this!'

Rivera and I didn't touch gloves. He backed away and I turned and stormed back to my corner. When I turned around a moment later the arena was going ballistic. I got into a fighting stance and let my body sway as the arena rumbled like an earthquake. Just 20 feet in front of me, Rivera stared from behind a high guard. His court jester was outside, hollering something.

It felt like I waited another eternity but, finally, Goddard started the fight.

Rivera had clearly been brainwashed by the pre-fight narrative that a) I was especially vulnerable to right crosses and b) that he possessed the best right cross in the history of the UFC.

He threw five right-handed haymakers in the opening minute, all of which I saw coming before he'd even balled up his fist. To settle things down, I shot for a takedown. It was completed with ease. Rivera confirmed my suspicions about his limitations as a grappler; all he knew to do on the ground was deploy a vicelike grip as a defence. I let him back up and clipped him with a left hook as he climbed to his feet.

'Is that all you've got, mother-fucker?' Rivera began his attempts to draw me into a brawl.

He went for three more lead right hands, all loaded with everything he had. All of 'em missed. I flicked a leg kick and a jab and took him down again. His only defence to my ground and pound was to grab hold like an aunt getting rescued by a fireman. Doing that would burn his shoulders and torch his speed of punch, I knew.

After changing the angles on him to give his arms a proper workout, I stood up in his guard and threw a big right hand to his jaw. Then a left and another right landed hard. Now I wanted him to again use up energy. I stepped back. As he began to rise I kneed him in the forehead. The realisation of what I'd done hit me before referee Goddard jumped between us.

Damn it!

The knee had been illegal. Under the rules, a fighter who had any part of his body other than his feet in contact with the canvas was considered a 'downed' opponent. Striking a downed opponent with a knee was prohibited.

The referee signalled he'd taken a point from me. Outside the Octagon, the wannabe was yelling obscenities. I flipped him the finger. Rivera took two of the five minutes he was allowed to recover, and the fight continued.

He went for broke. He threw a cross that came close and a couple of left hooks. He then pumped out several one-two combos and even turned southpaw. He stuffed one takedown attempt but I took him down on the second. He only had muscle on the ground; muscles that I could feel becoming swollen and weakened. I repeated the game-plan – ground and pound, make him get up, and pounce. I landed three very solid shots to the head which took a lot out of him. Again he went for a series of right crosses, but he was button-bashing now.

The round ended and Rivera and I exchanged words as we crossed paths back to our respective corners. He knew what I knew, though. After all his taunts and boasts, he'd realised far too late that, yes, I was an elite mixed martial artist.

My corner had seen exactly what I'd detected up close. 'More combinations,' they said. 'Don't let him catch his breath.'

Round two began – and Rivera finally landed the right hand he'd been looking for. A ringing sound erupted in my left ear and I needed to put my hand down on the canvas for a split second. Thinking I was hurt, Jorge charged after me, but I dodged his two right hands, tied him up and pressed him against the fence before extinguishing his ambitions with a knee to the body.

Even when I stepped back, Rivera seemed reluctant to follow me away from the fence. It took a second to realise it but, barely 40 seconds into the second round, he was hurt and out of ideas. Just to make sure, I stabbed him with an inside leg kick. Then I used a lead right cross and a jab. He was gasping for oxygen. I could see him pulling his lips back around his mouthpiece and dragging breath back.

This was it, I knew. I sat down on my shots. A left hook to the head buzzed him. A right cross staggered him. The end was near. I planted my feet like the roots of an oak and drove my gloves into Rivera. Then my knees. Then an uppercut. A hook. Another right cross.

After dropping to one knee, Rivera covered his face with his palms; and not like a professional fighter biding his time behind a defence. He was like someone's sister watching a horror film. He couldn't have seen the final three punches coming and was still covering his eyes in surrender as the referee waved it off.

'Go home, loser,' I told him.

The wannabe boxing coach leapt up on the apron of the Octagon. His face was contorted, his finger pointing like a gun and he was still screaming obscenities like he'd been all week. I'd fucking had it with this prick.

The euphoria of winning and the adrenaline of the fight overthrew my better judgement and I stormed towards the fence to get closer to him. He screamed some more at me, clearly threats and bullshit. I began to shout back at him, but there was no way he'd hear me. So I spat on the ground between us, the ultimate show of disrespect. Within moments my temper had evaporated and I regretted it.

Real contempt isn't often seen in sports. The pantomime put-downs of the press conferences are shrugged off as 'hyping a fight' but, confronted with a genuine dislike between two fighters, some sports writers pretended it was beyond the pale.

I had to talk about the fight over and over at the time, but one thing I want to make very clear now – I didn't intentionally knee Rivera illegally. I was winning every second of the fight. Why would I purposely hand him a point on the scorecards and give him up to five minutes' rest? No, I intended to knee him in the face – as hard as humanly possible – *legally*.

These were my actions in the heat of the moment. They followed me around for a long time afterwards. I regret how I acted after the fight, that's not how an athlete should conduct himself. But, I have to be honest, mostly I hate the fact I let those arseholes wind me up so much.

The Rivera fallout caricatured me as a 'brash British bad boy' in the United States, seemingly forever. The US media reacted like we'd reached the End Times or something, rather than one fighter letting himself down for a few moments. ESPN – who would hire me as an analyst a decade later – replayed my flying saliva more than any flying knee in the history of their UFC coverage.

'We'll have to see what the UFC wants to do with Michael Bisping now,' one hand-wringing broadcaster signed off.

The UFC knew exactly what to do with me. Same thing they'd done the last time I'd become a public enemy in the United States – they capitalised by having me coach *The Ultimate Fighter* again.

CHAPTER THIRTEEN

ANY TIME, ANY PLACE

If the theme of *TUF 9* was patriotism then the theme of *TUF 14* was aggravation.

The whole premise behind the UFC's casting of Jason 'Mayhem' Miller as the other coach, I knew damn well, was that Miller would annoy the hell out of me. The UFC newcomer had already caused a literal riot on live television during his run in the Strikeforce organisation. 'Let Miller wind Bisping up – it'll be great TV' – I knew that was the whole idea.

Now, I want to be a little careful with my words here, because since we did the show together and fought, it's become obvious that Jason Miller is not entirely well mental-health wise. He's been arrested half a dozen times for crazy things like smashing up a tattoo parlour, breaking into a church naked and picking fights with random police officers. There was an incident where he live-tweeted a day-long stand-off with armed police. By the time you read this it's possible Miller will have been sentenced to prison for a long time.

There's no way to avoid saying it, though. Mayhem Miller annoyed the hell out of me. He had all the charm of a burning dog-rescue shelter. He was just awful, and I so badly wanted to punch him in the face by the end of filming.

Coaching *TUF* for the second time was fun. I was a much more relaxed guy than I'd been just two and a half years before. Also, I was coaching a mixed group of Americans, Europeans and a Brazilian. I wanted my guys to win just as much as I had during *TUF 9* but, of course, I'd had a different kind of relationship with the British team.

I also had a completely different coaching staff with me. My relationship with the Liverpool gym had come to a head, again. I'd been owed sponsorship money from a supplement company who, according to everyone else they sponsored, paid on time every time. When my manager decided to base Rampage Jackson's entire camp for his challenge to UFC light heavyweight champ Jon Jones in the same sponsor's training facility, I pressed the issue.

'Have you gone and spoken to them yet?' I asked over the phone from Vegas.

'Not really,' was the predictable answer. 'I've just been so busy here with Rampage, when he's not training he's doing interviews so there's been no time for me to talk to them about your money.'

'Well, you're not training yourself, though,' I said, having no more of this bollocks. 'And you're not doing the interviews. Can you please go and speak to someone then?'

'You fuckin' what? What did you fucking just say?'

And there was that tone. The tone from *UFC 85*. I was so done with these people.

I called Dana and said that I would have a different coaching staff with me this time. I brought in Tiki Ghosn, a well-connected fighter I'd become mates with, his BJJ coach Brady Fink, who would in time become one of my best friends to this day, and 'Razor' Rob McCullough, the former WEC lightweight champion who was a similar size to the *TUF 14* contestants.

The top featherweight on my team was a teak-tough Brazilian named Diego Brandão. He buzzsawed through the competition and, in the finale, won the *TUF* trophy along with Fight and Submission of the Night bonuses. Also on my team was bantamweight T.J. Dillashaw, who I knew was a massive talent. He lost the finale match to John Dodson, but went on to be UFC champion.

With the filming done I flew home to England to be with my family. Like in a lot of families where one parent spends time away from home, the dynamic in the Bisping household is that when I get back from spending time away it is party-time for the kids. This time, though, instead of a family vacation Rebecca and I took a long weekend in Paris. It's important in any relationship to make time just for the two adults who started the family, y'know?

It was a warm September night in the French capital and I'd surprised Rebecca by taking her to Maxim's, arguably the most famous restaurant in the world. There are only a dozen tables served a night and I had to strongly economically encourage the concierge to get us a table at short notice. The place was amazing; everyone from Victorian Era royalty to famous poets and playwrights to today's celebrities have been there and I was really looking forward to spoiling Rebecca after being away from her for two months.

Located at No.3 Rue Royale, Maxim's has been open since 1893 and retains the over-the-top affluence of that age. It also works hard to echo the social culture of the era; my menu included prices while Rebecca's did not. It was like a scene from a romance novel sitting there among all the gold refinery, drinking wine with the woman I love. But I was distracted.

'You know what,' I suddenly announced to my partner, 'I'm not doing this any longer. I'm not having these people take the piss and disrespect me.'

She knew what I was on about. 'Your management?'

'Yeah,' I replied, and I told her about the latest phone call. 'I'm not going to put up with these people any more. The contract I signed – the one I never got a copy of – it's up now and I won't be signing another one.'

With that off my chest, me and Rebecca had an amazing experience at Maxim's. The waiters came around and performed tap-dances wearing turn-of-the-century clothing and hats, the old movie-blonde lighting made the oil paintings blend in the walls – it was like stepping back in time.

And then we came crashing back to the twenty-first century, when they gave us a bill that, if cashed in 1893, would have bought half the street.

When I got back to England a few days later I sat at my computer and typed out an email to the Liverpool gym. I was professional, polite and thanked them for everything they'd done over the years, but made it clear that I was moving on.

'Babe, let's just book the flights and go,' I said.

Rebecca looked up from the living-room couch where she was reading on her iPad. She knew exactly what I meant.

'Really, Michael? You sure this time? Because we've talked ages already …'

Yeah, I was sure. We were going to move to America. Australia had been on the cards for a while, but in the end I realised I would still need to go to the US to get the level of training and sparring I needed. I had a lot of friends and contacts in

California. Plus, Rebecca's parents had moved to the Far East, most of her friends had moved away, and I was gone for weeks on end throughout the year. She wanted to move somewhere warm. Plus, I was breaking into television work and had landed a few parts in action movies. Plus, we'd had a vacation in Orange County and the kids loved it there. Everything just lined up and pointed to making this move.

'We've got the works visa,' I reminded my partner. 'There's nothing stopping us. Let's not keep talking about it – we've talked about it for a year now. If we're not going, let's stop talking about it. Let's go – try it – and if we don't like it, guess what? Planes fly both ways over the Atlantic, and we'll come home.'

Rebecca began bashing away at her iPad and, there and then, booked a flight for five days later. Just like that, the Bispings were moving to Orange County, California. We packed up clothes and things we could carry and were in a rented house in no time. We left for the airport in a taxi, leaving the Mercedes E-Class in the drive.

We left it to my dad to send over our stuff from our old house in the UK.

'Right, Dad, I've gone through the house,' I'd told him. 'There are Post-it notes on every piece of furniture in the entire gaff. Follow the instructions on those Post-it notes carefully – some of the stuff, like the big table, we want to have in America. But most of it you can either sell or, if you can't, give or throw away.'

What did my old man do? He sent everything with a Post-it note on to us. Yep, even the stuff clearly marked 'THROW AWAY'.

My ex-manager continued to reach out, but now in a less aggressive manner. I agreed to meet him while I was in Las Vegas for a few days. The irony that he'd finally met up with me at the Palace Station, five Decembers after he was supposed to have for *UFC 66*, didn't escape me.

We sat down at the café and he was apologising before his arse hit the seat.

'I'm sorry, Mike, I was just so stressed with Rampage's camp,' he began. 'I'll never speak to yers like that again.'

He's a charming, charismatic guy, I'll give him that. Against my better judgement, I listened to what he said and agreed – on a trial basis and at a significantly reduced percentage – for him to represent me.

The fight with Miller was scheduled for the *TUF Finale* itself, 3 December 2011, at the Palms Casino in Las Vegas. The set up was similar to the last time I'd appeared on a TUF Finale, a decade ago.

Putting the fight on the Spike TV cable channel was a going-away present from the UFC, who had signed a new seven-year massive-dollar deal with Fox Sports beginning in 2012.

Remember what happened with my manager no-showing at *UFC 66*? Same thing with the Mayhem Miller fight.

'We'll be there the week before the fight ... week of the fight ... tomorrow ... no, tomorrow ... for the weigh-in ... for the fight,' and then a no-show.

Lawsuits were filed and court dates attended, but I never worked with those people again. The only negative was that my friendship with Rampage was over. They poured poison in his ear about me, and my mate – who'd been a great mentor and supporter to me since my second fight in the UFC – began to repeat their bullshit in interviews.

Years later, Rampage came to the same realisation I had about those people. We had a long text exchange one night where he acknowledged they'd bullshitted him about me. We didn't rekindle our friendship but the final texts between us were:

Me: So, we cool?
Rampage: You and me are cool.

You're supposed to walk to your corner upon entering the Octagon. I refused. I stood near the centre of the canvas, hands on hips, staring at Mayhem Miller until his eyes met mine.

'Two minutes,' I mouthed at him. Two minutes and I'd put my fists on him.

He tried to morph into his cartoon-character persona, but it was too intimidated to make an appearance. Miller had a good ground game but his punches were so weak, Italian soccer players would have hesitated before taking a dive from them. He took me down and held onto my legs for a while but once I got up I battered him from one side of the Octagon to the other. I finished him in the third round with an avalanche of 69 strikes.

Dana called the fight the most one-sided in UFC history. It might have been but on the night I was overly harsh on myself and told the media that, on that performance, I wasn't ready to challenge Anderson Silva quite yet.

Dana came to see me in my dressing room after the fight. He was wearing a silver suit and white shirt. He always wore suits at live events but it was always a little strange seeing the multi-millionaire promoter out of his jeans and T-shirt.

'Could you be ready to go again by January 28?' the UFC president asked.

'I could be ready to go again in twenty-eight minutes,' I said.

Dana laughed. 'We want you to fight Demian Maia on Big Fox.'

'Big Fox' was what Dana called the Fox television network. It was the US equivalent of fighting on BBC1 and meant I'd be fighting in front of one of the biggest audiences in the history of the sport.

'Sounds great,' I said. 'Email the contract directly to me.'

Eleven days before the fight, two days before I was scheduled to fly to Chicago where the event was taking place, I got a call from White.

He explained that Mark Muñoz, who was scheduled to collide with No.1 contender Chael Sonnen in the co-main event of *UFC on Fox 2*, was out of the Chicago event injured.

'What we want to do is pull you from the Maia fight,' the UFC boss explained. 'How would you feel about fighting Chael Sonnen in Chicago?'

Sonnen had given Anderson Silva the fight of his life the previous summer. The self-styled American Gangster had swept the first four rounds from the defending champion before making a massive mistake just minutes away from a historic victory. When Sonnen returned to defeat the dangerous puncher Brian Stann, a rematch seemed all but inevitable. The Muñoz fight had been seen by many fans and critics as unnecessary; Chael was clearly the No.1 contender.

'So,' I asked Dana, 'Chael Sonnen is the number one contender. If I beat Chael next week – what does that make me?'

Dana's answer was unambiguous. 'The winner of this fight goes on to fight Anderson Silva for the UFC middleweight title.'

That was all I needed to hear, but there was more. Dana and the UFC execs had mapped out two version of 2012 – one where Chael went on to fight Anderson again, and one where I earned the title shot.

The UFC brass told me that if I beat Chael and went on to fight Anderson, I'd challenge for the title in the UK. 'We're looking at maybe a soccer stadium in the summer,' White dangled.

Travelling doesn't feel glamourous when your alarm goes off at 3am and you know you'll find yourself in three airports before you sleep again but, no doubt about it, the chance to travel around the world is one of the best side-benefits to my career.

The fight, the co-main event, was to take place at the sold-out arena where the Chicago Bulls basketball team played. Chicago, Illinois, is one of the most amazing cities I've ever visited. There's a reason it's used as a backdrop for so many major movies and television shows. The sheer scale of the place, the heights of the buildings, how wide the streets are and, yes, how windy and cold it is in that city in January cannot be exaggerated.

The suite that I was put up in for the *UFC on Fox 2* event was beautiful. It was a 2,000-square-foot suite on the 34th floor of the Hard Rock Hotel, located in the famous Carbide and Carbon building. The whole place was incredible. I had my own bowling alley, my own pool table, several coffee tables with built-in video games and there was a guitar mounted over my bed that had been played by Joe Perry during a 1989 Aerosmith concert.

But it was the floor-to-ceiling window on one side of the suite that was the real jaw-dropper. I couldn't get enough of the view from 450ft above North Michigan Avenue. During the day, the only architecture visible above the cold fog was the last 15 or so storeys of the other skyscrapers sticking out of the swirling white below. At night the view was literally right out of the Christian Bale *Batman* movies. I was so blown away by it I ate my breakfasts that week sat in a chair by the window. I also called Rebecca back home in California and told her to take advantage of her parents' visit and join me for a few days.

Chael Sonnen was one of the biggest, if not the biggest, stars in the sport. In 2010 he had beaten Anderson Silva up – landing 320 strikes and taking the champion down at will – in a fight so one-sided it defied belief. Then, with only 100 seconds to go, Anderson caught Sonnen in a triangle choke and saved his title.

As if that performance wasn't enough, Chael had a wit and charisma all of his own. He maintained a persona of 'The American Gangster' all times. The joke – made all the funnier because everyone was in on it – was that Chael hailed from an affluent part of Oregon.

'Yeah, we had a maid,' he shrugged, completely in character, when asked how hard his upbringing could possibly have been, 'but she only came three times a week. What do you think happened on the other four days? I grew up witnessing things you couldn't even believe, jaywalking, littering, bad manners – you name it. You've never walked in my shoes. You've never seen what my eyes have seen.'

The ribbing stopped when he fought. And as a fighter, Chael could be as tenacious as a harbour shark. He threw in volume, not unlike me, and was similarly relentless in his attacks. While I had an advantage over him in striking, he was one of the best wrestlers in the sport.

'If I'm gonna be champion, I need to be able to beat these guys,' I said during a radio interview, conducted over the phone from my rock'n'roll penthouse three days before the fight. 'I'm not going to sit on the sidelines, twiddling my thumbs, hoping everyone beats each other and somehow I get a title shot almost by fluke. If I beat him, great, I go on and fight Anderson for the belt. If I don't beat Chael then I don't deserve the title shot. Simple as that.'

As was expected of us, Chael and me exchanged a few insults in the pre-fight press conference but there really wasn't any time for me to develop a dislike of the guy. Chael works hard to entertain whenever he has a microphone in front of him and in Chicago he carried a replica UFC belt around all week and deadpan insisted he was the legitimate champion.

For my part, I didn't need to work myself up into a feud to be motivated for this fight. The chance to finally earn No.1 contender status was all the incentive I needed.

As I expected, Sonnen shot across the canvas at me in the opening seconds of the fight. I landed a right cross, then he managed to take me down but I got up. All of that happened in the first 13 seconds of the fight and the pace barely slowed down from there.

Chael continued to skip forward, his gloves and elbows held in a very high guard. I landed a one-two combination which backed him off (he later informed me the combo badly rocked him – but his poker face was perfect). We grappled on the feet, our backs rolling against the fence. We were cheek to cheek, battling for control of each other's wrists and spiking each other with knees to the stomach.

The second round was the best of my night. I landed a lot of significant strikes at range and when we fell into clinch work against the fence, I continued to boss the fight. Rogan told the six million Americans watching live on Fox, 'Michael Bisping is imposing his game far more than Chael's been able to impose his. Chael's not been able to take Bisping down or hold him down.'

Chael took the third, taking me down and keeping me on the canvas for much of the round, working with punches and submission attempts.

'Chael Sonnen has to submit Bisping here to get that title shot and rematch against Anderson Silva,' was Rogan's opinion. 'He's winning this round but he didn't win the first two.'

I did what I could from the bottom – landing strikes of my own – but by the time I got up there was only seconds remaining. Still, I managed to take the All-American wrestler down and land three big elbows before the fight ended.

Before Bruce Buffer made the announcement, Chael and I shook hands.

'So,' he asked, 'what do you think?'

For the first time all week, I found myself speaking to Chael the bloke and not 'Chael P. Sonnen, American Gangster' the character.

'I think I got the first two,' I said.

With unanticipated honesty, Sonnen answered, 'Yeah, I think you did, too.'

But I hadn't. Not according to the only three people whose opinion counted. Two of the judges saw it 29–28 for Sonnen while the third, some cornflakes for brains named James Goodman, gave Chael every round.

There's always disappointment in losing a big fight, but here I'd lost a final eliminator for the UFC middleweight title that no one, including my opponent, felt I actually did lose. I focused on the positives; there was nothing else to do.

You are waiting for me to talk about Chael's history with performance-enhancing substances, aren't you? Or rather his history and *future* with them, because he'd been suspended for artificial testosterone usage before we fought and he'd be suspended for human growth hormone (HGH) and recombinant human erythropoietin (EPO) after he fought me.

Honestly? I wasn't bitter then – I'd accepted the fight because I thought I could beat him and become the No.1 contender. And I'm not bitter now. Yeah, I could muster the emotions if I really wanted to, but I actually really like Chael. He cheated, got caught and 'fessed up.

Chael went on to challenge Anderson Silva at *UFC 148* on 7 July. Round one of fight two saw the American dominate from start to finish but a single mistake sank Sonnen in the second.

Meanwhile, I was recovering from orthoscopic knee surgery. My left knee – which I first hurt back in 2006 – had begun to seize due to a torn meniscus and loose bodies in the joint. I was forced to sit out the summer but it meant I got extra time with the family as we settled in Orange County. Ellie and Callum soon became minor celebrities at their new school, learning what I'd already come to terms with – to an American ear even the most northern of accents sounds sophisticated. The kids – including young Lucas – loved their new house. That was no accident. Rebecca and I knew it would be an easier transition for them if their new house had a big pool.

Because of my experiences with the Liverpool lot, I was very reluctant to join one of the big MMA teams in the US. Especially as most of the gyms within driving distance of where I now lived had UFC middleweight – potential future opponents – already established there.

By this stage in my career – 27 pro fights and counting – I was a difficult guy to coach. I'd gone through years of trial and error to know exactly how to prepare for a fight and could recognise charlatan trainers a mile off. I needed a coach that I respected, someone who wasn't afraid to give me hard truths even though I was paying him.

That someone was Jason Parillo, who I called up for a session after he was recommended to me.

'You are left-handed,' he said after I'd pop-pop-popped maybe six combinations into his hands at the RVCA gym at Costa Mesa.

'Yeah,' I answered, and boomed the jab-jab-hook combo Jason had silently called for with the positioning of the target pads.

'Bring your feet with you a little more when you step in to throw the right hand,' he told me, and immediately I felt the difference.

'You have a lot of power on the left hook,' Jason added a minute later. 'I can help you put more on it.'

Jason Parillo is a former pro fighter himself and the son of a motivational speaker – he not only knew what he was talking about but also exactly how to say it.

Bringing Jason onboard as my coach was the best move I ever made. Even more important than the technical refinements Jason made to my game was what he did for me mentally.

A few months after we began working together we sat down on the ring apron sipping from our plastic Blender Bottles. Other than the creaks the tight new BJJ mat made under the feet of a solitary shadow boxer, the gym was pretty quiet.

'You're a natural fighter, Mike,' Jason said. 'By that I mean you've been fighting on natural talent, heart, your speed and all those years of experience. I'd say you are one of the top natural talents I've worked with.'

I thanked him and waited for the rest.

'You let your emotions control you and anger you,' he added. 'That's part of who you are as a fighter – and it has taken you all this way – but it won't take you much further.'

I nodded slowly. I'd thought this myself in my last few fights, but now one of the best coaches in the world was saying it out loud.

'If we can reprogramme you to control the fight with this [Jason tapped his head three times] you can become champion.'

My next fight – my seventeenth on the UFC – didn't come until 22 September 2012, at *UFC 152* in Toronto, Canada. I was matched against former US Marine Brian Stann, a powerfully built hard-hitter who'd won the Silver Star medal on active service in Iraq. The UFC was yet to introduce official rankings but most credible ratings had me at No.3 or 4 and Stann at No.6. A win over the WEC veteran, I believed, could well be enough to secure the title shot.

I actually suffered a neck injury while going for a takedown in the gym during the Stann camp but it would take several years before I realised just how much damage I'd done. I flew to Canada feeling very confident.

The PR build-up was great. Brian is another old opponent who I became friendly with after we fought, but it was obvious which buttons to press to rattle him during the final weeks before the fight. Brian had discovered his talent for MMA while serving in the US Marines and – rightly so – was very proud of his service. I knew that was a pressure point.

When Brian vowed to put me asleep, I fired back, 'Are you going to tell me some more boring war stories? Listen Captain Cliché, I was fighting in the UFC while you were peeling potatoes and getting called a maggot by your drill sergeant. There's no tanks, no bombs, no guns, no unit backing you up,' I continued, addressing the audience now. 'This is a sport, not war. It's an individual sport and on Saturday night I will individually kick his arse.'

Here's what I said just two days before the fight: 'Stann is one of the best fighters in the division, and I know he's going to look to knock my head off with every shot just like he did with Chris Leben and the others. He's also got some nice leg kicks which I expect he will try to use to slow me down, because I am clearly the faster fighter.'

Those words were prophetic. Brian had his moments in the opening round and his leg kicks were nasty, but my speed, variety and overall skillset saw me out-strike and out-grapple the 'All-American' hero over three rounds. I won 29–28 on all three scorecards.

At the post-fight press conference at the Canada Air Arena, Dana uttered these words: 'Bisping and Brian Stann was a great fight, me and Joe Silva were talking earlier tonight and I said that Bisping versus Silva is an interesting fight. Bisping always brings it, he always fights hard. We think Bisping and Anderson will be a great fight.'

When I was asked to respond to Dana's comments in a one-on-one interview afterwards, I said, 'In the three years since *UFC 100*, I'd won six fights, half of them via stoppage. My only losses in that time had been to Wanderlei Silva, who I thought I'd beaten, and Chael Sonnen, who everyone including Chael Sonnen thought I'd beaten. I feel I've more than earned a title shot by this point.'

Unfortunately, the title shot against Anderson never materialised.

Getting title fights, I was now sharply aware, depended on many factors I couldn't control. One of the most crucial – and obvious – is the availability of the champion. It didn't really matter that I was ready to fight for the title if Anderson wasn't ready to defend it; and the Brazilian didn't put his belt on the line until the following July against Chris Weidman.

The UFC was putting on more and more shows, sometimes running events in two different countries during the same weekend. Between me beating Stann and Anderson's next title fight, there were 24 UFC events.

Before long, Dana called me to offer a fight to headline one of them.

'Vitor Belfort,' the UFC president said, 'January 19 in Brazil.'

Even with the promise of a title shot if I won, this was the only time in my 29 UFC fights where I paused before accepting a fight.

With Dana on the phone, I weighed it up.

Like everyone else in the sport, I considered Belfort to be the most despicable performance-enhancing drugs (PEDs) cheat in the history of mixed martial arts. His physique was ridiculous; tubular veins stretched from slab after slab of square muscle and held in place by stretched skin. And it wasn't the lumbering bulk of a weight-lifter; Belfort's inhuman physical structure was packed with fast-twitching fibres which gave him menacing speed as well as strength.

Belfort had already been caught using anabolic steroids (by the Nevada Athletic Commission in 2006 vs Dan Henderson) and on another occasion walking around with almost double the normal levels of testosterone bouncing around his veins. There was no doubt in my mind I'd be facing a vastly more physically powerful opponent if I accepted the São Paulo fight.

And yet ... I also felt Vitor Belfort was mentally weak. Whatever the bullshit excuses they come up with, people like Belfort didn't take steroids because they were confident in their abilities, they took them because they weren't confident. Belfort had psychologically collapsed several times when faced by someone who fought back – he was terrified of Anderson Silva in 2011 – and I knew damn well I'd fight back.

That's who I was, wasn't it? I was the guy who never once said 'no' to a fight. I'd never ducked any opponent – and I never would.

'Yeah, I'll fight him, Dana,' I said.

The Brazilians I met out and about in São Paulo couldn't stand Belfort. Some of them didn't know much English but they knew enough to tell me how they felt about my opponent: 'Belfort – cheat!'

And not only a cheat, but one who used his sanctimonious Bible-thumping to excuse his cheating. When he was asked at the press conference to explain how it could be fair that he, a former PED abuser, got to now use Testosterone Replacement Therapy (TRT), Belfort had the gall to say, 'Like Jesus said, throw the first rock who never did anything wrong. I believe everyone in the world has done something wrong but that's not a reason to crucify them.'

When MMAJunkie.com reporter John Morgan pressed for a legitimate answer, Belfort asked for volunteers to beat John up. How Christian.

Belfort was insanely jacked at the weigh-in at the Ginásio do Ibirapuera arena the day before our fight. You could virtually hear his skin creaking against the bulging muscles and veins. He looked like the Incredible Hulk squeezing his penis.

My plan in the fight was to take over after the opening rounds. I felt good in the opening round, which was essentially the boxing match I'd anticipated. But in the second, I was stunned by a head kick to my right orbital socket. Belfort followed me to the ground and attacked with hammer fists and the referee stopped it. I thought the stoppage was early – I was fine – but it was what it was.

Twenty minutes after the fight, me and Belfort were lying down backstage on two gurneys about ten feet apart. The space we were in was curtained off and we were both getting cuts on our faces sewn. I always preferred getting stitched by the medical personnel at the arena rather than at a hospital when the adrenaline of the fight has worn off.

'Hey, brother, we both came out okay,' Belfort said. 'This is great; we are all happy and safe. God took care of us both.'

I made a joke about it being easy for Vitor to say that because he'd won the fight. The fight was over, y'know? We shook hands and went our separate ways. Before I left the arena, I checked my fresh stitches in a mirror.

The eye didn't look bad.

The flashes came later. The first thing I noticed was my fingers turning invisible in restaurants. The first time it happened I was reaching for my drink and my hand became a stump. I moved my hand a little closer to the centre of my vision and everything looked fine. *That's weird*, I thought, before carrying on eating and chatting away with Rebecca.

My professional record now stood at 23 wins and 5 losses. I didn't like the look of that '5'. I texted Dana White saying I wanted to fight again as quickly as possible. The match the UFC came back with was one that had been talked about, at least by my opponent, for over five years.

Alan Belcher had been vocally campaigning to fight me since I first moved down to middleweight.

'I'll have a fight with Alan Belcher on the way to the car back to the hotel,' I answered a fan question at the *UFC 152* press conference, 'but he should stop worrying about me and arrange a fight with whichever tattoo artist drew that abomination on his arm.'

Poor Alan's enormous tattoo of (allegedly) Johnny Cash, which covered the entirety of his upper left arm, was great for piss-taking. It's awful; the condensed forehead and elongated jaw makes it look like the result of a union between Roseanne Barr and Tim Sylvia. It was the worst ink job this side of that fat pervert in *The Girl with the Dragon Tattoo*.

Belcher had been on a good run while calling me out, beating Denis Kang (submission), Wilson Gouveia (TKO), Patrick Cote (submission) and Rousimar Palhares (TKO). He was coming off a loss, like me, so the fight made sense. The Arkansas striker did his best to talk up the fight but at the *UFC 159* weigh-in at Newark, New Jersey, I could see in his face that his confidence was wobbly.

'You are shitting your pants!' I told him. He confirmed my suspicion by shoving me in the chest.

Belcher had wanted to fight me for half a decade but, half a minute in, it was dawning on him that we were operating at two different levels. He was significantly slower than me. I felt like I had ages to get out of the way of his strikes. At one point I slipped a kick and actually said to him, 'What the fuck was that?'

We had a pure kickboxing battle. I landed triple the shots he did until, inadvertently, one of my fingers cut his eyelid and we went to the scorecards 29 seconds before the scheduled end of the final round. I won 30–27 on two cards and 29–28 on the other.

The next day I was getting a coffee from a Starbucks in the hotel and saw Belcher with his team waiting to be picked up to go to the airport. I went over to check if Alan's eye was okay and we spent about ten minutes chatting and laughing about the insults we'd thrown at each other over the years.

Despite being only 29 years old, that was the last time Alan Belcher competed in MMA. It was very nearly the final fight of my career, too.

'Oh, you're doing that crazy thing again,' my mate Damien said.

And I was. I was slowly moving my right hand side to side along the restaurant table, wiggling my fingers slowly as they disappeared into thin air. It was always in dark restaurants or watching the TV at home at night. Whenever my right hand was 45 degrees from my line of sight, I couldn't make out my fingers. They disappeared behind a grey curtain. Then I'd move my hand closer to my line of sight and my fingers would reappear. My eye didn't hurt at all, so I didn't go to see a doctor. I can be stupidly macho like that.

A few weeks after the Belcher fight I noticed my whole hand would now vanish if I moved it more than 40 degrees into my peripheral vision. The grey curtain had moved inwards. Then it was 30 degrees. Then 20. And then I was sitting at the kitchen table one night when I realised I couldn't see anything out of my right eye. Nothing at all.

I spun into a panic.

I googled the symptoms – hit after hit suggested one thing. I then googled 'best eye doctor' and telephoned the first one with a five-star rating.

'Hello, I think I may have a detached retina,' I said when they picked up. I explained I was a professional fighter who'd been kicked in the eye months before, and described my worsening symptoms.

I was put on hold for 40 seconds before the receptionist came back on the line. 'We were due to close in twenty minutes but I've spoken with the ophthalmologist and he wants to see you immediately. Do you have our address? And is there someone who can drive you here?'

Rebecca drove. When we got there I was laid down on a white examination table in a white room with a bright white light shining down. Drops were used to dilate my right eye and they swung some sort of viewing apparatus over my face which streamed images to a screen.

He wasn't looking for more than 30 seconds before he removed the apparatus from above my face. 'You do have a detached retina,' he said. 'Do you know what that is?'

'Just what I read on Google ...'

'The retina is what we call the thin layer of light-sensitive tissue at the back of the eye,' he explained. 'It is attached to a layer of blood vessels which provide the eye with oxygen and nutrients. If the retina is torn away from those blood vessels – in the case of your right eye now – not only is vision impaired but the eye is starved of that oxygen and those nutrients. I need to perform what is called a scleral buckling procedure, immediately.'

The surgery lasted an hour and it involved injecting oil into my eyeball to push the retina back against the blood vessels. The retina was then lasered back in place and, finally, a silicone sponge was positioned on the outside of my eyeball to help take the pressure off the tear while it healed.

Even though I'd left it for *months* before seeking medical treatment – and had even fought with the injury – the operation was a success. My eye definitely looked a little different with the oil inside it, but until the last couple of decades a detached retina was the absolute end of any sporting career, so I was happy that treatment was available.

I flew to London to film a movie called *Plastic* and then accepted a fight in Manchester vs Mark Muñoz on 26 October. Muñoz – who's now a real mate and our kids are friends – is a two-time All-American wrestler, so I supplemented what I was doing with Jason and Brady by working with MMA pioneer and catch wrestling legend Erik Paulson.

My camp was going so well, but looking back both Jason and Paulson commented that I was sparring far too hard. I wanted to send a message in the Muñoz fight, though, and kept pushing it hard. In late September I was driving the five miles from Erik's CSW Training Center in Fullerton to my house when a grey darkness skated from across my eyes as slowly and deliberately as electronic curtains in a posh hotel room.

It was a super-creepy experience. I knew exactly what had happened. My retina had detached again. I called the same ophthalmologist I'd seen just three months before and was scheduled for an operation the next day. I called Dana and informed him.

'Hey Dana, I've got some bad news but it will be okay. My retina has re-detached but I'm still going to be able to fight in Manchester because—'

'Wow, stop.'

'I'm having an operation tomorrow – I'll be in and out in an hour and—'

'Stop, stop.'

'… I reckon that if I rest for two or three weeks—'

'Mike! Stop!'

'… I'll be fully healed and I'll be able to fly to the UK and do the fight.'

'Stop! What are you talking about? Bro, you just told me your retina is detached. The fight is off.'

The UFC has always been great with anything to do with injuries. Dana had the UFC's medical adviser, Dr Jeffrey Davidson (known to everyone as 'Dr D'), liaise with my ophthalmologist as I prepared to go into surgery and I gave permission for Dr D and the UFC to be kept informed of my progress.

The day after the surgery I was in the passenger seat of our family car. Rebecca and I had dropped the kids off at school and had stopped off at a local Target (kinda like a giant Asda or Tesco) to pick a few things up for the house. I was dressed in a tracksuit and wearing a black eyepatch over the white bandages around my right eye. My phone rang.

'It's Dana,' I told Rebecca as she pulled out of the supermarket car park. I answered and said hello.

'I just got off the phone with your doctor,' Dana said. 'I'm so sorry, it's not good news. You're probably not going to fight again. Your doctor says there's too much scar tissue back there. He said you've been unlucky; the scar tissue has pushed the retina to detach again. In his opinion, he can't see how you get to fight again.'

CHAPTER FOURTEEN

EYE OF A NEEDLE

I pushed the news away from me. I wanted nothing to do with the idea that my fighting career was over. There was no way I was done fighting. No way.

But the nightmare had only just begun. The worst day of my life came a few weeks later. It began when I woke with a headache. Going for a walk with my dog Ditto and Lucas didn't help, it was getting progressively worse, and when we got back it was so bad I lay face down on the floor.

The pain just kept getting worse and worse. Over the course of an hour in the afternoon, I went from 'Agh, agh, this really hurts!' to screaming – *screaming* – in agony.

Rebecca called my ophthalmologist, but he was in surgery and so I went to the emergency care hospital at Garden Grove. There, I was diagnosed with a condition known as acute angle-closure glaucoma.

Basically, the eyeball is kept wet by the constant secretion of a clear protein-rich fluid that moisturises both the front of the eye and the chamber behind it. The chamber behind the eyeball is called the posterior cavity and the normal 'water pressure' (called IOP) in there is 9–20mmHg of pressure. Sometimes the drain in the posterior cavity becomes blocked, flooding the cavity and increasing the pressure on the eyeball.

Any IOP of 22 or over is considered high pressure. The worst case of acute glaucoma Garden Grove had ever seen was 60mmHg.

My eye pressure was 89mmHg.

'Think of a water balloon on a tap,' one of the doctors said. 'The water will keep filling the balloon until, eventually, the pressure will cause the balloon to burst. That's what's happening behind your eye.'

They treated it there and then with a laser – burning a tiny hole to let the fluid drain. They gave me pills for the symptoms and another set the size of Big Macs for the pain. Then they sent me home to rest. The pills knocked me groggy but didn't land a glove on the pain. When we got home, I lay face down on the living-room floor. I went to bed around 5pm. I shut the curtains because the light was painful. Rebecca checked on me every half-hour, growing more concerned that, despite the laser, despite the meds and the painkillers, I was still groaning with discomfort. Around 2am, I began screaming in white-hot agony at the top of my lungs.

The pain was now almost indescribable. I didn't know humans could suffer like that without passing out. It was like a rat was eating my eyeball from the inside out.

Rebecca dialled my ophthalmologist – who picked up but was about to go into an emergency surgery. He was extremely concerned that I was in such agony again. He instructed us to go to the nearest hospital immediately.

'They will be waiting for him,' he told Rebecca. 'Get him there right away.'

We threw some clothes on and Rebecca drove there as safely as she could with me screaming and howling behind her in the back seat. When we arrived the pain was so searing I'd have gladly shot myself in the head – anything to make it stop.

There was a doctor, a bald guy with a moustache, and a nurse in her thirties, waiting for me outside. My ophthalmologist had briefed them on the phone. I was awful to them, screaming and swearing as they tried to get me to answer a series of questions. 'DO SOMETHING!' I shouted, over and over.

'Michael,' the doctor said evenly, 'your IOP eye pressure is greatly elevated again. I can relieve the pain now but I need you to lay down on that bed and hold very still. Do you understand? Hold *very* still?'

'YES! WHATEVER IT IS, DO IT! NOW! JUST FUCKING DO IT!'

I locked my spine in a line, squeezed my fists as tight as I could and pressed the back of my skull into the bed I was lying on. The nurse stood behind me and braced my temples with her palms. My good eye darted anxiously about the room, trying to see what was coming. The doctor appeared above me with a needle. He moved fast. There was a stab of pain and – the relief was instant and overwhelming. I moaned ...

The doctor and nurse stepped back and told me to sit up. The pain had vanished like a childhood nightmare when the light's turned on. I spent 20 minutes apologising to both of them for the screaming and cursing.

The doctor then showed me a tiny rounded silicone device, maybe an inch in size. 'We need to insert this into your eye,' he said. 'It is an artificial drain and this will prevent the pressure from building again. Your eye isn't draining on its own.'

'Okay,' I said, now capable of a rational discussion once more. 'But I'm a professional fighter – can I fight with that in my eye?'

'Your only concern tonight is with your eye,' the doctor said. 'Patients lose their sight due to glaucoma and we don't want that happening.'

'No, I need to know,' I pressed. 'Fighting is how I take care of my family – it is how you are getting paid. I can't have a procedure done if it will end my career.'

The doctor relented. 'You can fight. I fitted this on a heavyweight boxer several years back and he resumed his boxing career afterwards.'

'Let's do it,' I said.

But the operation didn't go to plan. First, I came out of the general anaesthetic early, while the operation was still ongoing. I began convulsing uncontrollably until I was put back under. When I woke up again I was still in pain, pain that quickly boiled like a kettle until I was screaming again.

'Is it the same pain as when you came in tonight?' the doctor asked several times as I howled in agony.

'WORSE! MUCH WORSE!'

I was put under again. Adjustments were made to the positioning of the drain. After three procedures in one day, I went home exhausted, drugged-up and concerned about my future.

The eye injury not only torpedoed my MMA career but, I feared, would hurt my budding acting career. On top of that, I was fighting a ridiculous lawsuit brought by the Liverpool gym people back in England. It was a stressful period for me and one of the times my Rebecca and the kids rallied around me.

The doctor who'd performed the surgery had referred me to another doctor, who I saw every Tuesday at 11am for check-ups. It was an 80-minute drive there. It was an 80-minute drive back.

'We're going to keep you under close observation,' the new doctor said on my first visit. He was a middle-aged fella, balding on the temples and with the long physique of an enthusiastic amateur runner. 'Our main concern is around the scar-tissue area. We need to keep a close watch that it isn't pushing at your eye and tearing the retina once again.'

Asking for a timetable on returning to the Octagon was pointless at this stage, I knew that. I understood why sparring was out, too. So I asked him if there were any other exercises I should avoid while I ticked over waiting for my eye to heal.

Without looking up from his computer terminal he told me *any* physical exercise was out.

'Increasing your heartrate will cause an increase in blood pressure, and we need your blood pressure low if we are interested in this retina staying where it is.'

This became an impossibly boring, frustrating and worrying time in my life. Most days I'd come home from dropping the kids off at school and lie on the couch until it was time to go get them again. I spent a month watching *The Sopranos* all day, and at night I would drink more – much more – than I had since 2003.

Over the next few months, I grew to hate that doctor's office. I couldn't stand that I was the only patient under the age of 60, the waiting room was annoying, I loathed going through the conveyor belt of tests, getting the ink squirted into my eyeball, the light and air blasted into my iris and the waiting around to do the same binocular screen test. Most of all, I hated having the same conversation with the doctor at the end.

'There's no change, which suggests it is healing,' he'd say.

But I couldn't train.

'There's some improvement,' he'd say.

But I couldn't train.

'There are reasons to be optimistic,' he'd say.

But I couldn't train.

He wouldn't be drawn on any time frame for recovery.

'Your eyesight may never improve enough for you to resume your fighting,' he'd say, never realising what that meant to me. 'But it could also improve dramatically next week.'

The doctor thought he was dealing with a lunatic. 'A twice-detached retina is enough for anyone,' he said during one appointment.

'I can still fucking fight,' I told Rebecca walking back to the car many times. 'I am *going* to fight. I'm *going* to. I can fight with one eye if this one doesn't get better.'

To be granted a licence as a professional mixed martial artist by almost every major sanctioning body in the world, you must have uncorrected vision (without glasses or contacts, for obvious reasons) of 20/200 or better.

It's not a particularly high bar to hit, believe me: 20/200 vision means you need to be 20ft away from an object in order to see what 'normal-sighted' folks can see from 200ft away. It means you can't read newspaper headlines clearly. If you can't meet this standard even when wearing glasses or contacts, it means you are, in fact, legally blind. (There's also an argument that measuring how well fighters can see objects 20ft and more away is a stupid way of testing their eyesight for a fight.) But, week after week, my right eye failed to hit the 20/200 minimum.

The UFC brought me in as a guest fighter for the huge *UFC 168* event in Las Vegas, Christmas week 2013. I'd looked forward to it but when I got there and felt the excitement of a major UFC fight week, it was rough.

I'd been drinking way too much for months and the night before the fight in Vegas was no exception. It wasn't happy drinking, either, and it wasn't a happy hangover I brought to my ringside seat at the same MGM Grand Garden Arena where, seven years almost to the day, I'd won at *UFC 66*.

It didn't feel like the party was over. It was more troubling than that. The sport was getting bigger and bigger all the time. As I sat there watching Uriah Hall blast Chris Leben out in one round in what was the final fight of my old rival's career, and Ronda Rousey and Miesha Tate tear the house down in the second women's title fight in UFC history, it felt like the party was just beginning. But maybe I had to leave anyway.

While I'd been contemplating that someone sat in the row behind me had kept pushing my shoulder.

And again, and once more. I turned my head, just to let whoever was doing it know they were bothering me. Then it happened again, harder, and I heard laughing. I turned all the way around and saw it was Mark Coleman, a UFC heavyweight champion of the late 90s who few in the sport missed.

'You one-eyed bastard!' he laughed.

'Fuck you, pal,' I said.

There was more snickering, high-pitched like a child's, further to the right. Dan Henderson was sat two seats down from Coleman. He was giggling away, loving it.

'And you – fuck you, too!' I told him.

I got up and walked towards the exit to the backstage area. I needed to get out of there before I did something embarrassing in front of a lot of people.

On the way out I bumped into Dana, who was returning to his seat as the main card began. He asked me how I was doing or something. I stormed right past him and into the backstage area. Once I was away from the cameras and eyeline of the fans, tears raged from my eyes. I was angry and unsure what the future looked like.

Burt Watson spotted me. 'Come with me, Mike.' He put his arm around me and led me into a small dressing room which was going unused that night. Burt spent five minutes talking me off the ledge.

'You stay here as long as you need, baby, as long as you need to get your shit together,' he said in that almost musical voice of his. 'You do not want to go back out there like this – do not give those guys you are talking about the satisfaction of seeing you all emotional.'

I stayed in that tiny room for ages, listening to the noise of a full UFC house through the walls of the arena.

I felt better when I got off the pain medication. With a clearer head, some perspective returned. Instead of sitting in front of the TV (I'd finished *The Sopranos*, anyway), I'd drive to the park with Ditto and go for a long walk. Then I'd go home to my amazing family and our big house with its own swimming pool. Life could be a hell of a lot worse; I never lost sight of that.

My agent called with great news: I'd been cast in the major US TV show *Strike Back*. Things were going to be okay, no matter what happened with my eye.

The weekly eye-doctor appointments continued. Every week, Rebecca would drive me the 80 minutes there. We'd sit in the waiting room with the polished floor and black-and-white photographs of trees, the grey door would open and my name would be called to signal the battery of tests, the oil drops, air blast and the inevitable answer when I asked if I could train yet.

On one such soul-singeing visit in February 2014, I'd gone through all of that and was waiting in the doctor's office as usual. When the door opened, in walked an Asian man about 5ft 6in tall with salt-and-pepper hair. He had a real presence about him, and the kind of strong Californian accent that you hear in car commercials.

He shook my hand and introduced himself by his first name. I could read his credentials – there were a lot of them on the ID he was wearing on his lapel.

'Your doctor is away for a couple of weeks so I'll be looking after you today,' he said with a smile.

He was just the coolest fucking guy I've ever met. He was charismatic, funny, very intelligent – obviously, he was intelligent to be an eye doctor – but also worldly wise with it. He engaged with me, the person, not the injury. After taking a look at the day's test results, he swung a medical stool on its wheels and sat directly in front of me.

'Everything is looking fine,' he said. 'The repair looks good, no swelling, and vision has improved to 20/200.'

I asked him if that meant I could train again. Before he answered I started selling him on how important it was that I exercise.

He nodded away as I spoke. 'Yeah, sure, yeah.'

'Sorry, you mean I can work out?'

'Yeah, sure.'

'Any restrictions or—?'

'No, no, don't worry about that. Go do what you want to do.'

'Really? The other doctor said it wouldn't be safe ...'

'I can't imagine that cage fighting is safe,' he smiled. 'But you are at no increased risk than anyone else in your colourful profession.'

'Wait, wow.' I looked at Rebecca for a second – she was stunned, too. 'Are you saying I can *fight* again?'

'Yeah, sure. Call the UFC and book a fight.'

'Oh my God,' Rebecca said, knowing what this meant to me.

I struggled to take it in. It was like the world was re-ordering itself.

'So ... I'm at no extra risk of hurting my eye?'

The doctor used his feet to paddle his stool closer to me.

'Whether or not your retina will tear again, I can't say. No one can tell you that. What I can say is that your retina is fine today and your vision is sufficient to be licensed as a professional fighter in the state of California.'

Oh, fuck.

'Michael,' the doctor added, 'my father always said to me there are two types of people who live in the jungle. The first are the kind who go steadily when they're swinging through the trees; these people don't let go of one vine until they have a firm grip on the next. That's safe, that's very practical. But it may not get them to where they want to be in life before it is too late.

'Then there's the second type, the ones who swing as fast as they can go, letting go of one vine and stretching as hard as they can for the next. These people aren't as safe but they just might get to where they want to be in life. Something tells me that you are very much the second type of person in the jungle.'

'I am, Doc,' I said. 'That's exactly what I am like.'

'I know you are.' And he smiled again. 'Call the UFC. Tell them to book your next fight.'

The call was placed to UFC matchmaking that very day. The return call from Joe Silva came three days later.

My opponent was Tim Kennedy, a former US Army Special Forces sniper and 12-year MMA veteran who was coming into his own as a contender. He was coming off a first round KO of the in-form Rafael Natal. His only loss in three years was on points to Luke Rockhold for the Strikeforce organisation that had recently been absorbed into the UFC.

I knew him well. He was part of the same group that produced those juvenile videos with Jorge Rivera for *UFC 127*, and had a long-standing resentment of me.

The fight would be the main event – meaning a five-rounder – of a Wednesday night event in Quebec City in Canada. The event would be taking place on 16 April 2014, which gave me only seven full weeks of training after having little exercise for the best part of a year.

The first few weeks back in the gym were challenging, but I was just happy to be back doing what I loved to do. Kennedy had plenty to say to promote the fight. I'd missed every aspect of being a UFC fighter, including firing one-liners at opponents, so happily returned fire.

As great as it was being back, I absolutely hated the fight itself. Kennedy came with a game-plan of taking me down and holding me there, and that's what he managed to do for long stretches of the match. And it was a 'match' because, for me, it wasn't a UFC fight as much as it was a rough freestyle wrestling match.

Takedowns are supposed to lead to something offensive – like a submission attempt, an elbow strike, hammer fist – something. Only, Kennedy didn't go for any of those things and, having underestimated his wrestling ability, I needed him to do so to give me the space to escape and get back to my feet. At one point Kennedy was holding me down right in front of my corner and Jason and Brady were saying, 'Get up, Mike,' to which I could only answer, 'I'm fucking trying.'

Kennedy never hurt me, but it was incredibly frustrating. Before long boos were churning around the Colisée Pepsi arena. By the time he was announced a unanimous points winner I was disgusted with the fight, and myself for allowing him to do that to me.

This wasn't the return I'd wanted and I was happy to learn that my next fight would be against an opponent who wouldn't be looking to lay and pray.

That summer, Rebecca and I were married in front of family and friends in a beautiful ceremony not far from our home in California. We'd long since made a life-long commitment to each other, of course, but it was one of the proudest days of my life when we got around to the ceremony.

Bruce Buffer served as an unforgettable MC, introducing both me and my stunning bride as we walked into the reception.

Most marriages are a celebration of a life two people are going to build together; me and Rebecca's was a celebration of the life we were living.

'Hey, buddy, all your interviews done now?' I asked as I returned the fist bump offered by Cung Le, my next opponent.

'Yeah, now I'm ready to eat,' the former Strikeforce MMA and multiple-time world kickboxing champion answered.

We took our places around the circular glass table. It was a weekday in early June and we were in a private dining room at the Lung King Heen restaurant at the Four Seasons hotel in Hong Kong. The room, the restaurant and the hotel itself were all absolutely incredible, an award-winning kaleidoscope of Eastern style and Western money. There were some seriously wealthy people in there. I spotted at least three watches that would have set their owners back over $200,000 and women with diamonds on their fingers the size and shape of Quarter Pounders with Cheese.

Typically, UFC fighters who are scheduled to fight don't break bread together, but me and Le had gotten along great during our three-day trip to promote our 23 August main event. We were to headline a card due to take place 55 minutes across the South China Sea in a casino in Macau. And, y'know, you don't turn down a private room in a restaurant like Lung King Heen when someone else is paying.

Cung had a background right out of the martial arts movies he appeared in from time to time. Born just days before the fall of Saigon, when Communist North Vietnam captured the capital of South Vietnam, Cung had been smuggled out by his mother under heavy machine-gun fire. His family eventually settled in San José, California, where bullying led Cung to begin training in martial arts at the age of ten. He would become one of the best kickboxers in the world, and after dominating that sport, he moved to MMA in 2006. His flashy striking had beaten the likes of Frank Shamrock, Patrick Cote and, most recently, he'd slept former UFC middleweight champ Rich Franklin in the most devastating one-punch KO of 2012.

As we ate our ludicrously expensive – but also free – gourmet meal, Le and I traded stories about breaking into action movies and showed each other pictures of our families. Other than him name-dropping actor Channing Tatum several times more than anyone could be expected to feign a polite interest in, I enjoyed his company.

The next morning I flew home to get ready for a fight against a fellow martial artist, a fellow striker who I respected and actually quite liked.

A few weeks later Callum stuck his phone under my nose and showed me a UFC fan Q&A with Cung and Luke Rockhold that had taken place that day.

My eldest son had developed into a hardcore UFC fan. He watched not only every fight, but watched and read every piece of UFC content he could get his hands on. (He even visited the fan forums, which had me joking that he'd develop a very unfavourable opinion of his father if he believed what he read there.)

Callum pressed play and, wouldn't you know it? There was my Hong Kong dinner date, Cung Le, joining in a bit of Bisping bashing.

There was an adjustment period as I adapted to the diminished eyesight in my right eye.

Can you see your nose? No, you can't. It's always in your field of vision but your brain perceives it as a distraction; and so it filters the image out, and replaces that part of your vision with information from your opposite eye.

My brain perceived the less detailed information from my right eye as a distraction, and was filtering it out in favour of the 'better' data from my left eye. This threw my depth perception off a little and I found that my jab, for example, which had been a key weapon for me throughout my career, was now often half an inch or so off target. If you look at my punch stats pre- vs post-eye-injury, you can see that I went from landing dozens of jabs in each fight to barely a handful.

I'll figure it out, I told myself. *You did this before in the middle of the Akiyama fight.*

I'd begun training regularly with my old mate Kendall Grove. My fellow *TUF 3* winner had left the UFC three years before and was preparing for a fight in the Bellator organisation. Having him around was great, I'd managed to put a terrific team around me in California – and that included my new management team. I'd begun working with Paradigm Sports, an Irvine, California, agency founded by an Iraq-born former college athlete named Audie Attar. We'd started on a fight-by-fight deal (I wasn't going to sign anything long term after Liverpool) but Audie was doing a great job by me.

I made a lot of progress during the summer of 2014. I'd adapted my style and found a group of people who had my back. I got back on the plane to China determined to remind the whole MMA world what I was capable of.

'Are you sure that Cung Le isn't on TRT, Dad?' Callum asked via email.

I was sat on my bed in my suite back at the Four Seasons. During the time I'd been in the Far East ticking down to fight day, I'd seen headlines about my opponent looking 'ripped' and in 'insane' shape in an Instagram post, but until Callum emailed me the link I hadn't seen what the fuss was about.

A click later, I saw. There was Cung Le photographed from the waist up, wearing nothing but a gormless grin, looking for all the world like a condom stuffed with Lego bricks.

The recriminations from the MMA community were well under way. Some media and fans were wondering how on earth Le had gained so much lean muscle and trimmed all excess fat after the age of 40. Other weren't wondering at all – they were flat out stating their belief such a transformation had required the use of banned substances.

If Le had posted that same picture five years before, I believe, he'd have gotten exactly the feedback he was obviously looking for. 'Wow! Cung's in amazing shape for Bisping!' 'Holy cow! Le is shredded!'

Times had changed, though. Cheaters like Vitor Belfort had made everyone who followed the sport a reluctant expert on the effects of performance-enhancing drugs.

When Jason Parillo clocked Le in the hotel lobby four nights before the fight he walked straight up to him and said, 'You are looking very vascular, Cung. Trained hard for this?'

If my opponent's head coach had flat-out accused me of doping, I'd have told him to fuck right off. Cung didn't do that.

Here's what I said about the now-infamous picture when asked at the UFC press conference three days before the fight.

'It's funny how Cung's genetics have finally kicked in now he's forty-two,' I told reporter John Morgan. 'He's trained hard his entire life, but he's never had a physique like he's got now. Now, maybe he's just really applied himself like never before. I hope he has. I hope that's the case because if he pisses hot on Saturday night, that throws the whole fight into disrepute.'

Morgan, seemingly present at every MMA event in the world, asked his follow-up question: 'Does it give you pause, though? Given your track record with guys you fought on—'

'I would love to do a blood test Saturday night,' I answered quickly. 'A urine sample isn't enough for me. I would happily do a blood test and a urine sample.'

Morgan walked across the thick carpet of the function room and relayed my comments to Le. They say only a guilty man runs when no one chases, and Le's rambling three-and-a-half-minute answer did nothing to abate what had become a full-on PR nightmare for the previously well-respected fighter.

Here's just some of the explanations that came rambling out of his mouth: when the picture was taken, he'd just lost 'six-and-a-half pounds' in a 'hard-ass workout', the picture was taken in 'perfect light', he'd always been veiny (y'know, apart from the entirety of his MMA career, where he'd always been borderline soft), back in his younger days he used to 'eat fries with double cheeseburgers' – '*triple* cheeseburgers', even! – *before* his training sessions, but now, over two decades into his competitive martial arts career, he'd finally bothered to figure out a proper diet … he was now finally injury-free and able to train hard … etc., etc.

At no point in this barrage of bullshit did Cung Le deny taking performance enhancers.

It's just not in my nature – or any real fighter's nature – to pull out of a fight purely on the suspicion that an opponent is doping. Whatever it is in our brains that allows us to fight in cages for a living in the first place doesn't switch off when the word 'steroid' is mentioned. I thought I could beat Cung Le, on steroids, on HGH, on Captain America's Super Serum – whatever he liked.

That said, after losing a world-title shot to Dan Henderson (who'd since been outed as the OG of TRT in the sport), Wanderlei Silva (who the Nevada Athletic Commission wanted to ban for life for literally running away from a random drug test) and Chael Sonnen (since banned for two years for multiple failed tests) and almost losing an eye to Vitor Belfort (biggest cheating scumbag ever), I was done with tiptoeing away from this issue.

I found Dana White and said I wanted to be tested 'to the max' along with Cung Le.

'Not just a post-fight urine sample, Dana,' I said. 'Pre-fight and post-fight, blood and urine. You can literally test the piss out of me – I'm clean.'

I let the implication hang in the air for him to pick up.

'Good news for Michael Bisping,' Ariel Helwani reported on Fox Sport's *UFC Tonight* TV show in the US an hour later. 'I spoke with UFC president Dana White from Macau and he told me that Cung Le and Michael Bisping will be subjected to enhanced drug testing. Blood and urine testing after the fight.'

Whether or not Le was running on Super Unleaded or not, I put it out of my mind. This fight was about me, not him.

The words I recorded for the UFC's opening promo were:

I'm not finished. I ain't going nowhere. I still want to be the world champion. While there's still life in my body, that's what I will try and achieve. There's a lot at stake in this fight for me. My back is against the wall, I know that. I've got to prove I'm still the fighter that I've been proclaimed to be. I need to go out there and finish Cung Le.

My performance against Cung Le in Macau on 23 August 2014 was one of the best of my entire career. Although Le had been a collegiate wrestler, his MMA style was almost entirely strike-based; without having to split my focus on defending potential takedowns, I was able to use the full compass of my own striking ability.

From the moment the fight started, it was all about pressure. I went out there to absolutely destroy Le. He started off confidently, marching forward while throwing out some of the tricks he was famous for. He went for a spinning back fist, he landed a hard right hand to the body, he threw back fists. But I found my rhythm quickly and it was my spinning heel kick that landed halfway through the first round.

Le had broken Frank Shamrock's forearm clean through when the former UFC light heavyweight champion blocked one during their 2008 fight. They were powerful kicks and I fired combinations as soon as Le was in range to discourage them. Le landed the same right hook that knocked out Rich Franklin in his last fight, which got my attention, but I soon landed a hook of my own to underline that I'd won the first round.

I began to open up a lead in the second. I read Le's attacks like a book and began to walk him down, throwing and landing far more kicks than in my recent fights. A right cross raised a huge welt around Le's right eye and he began to look distressed. I hit him again in the eye, and the bruise was burst open. Then I cut him with a hook and right cross to the left eye. Then I ripped his bottom lip apart. From then on, Le fought covered, brow to beltline, in his own blood.

'Cung Le is a mess,' understated commentator Kenny Florian.

The referee called the doctor in to check Le could see. He could, but he was insisting – incorrectly, as confirmed by replays – that I'd poked him in the eyes.

Le continued to fire his heavy artillery. A spinning back fist into a roundhouse kick; a hook kick chased me back to range after I landed an uppercut. I landed another lead right cross to the face and Le's blood literally splattered on my forearm. I was two rounds up, dominating.

There was no poker face on Le in the third. His features were slippery with blood and, behind the red, black bruises were contorting his face even more. He couldn't hide the pain he was in – but he wasn't beaten yet. His corner had instructed him to fire the right hook and he did until one landed on my jaw. As I stepped back for a second, Le landed a spinning heel kick to my stomach.

I had to take in some deep breaths because that one really hurt. I returned fire with a shin to the ribs; Le answered that with one of his own. I closed the distance and dug a three-punch combination into Le.

We were putting on a true mixed martial arts contest in front of 7,022 smartly attired Asian fans at the Cotai Arena. China is in many ways the birthplace of martial arts and I was in a real-life *Bloodsport* or *Big Boss* movie.

I hurt the former Strikeforce middleweight champion with a right hook in the last 90 seconds of the third. His legs shuddered for the first time.

The fight was mine to lose going into the fourth. Le's face looked like the front cover of a horror movie Blu-Ray. I'd swept the first three rounds and could certainly have made the calculation to play the percentages all the way to a clear points decision. But I'd not flown all that way to win via the scorecards.

A left kick to the temple bounced off Le. Then a jab stabbed at his now entirely closed right eye. An uppercut rocked him back on his heels and I sensed my siege of Cung Le had entered its final stage. I'd pushed him back to his last line. He was cornered, desperate; out of ammo and ideas. The aggression had drained from his eyes. He was pushing out strikes as pleas to leave him alone and let him rest. Another left shin to the head signalled a sustained attack of 15 punches – all of them with vicious intentions – and then a knee to the jaw sent him careering backwards half-unconscious. Referee John Sharp called it off 57 seconds into the fourth.

It was 4 months since the boring 25 minutes with Tim Kennedy, 6 months since I was told I could fight again, 11 months since my first eye surgery and 20 months since my retina was torn vs

Belfort ... but I was back! I'd put on an exciting and dominant performance when I needed to the most. The Kennedy fight was an aberration, everyone could see that now, it was the result of rushing back after a long lay-off. The real Michael Bisping was back.

'This is what I'm capable of,' I told Kenny Florian in the post-fight interview. 'Believe me, I am capable of better. I want to be world champion – I have the tools to do it. But I've got to back it up – this was the start of backing it up.'

Knocking out Cung Le was my 15th win in the Octagon. No other fighter in the history of the UFC had won so much without getting a title shot.

There's no better platform a UFC fighter is afforded than those few moments after a big win, that's when you are able to craft your own narrative, when you can't be misquoted and you have everyone's full attention. I knew what I needed to do.

'There's an idiot called Luke Rockhold who can't stop talking about me – I think he's got the hots for me, to be honest – Rockhold called me out. You want it? Let's dance. I'll beat Luke Rockhold and then I'll take the title.'

I knew Le's pal Rockhold, the last man to hold the Strikeforce title, was in the front row. He'd been calling me out for a couple of years and, I knew, a fight with the UFC's answer to a Ken doll would land me right back in the top three.

My dad came to all but two of my professional fights. He couldn't make *UFC 66* or *UFC 127* – he was at every single one of the rest. It's one thing to tirelessly travel up and down the British motorways, and another to fly from England to North American a dozen times, to Australia and China twice and Brazil, especially when you're as tall as my father is.

My dad's best mate – Mick Warburton, aka 'Little Mick' – travelled with him to most of my fights.

The morning after I beat Cung Le, my dad, Little Mick and I were enjoying an awesome breakfast of eggs, turkey and apple sausage, toast, mushroom and tomato sauce (because that's what Englishmen eat for breakfast when they travel to China) in the hotel when we were interrupted.

'I'm going to beat the fuck out of you!'

There was Luke Rockhold.

'I'm going to destroy you. You want to fight me? I'll fucking retire you!' he raged, attracting whispers and worried looks from a restaurant full of the sort of people who wear dress shirts to breakfast.

'What are you doing, Luke, you idiot? I'm having a quiet coffee here with my dad and mate,' I explained. 'I don't fight in restaurants, and you shouldn't promote a fight when there's no one else around. Stop making an exhibition of yourself, you knob, and I'll see you soon enough.'

The match was set for 8 November 2014, at the same arena in the outskirts of Sydney, Australia, where I'd faced Wanderlei Silva and Jorge Rivera.

The genesis of the feud with Rockhold began two years earlier, when I appeared on a TV show called *MMA Uncensored Live* and was asked about the Strikeforce middleweights being absorbed into the UFC. Should Luke Rockhold, the Strikeforce champion, for example, be automatically installed as the next contender for the UFC belt?

Jason Parillo had brought Luke to the RVCA gym a few months earlier to spar and, put on the spot and looking to entertain, I said,

'Let me put it like this: I've sparred with Luke Rockhold recently and let's just say I'm the unofficial Strikeforce champion. Sorry, Luke!'

Now, me going on cable TV and bragging about kicking his arse probably wasn't the thank-you Luke was expecting when he did me a favour and came and sparred with me. But it was a joke, another joke in an interview that had been light-hearted and irreverent all the way through.

Rockhold took himself way too seriously to get over it. He dropped my name for the next two years and, finally, the fight happened at *UFC Fight Night: Rockhold vs Bisping*.

Almost every day – literally, not kidding, every single day – I'd have at least a few minutes spent worrying that my vision had dipped just 1 per cent below 20/200. The days leading up to an eye exam were almost unbearably anxious. My right eye had 20/200 vision on its best day; there was no margin for having tired eyes.

If I'd stayed up late watching the end of a movie, or if I had a bit of a head cold, or showed up on the day of the eye exam with a shiner – who knows?

As well as fretting about my eyesight declining on its own – I was now wearing glasses to watch TV at night – I fretted that some random doctor at a weigh-in would take one look at my right eye and consider his Hippocratic Oath demanded erring on the side of not sending a man with one good eye into a cage fight.

Worrying about an impromptu eye exam and having my licence to fight withdrawn – and potentially my whole career ended – became the opponent I faced every day in the gym and every second of fight week.

My anxiety in Sydney was through the roof. Just two days before I left for Australia – flying the 15 hours from LA and not the 23 hours from Manchester this time – I was cut on my good eye in sparring. I needed six stitches to close up the three-quarter-inch slice at the top of my eyelid.

'Mike, if you lose this fight, that's it, right? If you don't win this one then you'll never get another No.1 contender fight again, so it is fair to say your career is on the line here?'

'No,' I answered in a one-on-one interview after the press conference. 'I won't lose this fight but, even if I did, I am not going anywhere until I get my world title shot. Fair enough, if I lose to Luke, I will drop down the rankings again, but I'll dust myself off and try again.'

Tall with dark features, Luke Rockhold had been blessed with the good looks of a supermodel and half the brain power. He was also enormous for a middleweight, had a powerful kick and punch and was very good at submissions. He was the best opponent I'd faced in a long time and the sports books had me as a 2/1 underdog.

I arrived at the arena, now called the Allphones not the Acer, and was ambushed by two frantic UFC staff. 'The commission doctor needs to see you immediately,' they said.

Oh, shit. 'Why?'

'Because of your eye.'

Shit, this is it. The moment I've been dreading.

In fact, the Aussie doctor needed to take my stitches out. I don't know why I thought it would be okay to fight with medical sutures, but at least I got the benefit of them right up until a couple hours before the fight.

It wasn't long enough. Barely 90 seconds into the fight Rockhold ducked down and his head collided with my face, re-tearing the sore flesh above my right eye. Referee Herb Dean saw the head clash and brought in the same doctor who'd removed my stitches earlier to check the cut out. The fight resumed, but I knew I was in trouble.

Blood was running directly into my left eye. Every time I blinked it was like using car windscreen wipers on mud. I tried using my fingers and gloves to clear my eyes, but nothing restored the vision in my good eye.

If you watch the fight back, it is obvious I couldn't really see. I'm trying to con Rockhold into staying away – firing kicks and punches into his general direction. It was like a video game: if I managed to blink 10 or 12 times I'd get a few moments of sight and be able to throw a one-two or block one of Luke's nasty kicks effectively. Then a red curtain would roll down the world and I'd be back to seeing lights and shapes again.

My corner did what they could between the first and second round but the whole thing was doomed. A minute into the fight resuming, Rockhold landed a whip kick to the left side of my face I barely saw coming and then he brought up a baseball bat of a left shin to the right side of my head that I didn't see at all. He landed a big right on the ground and pound. As I scrambled to get up, he clinched in a guillotine choke to win the fight.

Other than congratulate Rockhold and affirm the obvious – yes, the cut did affect me – I couldn't say too much more. I needed to avoid any talk of why blood in one eye changed the complexion of the fight before it'd even begun.

I had to. Because, just like I told that reporter earlier in the week, I had every intention of dusting myself off and trying again.

CHAPTER FIFTEEN
SILVA BULLET

When people say Anderson 'The Spider' Silva is the greatest pound-for-pound fighter in the history of the UFC, they are just reading a label that's been attached to the Brazilian since 2006. The term 'P4P' and even his statistics – record longest title reign in UFC history (2,457 days), record longest winning streak in UFC history (16), record number of knockdowns in UFC history (17) and on and on – don't really describe how good a fighter he was.

At his best – and his best could be summoned at a moment's notice – he was as good in our sport as Pelé or Ali were in theirs.

In speed, power, timing, the ability to take a punch, Silva was more than an equal for anybody in the middleweight division; but it was in the less obvious attributes that Anderson held all the X-factors. He had the timing of an orchestra conductor, sat-nav-like precision and uncanny spatial awareness in avoiding attacks. And in terms of imagination – using techniques on the biggest stage that most fighters would be apprehensive to attempt behind closed gym doors – there was no one like him.

Only those of us who've swapped talent and bad intentions with him can really explain how outstanding a prizefighter Silva really was. And we don't do it with words. Rich Franklin's misshapen nose, Chael Sonnen's crushed ego, Forrest Griffin's shattered pride and the zagged scar on the bridge of my nose tell you the story.

The first time I became aware of this slender, almost skinny, Brazilian who preferred to strike was during his four-fight run in Cage Rage. My Cage Rage debut came at *Cage Rage 7*, while Anderson's came at *Cage Rage 8*. Two years later we graduated to the UFC on two different Las Vegas cards during the same week; while I won the *TUF 3* tournament, Silva annihilated Chris Leben in 49 seconds.

Just 16 weeks later Silva was back in Las Vegas for the *UFC 64* pay-per-view, in a challenge to superstar middleweight champion Rich Franklin. 'Ace' Franklin was a former maths teacher at Oak Hills High School in Cincinnati but Silva gave him a lesson in trigonometry, finding the angles for shot after shot before subtracting Franklin's world title from him in 2 minutes and 59 seconds.

Silva was just getting warmed up. Over the next seven years, the Spider defended the middleweight title ten times, a record likely to stand for decades. He dismissed a generation's worth of contenders, often with the bored superiority of a big brother handing out Xbox schoolings.

During those seven years as champion Silva had no one to overtake on top of the pound-for-pound rankings other than previous versions of himself. There was no one in MMA's short history to compare him with. So most experts didn't even try; instead, they would make contrasts with the giants of the boxing ring like Roy Jones Junior, Sugar Ray Leonard and even Muhammad Ali himself.

Every time I checked where I stood in the middleweight Top 10, it was his name at the top. He was the summit I was working so hard to climb to and, quite honestly, I felt I'd give him a much better fight than several challengers who seemed overawed by Silva's reputation. I badly wanted to fight him.

I'd had my chances to fight him over the years. If I'd have beaten Henderson at *UFC 100*, I'd have fought Anderson Silva for the belt in late 2009. If the judges had acknowledged that I had beaten Chael, I'd have fought Anderson at *UFC 148* in July 2012. If I'd have beaten the Radioactive Man in January 2013, I was tabbed to fight Anderson for the title at *UFC 162*.

But none of that happened and, instead, Anderson's time as champion came to an end in those two bizarre fights with Weidman in 2013. Chris Weidman, 9–0 at the time, had apparently earned his title shot by staging a 12-month sit-in at his home in Baldwin, New York.

At *UFC 162* in Las Vegas, Silva acted like he'd had some Adderall crunched up into his morning protein shake the entire fight – yelling, pointing and even dancing while in range of the New Yorker's punches. Finally, Weidman capitalised and threw a left hook that the defending champion – the same man who made Forrest Griffin, Vitor Belfort, Dan Henderson and all the rest miss by millimetres – all but head-butted.

It was shocking. It didn't look like real life.

The rematch later in the year ended in even more bizarre circumstances – Weidman blocked/checked a routine leg kick and Silva's shinbone snapped clean in two. I was in the front row and heard the wet snap, like a whip hitting a puddle, and witnessed the foremost talent in MMA being carried out on a stretcher. He screamed in agony the whole way. It was awful.

It looked like the greatest career in MMA history would end on the cruellest and most painful of flukes but, to everyone's astonishment including my own, Silva returned just 13 months later and soundly defeated Nick Diaz in a super-fight. Both fighters tested positive for banned substances in their post-fight test, and

Silva's reputation took a hit as he was banned for a year for, he claims, taking an erection tablet a friend of his brought back from Thailand.

Yeah.

While Anderson was serving his time, I was clawing my way back up the rankings with two straight wins. I probably should have taken the time to get elbow surgery done on my right arm. Some cartilage tissue had broken off during training for the Brian Stann fight and had been floating around in my joint so long they'd become calcified. They were so big my range of motion was becoming affected. But I wanted to fight, to win, as soon as possible.

A good win over veteran contender C.B. Dollaway at *UFC 186* in Montreal on 25 April 2015 set me up for a headline fight back in the UK.

After years of teasing it, the UFC finally held an event in Scotland on 18 July. The SSE Hydro arena in Glasgow was packed with over 10,000 fans. A lot of my friends and extended family from Clitheroe, who couldn't fly to Brazil, Canada, the US or China on two months' notice, all made the drive to Glasgow.

My opponent was Thales Leites. It was another one of those fights where only the people who really follow the sport understood how tough an assignment it was. Leites was a legit third-dan BJJ black belt and, after losing to Silva in a UFC title challenge, had really worked on his striking.

The US-based Brazilian was on an eight-fight win streak and the odds-on favourite when he landed in Scotland to fight me. After the Rockhold loss, I'd been written off by some sections of the MMA world, I think that's fair to say.

But I knew things the critics didn't. First and foremost, I knew I was getting better.

Jason Parillo and the team were pushing me to another level. I was now one of the most experienced mixed martial artists in the sport and, because of the way I'd always trained, I could pair that experience with a level of aggression no one in the division could match.

But – even more importantly – I'd become a much more even-tempered fighter. That hadn't come about overnight. It took time and patience on Jason's part to round the jagged edges off my mindset when it came to my fight career. But, after eight fights and three years together, I trusted him implicitly.

One humid May morning, I pulled into the RVCA gym car park and chose a spot under the giant graffiti-style mural that lights up the outside of the white building. I was grabbing my gym bag out of the boot (I still couldn't bring myself to say 'trunk' quite yet) when Jason appeared.

Yours truly had been a little irate towards his training partners the previous few days. I'd lost my cool in sparring and allowed it to darken my mood. My coach wanted a word about it.

'There are a lot of good guys inside that gym who want to spar with you, Mike,' he began. 'They are all very, very good. But you're world champion calibre. I'd like you to go in there and *act* like the world champion we both think you are – handle them like they are the world champion's sparring partners. Don't let them get the better of you and your emotions. Go in there and dominate the room in a positive way. Set the tone, set the worth ethic. Can you do that for me?'

I nodded: 'I can do that.'

And I did that all through the camp and all the way to a win over Thales Leites. The only time my emotions spiked was when I hugged Callum seconds before I stepped into the Octagon.

As a main eventer, I was allowed an extra cornerman. I'd asked Cal if he wanted to do it. His eyes lit up and the grin on his face went from ear to ear. He had the best week, following me around during the PR stuff, collecting his official Reebok cornerman tracksuit from the UFC office. He was really professional as I went about my usual fight-week routine. I was so proud to have him with me and I thought this could be a regular thing whenever I was given a fourth cornerman.

Then it came to the fight. When I got to the Octagon steps and gave Callum one of those last-moment hugs fighters share with their team my emotions burst through like a dam. The whole reason I began this journey was to provide for Cal and Ellie when they were toddlers and the emotions were stirred up too much. It was an emotional distraction exactly when I needed one the least.

Leites and I had a hard five-round fight. He was very big and strong for a middleweight and caught me with some hard shots. As if he wasn't a tough night's work on his own, my right elbow locked up a couple of times due to those floating pieces of calcified cartilage, plus I suffered a crazy injury in the first round. Somehow, I caught the underside of my big toe on the edge of the sandpaper-like logo on the Octagon canvas and it sheared the skin off like a doner kebab.

You're going to have to take my word for it – every second my toe was on the canvas, it was like an electrical current of pain. One of the newspapers the next day had a close-up of it with the headline 'TOE-TALLY GROSS!'

Nevertheless, I landed great combinations on Leites in every round and mixed my shots up very well. In all, I landed over 30 more significant strikes than he did in a fight which was almost entirely spent striking. I won the decision.

My old opponent Brian Stann interviewed me afterwards and I reaffirmed once again I was coming for the title.

'UFC – I am still here ten years later,' I said. 'Weidman, Rockhold, Yoel Romero, line 'em up and I'll take 'em out.'

My next opponent was supposed to be Robert Whittaker, not a big name at the time but clearly a fighter who had a big future, at the massive *UFC 193* event in Melbourne, Australia. I was really looking forward to competing on the blockbuster indoor-stadium card; Ronda Rousey, by now the top star in the sport, was defending her women's title vs Holly Holm and a staggering crowd of over 56,000 would be on hand.

Then I got an email from the UFC.

'NOOO!' I yelled, making Rebecca jump as we ate breakfast at the kitchen table.

I read her the email. Because MMA had only just been sanctioned by Sport and Recreation Victoria State authority, after years of lobbying by the UFC, the local commission was insisting on all 26 fighters on the card retaking all their annual medicals once we got to Australia. That would mean heart tests, blood work, MRIs and, yeah, a full battery of eye tests.

I'd already seen at first hand the huge variance between medical opinions regarding my eyesight. One doctor insisted I couldn't even go for a jog; the next week another doctor had cleared me to actually fight. What if this random Australian doctor, assigned by an authority who until recently had refused to even sanction MMA, decided the baseline requirement of 20/200 wasn't good enough?

It wouldn't just mean I'd be taken off *UFC 193* and miss out on a payday despite completing and paying for a full training camp. If I was denied a licence to fight anywhere in the world, it would make getting a licence to fight everywhere that much more difficult. There was every chance my entire career could unravel.

Putting my entire career in the hands of some stranger who, for all I knew, could have been against MMA getting sanctioned in Victoria in the first place made me very anxious. It was all I thought about for several days; every scenario ran through my head all at once. The one I kept coming back to was a jobsworth doctor declaring me medically unfit.

'You can't go on like this,' Rebecca said. She was the only one in the world who I confided in. 'You're supposed to be focused on training and fighting, but all your mental energy leading into fights is spent worrying about eye tests.'

She was right, of course. From the Kennedy fight to my retirement, the mental stress I felt regarding my eye situation was unbearable. The fighting itself was easy in comparison; climbing into the Octagon for a professional fist-fight was a reward, a stress reliever almost.

Thoughts of my career coming to an end via the email of an Australian doctor plagued me. I was distracted and distant in training. During a wrestling practice I was taken down and posted my left hand awkwardly. The pain was enough for me to call time; when I stood up my arm was locked at 45 degrees.

'Guys, I can't move my arm,' I said as Jason and a few others gathered around. 'I'm trying to straighten it as hard as I can – it's not moving.'

I knew exactly what had happened. I dug my fingers into the joint and could feel one of those calcified floating bodies jammed deep in my joint. It was painful, but I wiggled it out and could move my arm again.

I saw a specialist that afternoon. Doctor Mora was of Peruvian descent and one of the best orthopaedic surgeons in America (he's also handsome enough to star on *The Young and the Restless*, or so Rebecca has informed me more than once). He told me the bits of tissue were now so big they would continue to get jammed up my elbow.

'These bodies are going to continue to calcify,' he said, 'which means they will get bigger and will interfere with your range of motion with increasing frequency.'

The news my arm could lock out in front of me at 45 degrees – like a German with a beer tankard – in the middle of a fight wasn't great, but the doctor had more.

'I encourage you to get this taken care of now,' she said. 'I know you have a match coming up. From personal experience, I can tell you it is not worth it. I had similar foreign bodies floating around my knee – I put off the surgery until the end of the season but my leg locked up in the middle of a meet. It is literally like throwing a spanner in the works. I damaged the joint so much I missed a full season.'

The next morning I called the UFC and pulled out of the Melbourne event, then I called the specialist back and confirmed I'd take the Thursday slot for the operation.

I hated pulling out. I prided myself on showing up and fighting but I think Rebecca had a point when she said the elbow injury was a blessing in disguise.

'You probably should have got the elbow surgery several fights back,' she said. 'There's a reason you didn't. Maybe something was going to happen in Australia with the eye exam.'

'I don't know how much longer I can go on doing this,' I admitted. 'The stress of the eye situation … and a random doctor could take it upon himself to overrule the others and end my career on the spot. I'm paranoid about people looking at my eye. Did you see me at the last press conference? I've taken to wearing sunglasses indoors!'

Rebecca looked at me with an exaggeratedly puzzled look. And I laughed.

'Yeah, I'm well aware of what I used to say about dickheads who wear shades indoors,' I sighed, appreciating her lightening the mood. 'And I wasn't wrong! If you wear sunglasses indoors, in the winter, then you are announcing yourself as a dickhead. Only difference is that I'm now one of them.'

It was Christmas Eve 2015 and I was sat on the couch at home with Ellie and Rebecca. Callum was playing with his phone across the room, and Lucas was lying on his back on the rug in front of me, watching the television upside down.

My elbow was fully recovered and the Bispings were ready for Christmas. In fact, after living in America for a couple of years we'd begun to use Thanksgiving almost as a dress rehearsal for Christmas, so we'd been ready for over a month. I was dodging most of the tasty food, though, because I was already in training to face Gegard Mousasi in London on 27 February 2016.

I'd be back in the gym on Boxing Day (or, as Americans call it, 'December 26' – they have no idea what Boxing Day is and, after years of trying to explain it, I realised that neither do I).

We were about to make a decision on whether or not to go out that night when my phone rang.

Dana calling on Christmas Eve? What could this be about?

He got right into it: 'We're thinking of changing things around on the London card. You versus Anderson Silva, main event, O_2 Arena. How's that sound?'

Wha—

'Hell, yes! I've always wanted to fight him.'

'Yeah, I know. Merry fucking Christmas.'

'Merry fucking Christmas!' I said.

We hung up. From the first ring to me putting my phone back down took less than 30 seconds.

'Who was that?' Ellie asked.

'Dana,' I said.

I just sat there. My family knew something was up. Rebecca and Callum leaned in. Lucas told me to be quiet – he was watching his movie.

'I'm fighting Anderson Silva in London.' I heard the words come out of my mouth. Just like that, after all these years, it was a reality. It actually felt like a Christmas present. Magical, almost.

I was already training very hard for the London event but from the moment Dana called my discipline became razor-edged. I didn't have a single 'cheat meal', cheeky glass of wine with dinner, nothing. I called Daz Morris, my old friend and one of the best Thai coaches in the UK, and added him to my team for this one.

No stone was left unturned – beating Anderson Silva was everything to me. This fight, I knew, would deliver the final verdict on my entire career. I knew the sport's self-appointed historians had already drafted the summary: *'Michael Bisping, perennial contender, BUT couldn't win the Big One.'*

Anderson Silva would be fighting for his legacy, too.

After getting chinned by a meat and potatoes left hook from Weidman, the uncontrollable agony of the leg-break rematch, the drug test ruining the Lazarus-like comeback vs Diaz and the embarrassment of the 'Thai erection pill' defence, Silva needed a resounding victory himself.

He wouldn't just be looking for a win; I knew that for a fact. His ego would demand the full restoration of his near-mythical status that only a spectacular knockout would deliver.

The UFC promoted the showdown as a decade in the making. We both had so much at stake, so much to win. For one of us to succeed the other had to fail.

'It took Chael Sonnen two years of non-stop bullshit to finally anger Anderson,' the Spider's manager Ed Soares said during fight week. 'It's taken Bisping less than two months.'

No doubt about it, I'd worked fast. You can guess which pressure point I focused on. Silva refused to discuss the doping failure, stating it was not 'relevant' and insinuating I was somehow being 'unprofessional' for bringing it up in media interviews.

When we did an open workout for the media and hundreds of fans at a UFC Gym location in Torrance, California, on 11 February, Silva learned that I'd bring his doping up to his face, too. I waited until the cameras were rolling and gate-crashed Silva's interview scrum.

'Hey – did it work?' I asked with the tone of a comedian about to roast a hapless audience member. 'Did the Thai sex pill work? Did you have an erection?'

During fight week in London, at the press conference, and at a photo-op shot on the banks of the Thames with Tower Bridge in the background, I wasted no opportunity to get right up in Silva's face.

At the weigh-in I held out my hand to shake his. He looked puzzled. I held it out further. 'C'mon, shake,' I said. He reached for my hand – and I withdrew mine, putting it behind my back. I leaned my face into his again. No respect. No quarter asked because none would be given.

Silva smiled, but his eyes were on fire.

Finally, when handed a microphone to address the 5,000 British attending the weigh-in, I had this to say: 'When I step into that cage tomorrow I'm doing it on behalf of myself and Great Britain. This man is a cheat! This man is a fraud! All the needles in your arse, all the steroids will not help you, you pussy!'

So, why did I go all out to piss off the most talented fighter of all time?

Simple, I respected him far too much.

There's no shame in admitting that I had massive appreciation, admiration, really, for Anderson as a fighter. I had to completely change that mindset to give myself the best chance of winning.

Silva preyed on respect. For years, I'd watched opponent after opponent fail to challenge him to the best of their ability because they went in going, 'Oooh, I'm in with the legendary Anderson Silva.'

The Rashad Evans loss in 2007 was caused by the folly of giving too much respect to an opponent. And so, I seized upon Silva's positive steroid test. That one event was the entirety of his life, in my mind's eye. He was a *fucking cheat*. Another Dan Henderson, another Vitor Belfort. He deserved contempt, not respect. Mentally, I diminished him until he was the size of a normal fighter.

This wasn't a trivial mental exercise. Silva was a master mind-gamer himself, often exchanging meticulous respect (the bowing and all that nonsense) to con opponents into 'respectful' martial arts contests that suited his style. Then, inevitably, he sprung the trap and smashed them to defeat as brutally as anyone in the sport.

My vocal disrespect sent the message none of that would work.

Between *UFC 120* on 16 October 2010 and the Anderson Silva fight in February 2016, there was a gap of five years, four months and ten days between me fighting in England. That was literally, almost to the day, half of my UFC career.

The atmosphere crackled with energy as I stepped into the Octagon. I was back in the fortress, ready to defend my undefeated record on British soil. Everybody I knew from Clitheroe was there, like my mate Burge, people I used to train with years before like Ian Freeman, my friends from the acting world like Noel Clarke, Guy Ritchie, my mum, my dad, Rebecca – everybody.

Referee Herb Dean brought us together in the middle of the cage for final instructions. When Dean was finished, Silva offered both gloves, stretched into fists. He also bowed in the traditional form of respect one martial artist shows another. I accepted the show of respect and said, 'Good luck.'

I meant it. Despite what I'd said during the previous two months, I respected the man and didn't want either of us to win due to some fluke occurrence.

The fans erupted as the moments ticked down to the opening buzzer. This was it. My title shot, my legacy and the final verdict on my 35 professional fights, 12 years as a professional, 25 years of training, thousands of miles of road work, hundreds of days away from my family.

There was no way to beat Silva on the back foot, I knew. I had to take the centre of the Octagon right away, be intelligently aggressive and push the pace. Silva would counter and hurt me, he'd play his gamesmanship and make me miss, he'd pretend nothing I did was working but – whatever happened – I knew I could not let him blunt my aggression.

I landed first, and not just a single shot but a combination. Silva switched from his natural orthodox stance to his preferred southpaw, back and forth, back and forth, and I could see him performing calculations behind his eyes. He threw – and landed – several punches. The speed was equal to the accuracy. I had no trouble landing on him, though. I kept pressing him backwards, landing ones, twos and even several three-punch combinations. I worked his lead leg and got the better of a clinch. He wasn't as hard to hit as I had expected, although hitting him with the same combination or set-up twice proved difficult.

As if a timer had gone off, Silva surged forward in the last 30 seconds. I had to stand my ground – and did – clipping him with a big left hook that staggered him as the buzzer sounded.

As the horn blared out to end my 10–9 round, Anderson attached a goofy grin on his face and came in to give me a hug. It was another one of his psychological set pieces. *Congratulations on winning a round against the great Anderson Silva*, his embrace inferred. I shoved him backwards – hard – with both hands and told him what he could use a Thai sex pill for.

You are not coming to my country and condescending me in front of my own people. I am just getting started with you – see you back here in one minute.

I sat down on my stool feeling good.

'Our round?' I asked Jason as he and the team worked on me like a Formula 1 pitstop.

'Our round. You're doing great. Don't let him bait you into bullshit,' was Jason's final instruction.

Anderson reached deeper into his bag of magic tricks in the second.

Silva's reflexes were extraordinary. He could go from nought to nuclear in a split second. But one of my long-held suspicions was already confirmed – he relied on discouraging opponents from throwing combinations as much as his own reflexes to avoid them. I'm a stubborn bastard at the best of times, and I trusted my cardio and skillset to land strike numbers three, four and five even if numbers one and two missed.

This was no unmasking, though. Silva was every bit as good as he'd looked during his championship reign. On several occasions, his anticipation of my attacks was so exact it gave me the disquieting sensation we were doing fight-movie choreography. I had to push such thoughts away as the imposters they were. He was just another fighter who I needed to keep the pressure on.

A minute into the second round, Silva backed himself against the fence, squared his hips into a normal standing posture and waved me in. 'Come on, man,' he said in that Michael Jackson voice of his, expecting me to play the game of firing punches while he dodged like Keanu Reeves in the *Matrix* movies.

Unfortunately for Anderson I'd seen this ruse before (most memorably vs Stephan Bonnar in 2012). His squared-up stance made dodging punches easier, not harder, and the proximity to the fence all but ensured no one would try a full-power kick and risk catching their toes in the chain links.

It was a con, not unlike those can't-win carnival games, and I'd have none of it. I stepped back three paces to the centre of the Octagon, put my hands on my hips and shot Silva an unimpressed look. *I'm not one of the overawed challengers you've clowned and beaten for years*, I said with my eyes. The British fans played their

My nose was broken and I was cut and bruised – but beating Anderson Silva in front of the UK fans was one of the greatest moments of my life. London, February 2016.

Shaking hands with Anderson Silva immediately after our fight. You can see I'd bled from literally head to toe.

Getting back from a run with Callum and Dito the dog, May 28 2016, the weekend before winning the UFC world title.

After a decade of chasing it, the UFC world title belt was wrapped around my waist after defeating Luke Rockhold on June 4 2016, in Inglewood, California.

My left orbital socket was broken in the rematch vs Dan Henderson at UFC 204 on October 8 2016, closing my good eye as the fight went on.

Kneeing Dan Henderson during our fight in Manchester.

An amazing aerial shot of me celebrating
in the ring, after my first round knockout
win against Rockhold.

Promoting the GSP fight during an appearance on Conan O'Brien's late night talk show, October 2017.

At the UFC 217 press conference at Madison Square Garden. I took to wearing sunglasses to prevent anyone taking a closer look at my damaged eye.

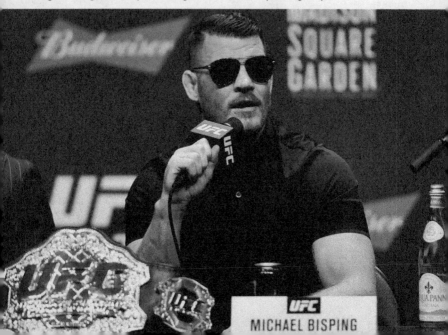

Landing a punch against Georges St.-Pierre during UFC 217 at Madison Square Gardens. NYC, November 4 2017.

Meeting British fans after the UFC Hall of Fame announcement at the O2 Arena, London, March 2019.

On May 4 2019, I made my debut as a UFC colour commentator.

On the set of Fox Sport 1's UFC Tonight show in Los Angeles, California, with Lucas.

With my daughter Ellie.

The Bispings on holiday in Hawaii. Providing a better life for my family was the reason I set out to become a fighter in the first place.

part, too, cheering my bravado and letting Silva know he was a long way from Brazil.

Because of my role as a TV analyst, I knew for a fact that Silva hadn't even attempted a takedown in over six years. Like with the Cung Le fight, that knowledge enabled me to bring a whole other arsenal of strikes to this fight. I used a push kick to position my opponent against the cage and a roundhouse kick to his right thigh.

While we were exchanging strikes, Silva caught me with a counter – an elbow to the ear – that was so fast commentators John Gooden and Dan Hardy didn't see it.

Despite taking that and several hard strikes, the second round was going even better than the first for me. Silva knew it, too, and in the final minute he dropped down off his toes and loaded more TNT in his gloves. Silva pressed forward but I sent him into reverse with a push kick. Then I flicked a jab on my way inside and – BAM! – a drum-tight left hook buzzed him badly. Before he could recover any equilibrium I twisted my hips into a right cross and then arched another left to the jaw. BAM-THUD-BOOM!

I'd decked him! He was down, hurt!

The British fans roared like the place had caught fire. I followed Anderson to the ground – taking an up kick from the lightning-fast Brazilian on the way down – into his guard and began hacking away at him like a madman.

(The up kick was incredible, I have to add. I could see in his eyes he was rocked – but this man is such an instinctual fighter he still fired and landed a counter.)

I had no fear of his BJJ guard. I wish I'd got him down earlier, because the 30 seconds of ground and pound were my most dominant of the fight so far. I smacked him with both fists and elbows until the round ended.

The fans went crazy at the end as I walked to my corner. I felt great. It was hard; I was a little bloodied already – but I was putting on the performance of my life. I was two rounds up, 100 per cent. I just had to keep focused like the edge of a scalpel.

'You're doing well,' Jason said. 'Stay focused. Rip the body when you find him open. You are getting close enough.'

For the third round, Anderson shot off his stool like a man determined not to lose a third straight round. He was coldly aggressive, less content to give ground and, after getting hurt and dropped by the left hook, he wore his shoulders locked in formation either side of his chin.

Silva's punches and kicks were as accurate and slicing as the strokes of a diamond-cutter. He is the only fighter in a quarter-century to have landed over half his strikes. He thudded a kick into my mid-section. I refused to back off. I chased Silva to the fence and landed three of a four-punch combination. Silva's right fist sent sweat bouncing from my head. Moments later I felt his nose stab between my middle knuckles as a right cross crunched into his face.

'This fight is living up to the hype,' commentator John Gooden stated.

BISPING! BISPING! BISPING! BISPING! rumbled around the arena.

Anderson slammed his left knee through my defences and into my guts. He chased me along the fence. We exchanged shots and, somehow, my mouthpiece fell out. I pointed the ref's attention to it, lying on the canvas, and Herb Dean went to retrieve it.

For a split second I thought about the long-term consequences of professional cage fighting. I wanted my gumshield back in before my incisors were knocked out or my face was grated from the inside out.

'Mouthpiece!' I said to the referee. The Spider read my preoccupation as a weakness and attacked – ripping in strikes to my head. He caught me in a Thai clinch and threatened a knee strike but I escaped and stepped back.

That was a lull in the action, as far as I was concerned, and the referee needed to step in and replace my mouthguard. 'Mouthpiece,' I turned and repeated to the referee.

Silva blasted into the air like a rocket and drove his knee directly into my face. I crumpled to the canvas with blood gushing from the bridge of a broken nose. Before I'd finished falling Anderson had landed, turned and was walking towards the centre of the Octagon.

BEEEEEP!

The round ended two seconds after Silva's knee had struck.

If that had been the end of the fight, it would have haunted me for the rest of my life. I'd fought an intelligently aggressive fight for 14 minutes and 58 seconds, hurting the GOAT in the first round, dropping him in the second and out-striking him 63–36. And then I'd completely disengaged from the task and invited a calamity to happen.

But it wasn't the end of the fight. My face felt collapsed but I was still with it. 'I'm not knocked out!' I told Herb Dean. 'I'm okay!'

One of those statements was more accurate than the other, but Dean confirmed I wasn't out of the fight.

'No, you're not knocked out,' Dean said to me clearly. 'End of round.'

Twelve feet away Silva had thrown himself into celebration. Somehow, his entire team burst into the Octagon to join him. Confused commissioners wandered after them; emasculated grandparents trying to persuade kids that it's bedtime.

Silva then leapt up and straddled the Octagon fence and celebrated even as officials on both sides of the mesh – including Dana White – pleaded with the excited Brazilians to accept the fight was not over.

Somehow, his manager Ed Soares was in the Octagon speaking with him but, at the opposite gate, Jason, Brady and Daz were refused entry by security. Some official brought me my stool to sit on and for several long moments I had three perfect strangers all talking at me. The referee told them to clear the cage. Bags of blood gushed out of the cuts and I badly needed the assistance of a cutman and my team. The cutman appeared above me momentarily, only to be marched away by some random official without so much as applying grease to my lacerations.

Finally, Jason and Brady sprinted over to me. They were told I needed to return to my corner (there's no such rule – but the Octagon was a complete clusterfuck by now).

'You've still got this,' Jason said calmly. 'You can still win – this is still your fight.'

When I raised my head once more the Octagon had been cleared. Anderson Silva was pacing for the fourth round to begin. I rose off my stool.

'Michael Bisping does not look like himself,' Dan Hardy told the television audience. 'He looks dazed. He looks confused.'

In fact, mentally/cognitively I felt okay – physically I was a car wreck. My right leg trailed behind me as I moved across the canvas; my full weight had collapsed on top of my bad knee and the bottom half of my leg was numb. My nose was broken and I couldn't breathe through its collapsed nostrils for the rest of the night.

But I wasn't done.

I can do this! I swore behind the blood and my bruised eyes. *I can do this!*

That's when I heard it. The roar.

The roar of the British fans rolling tighter and tighter until I could feel the soundwaves moving the hairs on my forearms. They still believed I had this, too. For a full decade, no matter what, they'd always believed in me. I can't describe what that cheer did for me. Whatever confidence Jason had instilled, whatever self-belief I'd dragged from the bottom of my soul – these people doubled and tripled it.

I let the referee's signal release me. I went out and took the fight to Anderson Silva all over again.

We had both reached the championship rounds hurt and tired. The fight had become a battle of wills. I expected Silva to pounce on me but, instead, he skipped around on the outside for a full minute. I continued to walk him down until I trapped him against the fence. I pumped out combinations: an inside leg kick followed by a foot stomp into a jab, a right cross, a left hook, a right hook and another left.

'Great work by Michael Bisping! His hands are really fast and Anderson Silva is struggling to keep up with him,' Dan Hardy said on colour commentary.

Silva remained against the cage, looking for a big counter, as I kept the pressure up. I switched up my attacks constantly, trying to make it harder for him to read what I was doing next.

BISPING! BISPING! BISPING! BISPING! BISPING! The fans were heard again.

In the inverse of my stance, Anderson is right-handed but fights as a southpaw – which makes his jab feel almost as hard as a cross. He speared at my face with it half a dozen times during the fourth round, puncturing my already bruised features above and below the left eye. With the cuts I'd already sustained, my entire face and neck were awash with blood.

Once again, he launched a lightning raid in the final 40 seconds. A corkscrew uppercut plus left cross combination buzzed me and opened the gash under my eye a little wider. I timed his next attack and sent him careering backwards with a right hand. The round ended.

The most ridiculously talented improvisational mixed martial artist ever had the same strategy for each opponent: 'Be Anderson Silva.' At the end of the fourth round he went back to his corner with the knowledge that wasn't enough. Not against me, not on that night. He'd emptied out his bag of magic tricks. He'd gone through his arsenal of special weapons. Yet I was still marching him down.

The fourth round was my most active of the fight; I threw 80 strikes, all but 12 of them power punches and kicks, and out-landed Silva by a third. I was sure I'd taken a decisive round.

'You are winning this fight, Mike,' Jason said. 'He's looking to counter with something big when you got him against the cage. Keep smart pressure on him.'

The cutman could do nothing with any of the axe wounds on my face. In the seconds before the fifth and final round I looked up at one of the big screens suspended 140ft in the air. There was my face, shredded raw.

The cut above my left eye was drowning my good eye with a constant pour of blood. Every blink smeared the blood across my eyeball. Whenever I was far enough away from Anderson's striking range to risk it, I'd scoop the blood on the tips of my fingers and then wipe it on my shorts.

Silva went for the knockout right away – I barely blocked two head kicks thrown just moments apart.

Unable to breathe through my nose, I had to curl my lips and drag air over my mouthpiece for long stages of the fight.

(Opening your jaw is a huge no-no in a fight; a strike to a slack jaw increases the effect of the strike and risks a broken jaw and broken teeth.) My oxygen levels must have plummeted, because I was more tired in that last round vs Anderson than in any in my career. The blood loss wouldn't have helped, either. Blood was landing on my shorts in such quantities the cloth could no longer absorb it. Red streaked from my face to my torso to my shorts to literally my ankles.

The Brazilian was fighting on fumes, too, I could see him biting down on his mouthpiece as he stalked forward, throwing every last watt of power into his strikes.

The referee brought in the doctor to look at my cuts, but I wasn't worried the fight would be stopped so late on cuts. 'Do you want to continue?' the doctor asked. Of course I did.

Anderson walked towards me with his palms open. We touched both our gloves in respect. It was genuine and hard earned.

The legend whipped a big left cross in. I matched him with a hooked right cross that sent him backwards against the cage. I gave chase but missed the follow-up and – BANG! – I was sent staggering backwards by something.

Silva had uncorked the front kick to the jaw that had so iconically laid out Vitor Belfort. I was hurt and Anderson went for broke. His knee thudded into my guts, then my chin. He kicked my nose and the already contorted cartridge felt like it snapped. Everything he sent into the air was intended to land with a fight-finishing detonation.

But I refused to go backwards for long. I landed a heavy one-two combination to his mouth. My left hook landed once, twice and a third time. Then he clubbed my jaw with that Filipino back fist. I heard him gasp as I swung a kick to his mid-section.

And then the round – the fight – ended. Exhaustion hit me like a tidal wave. I'd spent all of myself. Nothing was left.

You never know when close fights go to the scorecards, but all three judges scored it 48–47 for me. That moment was overwhelming. The swelling and blood gave my tears cover as they streaked out of my eyes. I was overcome with emotion. This was my world title win, the Big One.

When the critics least expected it and when I needed to the most, I produced the performance of my life. I took control of the narrative of my career like I had the narrative of my life 14 years before. *I was one of the best fighters in the world.* No one would be able to take that away from me again.

Dan Hardy was hovering around with a microphone in his hand to interview me but I ran out of the cage to my family. The first person I gave a blood-splattered hug to was my mum. Then I saw Rebecca, and the look of pride on her face. She knew what this meant for me. (Unfortunately, I didn't know what her new suede jacket meant to her. I got blood all over it – and to this day I have to hear all about it.)

I shared a brief moment with my family before turning back towards the Octagon. I'd run out of the cage seconds before but, with the adrenaline gone, I limped up the steps towards Dan.

'I wanted this fight for so long,' I told my old training partner. 'These people (I looked around the arena) – they give me the power. I'm just a guy, from a very normal background, and you guys have been in my corner every single time. Thank you so much.'

I addressed Anderson, who was stood just feet away putting on a tracksuit. 'Anderson, I know I said some things, but I worship you. You're the greatest martial artist of all time. That's why I am so emotional, this has been a lifelong dream. The respect I have for you cannot be measured. You inspired me when I was a cocky young kid, saying things I regret, and there was you … I wanted to be like you.'

The UFC didn't want me to go to the post-fight press conference. My fresh stitches had finally stopped weeping pink ooze but my face was a mosaic of black and deep red swellings. The medical staff was insisting I go directly to the hospital. I refused. I was going to get dressed and go to the post-fight press conference.

Desperate, the medical team asked a couple of UFC staff members who I had a lot of respect for and had personal relationships with to come and change my mind. They didn't.

'I've wanted to fight – and beat – that man for ten years,' I told Reed Harris, a silver-haired UFC vice president I'd always liked. 'If you think I'm missing the press conference about the biggest achievement in my entire career you've got another thing coming.'

The media room was crammed with over 70 reporters and crew clutching cameras, lights and laptops. It isn't supposed to be the done thing, but the media stood and gave me a round of applause when I took my seat at the dais.

Ariel Helwani waited until the presser was over to speak with me. 'Why didn't you call for a title shot?' he asked. 'You've been calling for your shot after every win for the last three, four years. The moment was perfect tonight. So why not?'

I didn't have a good answer for him. Calling for a title shot just never entered my mind while I was in the Octagon. I had too many people to thank, too many emotions to allow myself to feel. I'd reached the summit of a mountain few believed I could climb and I just lived that moment rather than moving on to the future.

I turned 37 years old two and a half hours after defeating Anderson Silva. I didn't know how many fights I had left in me.

CHAPTER SIXTEEN
ACTING HARD

In 2010, before I'd moved to the US, my T-shirt sponsor Tapout called and said they were putting up some money for a feature film entitled *Beatdown*. Tapout had cast several of its sponsored UFC fighters – including Mike Swick and Bobby Lashley – in the movie and, out of the blue, offered me a major part. I'd started martial arts in the first place because of beat 'em up movies so, terrified as I was, I jumped at the chance.

Director Mike Gunther – who'd worked on everything from *Sons of Anarchy* to *Grey's Anatomy* – and producer Stan Worthing helped settle me down when I arrived in Texas to shoot the film.

'I was kinda shocked you've not acted before,' Stan said after the first couple of days' filming. 'You've got real presence. I encourage you to continue with this as a side-career to your fighting.'

Upon my return to the UK, I continued taking acting lessons in Manchester. The first thing my coach did was get me bawling my eyes out crying by getting me to focus on my children, what had happened to my brother Konrad and other emotional touchpoints. I found the craft fascinating. I wanted to do more.

My second acting gig was on *Hollyoaks Later* – the annual five-episode spinoff series of the long-running British soap opera. Some of my mates had the time of their life taking the piss, but for me, it was about getting more time on a set, having more lines to learn, meeting more people who knew what was what in the industry. My villainous Nathan McAllister character also got one of the best on-screen deaths since Christopher Lee's Dracula – I was thrown off a rooftop into a giant vat of oil. My on-screen brother – played by Chris Overton – desperately drains the oil only to discover I'd been impaled on a spike. Chris and I are mates to this day and he went on to become an Oscar-winning director.

The move to California was for the benefit of my UFC career and so I wasn't away from my family quite as much but, obviously, for someone who had developed a passion for acting I couldn't have relocated to a better place. I hit up Stan from the *Beatdown* movie on email and he put me in touch with a manager, Aaron Ginsburg, who agreed to meet with me at his offices in LA.

I was five hours late to that meeting. I was entirely reliant on my car's sat-nav to get me there and it proved as dodgy as Vitor Belfort's protein supplements. Aaron, amazingly, laughed it off and agreed to manage me.

He helped me land a role in the big Cinemax/Sky One action series *Strike Back: Legacy*, based on the novel by SAS officer turned writer Chris Ryan. It was a hugely successful, big-budget show, and the cast featured people I'd seen in movies and TV. This was during the time my MMA career was supposedly over due to my eye injury, so getting cast on a major network show like *Strike Back* felt like a lifeline.

We began filming in January 2014 in Bangkok, Thailand. Nine years before I'd flown out there to work on my clinch work, and now I was back to get a crash course in shooting an action series.

The star of the show was Sullivan Stapleton, an Australian actor who'd just finished the sequel to the *300* movie. 'Sully', as everyone calls him, was just a great guy to be around and we hit it off right away.

One night after filming was done, a whole bunch of the cast and crew went out for a meal and a nightcap. We filtered into the street outside the club we'd been in and began flagging down rides back to the hotel.

Me, Sully and four others flagged down what's known as a 'tuk-tuk', an auto-rickshaw taxi. Three guys and a woman from production jumped in the cab while Sully and I stood on the thin bumper at the back and grabbed onto the roof.

The tuk-tuk was soon hurtling down Bangkok's side streets at 30mph when – BUMP! – the whole vehicle jolted forwards and then lurched into the air for several terrifying seconds. Sully was thrown into the air and slammed onto the asphalt behind us.

'WAIT! STOP! STOP!' I banged on the roof until the driver brought the tuk-tuk to a halt. Sully was still on the ground 50 yards back down the road. He was spread-eagled on his back and wasn't moving.

I sprinted over to him. A pool of blood was creeping out in a circle from behind Sully's head.

I dropped to my knees and tried to rouse him. 'Hey, Sully, Sully! You okay? Can you hear me?'

He was lifeless.

The others caught up and started freaking out.

'Sully? Sully? SULLY!'

My brain flew back to a bit of CPR training I'd had in Nottingham all those years before. I checked his pulse – but couldn't find one. The blood flow from Sully's head kept coming.

The knees of my jeans were soaked like blotting paper. I checked for breath, putting my cheek next to his mouth. No breath. I pressed my ear against his chest. No heartbeat!

He's gone – he's dead!

A muttering crowd formed around us. Mopeds beeped and honked and swerved. No one helped. Somehow, it was on me.

Copying from what I'd seen on television, mostly, I started pumping his chest and giving CPR. I did the one-one-thousand, two-one-thousand, three-one-thousand and breathed into him. Nothing. I did it again. Still nothing. And again. Nothing, nothing.

'NO! NO! COME ON, SULLY! DON'T YOU DIE! DON'T FUCKING DIE!' I heard my voice bark. I wasn't going to give up. I tried hitting his heart as hard as I could. I hammer-fisted his chest once, twice and then …

'Arck! Arck!'

He was breathing!

Slowly, I turned him on one side. I cradled his head and could feel breath pushing out on my wrist.

A white ambulance arrived seemingly a minute later. Two men leapt out and lifted Sully onto a blue stretcher and into the ambulance. My four colleagues piled into it along with Sully and within moments its whirling blue light was a mile away into the night. It then turned a corner and vanished, leaving me to walk back to the hotel covered in blood.

Everyone was in a state of shock the next day. Sully was in critical care. Then we were informed the local police were doing a full investigation into how a Hollywood actor had almost died on their streets. Everyone who was present at Sully's accident would have to go to a police station to be – I'm quoting here – 'interrogated'.

As if that didn't already sound dodgy enough, we were then told to say that no one in our party had been drinking alcohol. Why we were told that, I can guess, but I was having none of it.

'Yeah, I was hoping this would lead to more television work but starring in *Locked Up Abroad* wasn't what I had in mind. Lie to the authorities in this part of the world? Sorry, I'm not risking spending the next three years in the "Bangkok Hilton".'

That afternoon me and five others (none of whom would appreciate getting named here) were picked up and taken to a bunker of a police station located on a side street to nowhere. In a car park area to one side, thirty police in uniform were stood in a rank formation listening to a little man wearing medals and a moustache.

Directly across the road from the station was a breezeblock wall, unpainted and unrepaired, running down the street in both directions. It was covered in dozens of posters, not quite weathered enough for me not to see they were advertising English-speaking lawyers.

Everyone had heard horror stories about the Thai authority's corruption. Fake arrests to get bribes, that sort of thing. There was an American movie star in intensive care and I felt anxious as I followed the group inside the station.

There was no air conditioning, just humming fluorescent lights and cops with hair slicked back with sweat. We were taken – marched, really – down zigzagging narrow corridors. The place was way bigger than it looked from the street.

'Sit here.' A tall, skinny policeman gestured to plastic chairs lined against a wall. Then a windowless door opened to our right, and they took one of the guys inside to be interviewed. We sat in silence. The girl looked petrified and on the verge of tears. Sweat was streaming down my ribs and back. I was now sat nearest the door – I would be taken in next.

Twenty minutes later the door opened and out came my *Strike Back* colleague. I stood up and gave the police officer an expectant look.

'Not you! Sit,' the skinny policeman said. 'You talk last,' and, with that, another guy was taken in and I sat back down.

My paranoia kicked in. Were they looking to pin this on me? To get me to pay them so I could leave the country? To send a message that Thailand was tough on crime? Were they going to tell me to pay a ton of money or I was going to prison?

I really began to sweat.

'We find it very strange Mr Stapleton fell off the tuk-tuk so violently but you did not.'

Finally, I was sat inside the interrogation room with the two policemen. The room was small and I was sweating so much my forearms slid on the table.

'I don't find it strange,' I said.

'No? So, explain to us why he fall and you did not.'

'I can't explain that, can I? Maybe he wasn't gripping as tightly as I was?'

'When he was on the ground in a serious medical state, why did you strike him with your fists?'

And that's how it went on, for almost an hour. Finally, they were satisfied what had happened was simply a terrible accident.

When I got back to the hotel the call had been made to wrap filming. What else could they do? There were still no details on how Sully was doing for a while after I got back home. A short statement was put out, but that was it.

The truth eventually came out that my mate had fallen into a coma. When he woke he was kept under care for six months. Amazingly though, Sully rehabbed his way to a complete recovery.

Fourteen months after the accident we were all back in Thailand to finish the series. I dropped my bags off in my room and went to see Sully in his suite. It was the first time we'd been face to face since he'd been driven away in that ambulance.

We sat down on the balcony and he asked me what had happened that night. 'I can't remember a bloody thing,' he said. So I described it to him pretty much like I have to you.

He got emotional. Then he stood up and gave me the biggest hug. We've been brothers ever since.

A loud and abrasive personality gets you noticed in combat sports; if you can then back it up when it counts it can boost your career. That's not how it works in the acting world, where those traits will get you nothing but a reputation as hard to deal with.

That said, there are some attributes that made me successful in MMA that are helping me in Hollywood. Just like in the UFC, I like to think I'm earning a reputation as a hard worker who shows up prepared every time. I've also experienced a lot of great highs and lows in my fighting career that I can tap into when I'm playing different characters and, like my opponents found out, I'm not discouraged by setbacks.

And, of course, because I've trained in half a dozen martial arts since I was a small boy, I pick up fight choreography quickly. In fact, when I got my big break in *xXx: Return of Xander Cage* in 2016, they were interested in having my input in the fight scenes. It was really cool that massively experienced action-movie veterans

Vin Diesel, Donnie Yen and director D.J. Caruso were so openly collaborative in a huge summer blockbuster.

It was also ironic because, years before, on a tiny movie that may not have seen the light of day, I was informed I had 'little aptitude for martial arts'.

True story. It was on a small independent movie about kickboxing; I had a small part as the main character's sparring partner. It actually cost me money to do the project – I turned down two weekends of working as a TV analyst for Fox Sports' UFC coverage – but I wanted the experience.

And what an experience it was.

The fight choreographer – I'm going to call him *Sensei Guru* – was one of the most conceited and unbearable characters I've ever come across (and, remember, I've met Colby Covington).

There were five of us actors in the small dance studio in the outskirts of LA. We lined up in front of the mirrors and Sensei Guru got off to a flying start by introducing himself as 'the motivating dynamism behind the most successful people in America'. He listed off a bunch of big-name actors, pop stars, TV presenters and, I think, basketball players. 'These A-listers turn to me for enlightenment,' he said, 'and they leave with the courage to grab greatness.'

Then he got to his McDojo martial arts credentials. He was the first Westerner to be taught at 'the Temple' by some grandmaster in Japan, he'd won some super-secret tournament he's not supposed to talk about and, yes, he even mentioned the *dim mak*.

Over the coming week in that studio, we were assured, he would distil some of this knowledge for us lucky wretches. It was weird but, whatever, I was there to learn and so applied myself to doing exactly what was asked of me.

He barked orders like we were Marine recruits but I didn't so much as roll my eyes when he 'corrected' my stance over and over again. Nor did I utter a word, when he singled me out as 'doing everything one-eighty degrees wrong from how it works in real fights'.

'*Show* me a left hook!' he suddenly snarled at me. I did, but apparently not to his satisfaction.

Sensei Guru closed his eyes and whipped his head left and right like he was riding an old roller coaster. 'No! No! Wrong!' he howled.

He took two steps back to ensure everyone could see him clearly. Ancient martial knowledge was about to be imparted, I could just tell.

'*This* is how a left hook is thrown!' He demonstrated three times and then glared at me. '*See* the difference?'

I nodded and said, 'Absolutely, I can do that, no problem. It's the position of my fist you want me to change, yeah? I throw hooks with my thumb facing the ceiling rather than back towards my face – but I can do it your way, easy.'

'*My way* is the correct way,' he stated. 'I've no idea where you picked up *that*.'

This is the most bizarre day of my life, I remember thinking. *This would make for a hysterical hidden-camera prank.*

The studio was an hour's drive home – two hours if I hit traffic – but I had barely got halfway before the production company called.

'The fight coordinator says he can't work with you,' I was told.

'What?' I asked over the car's hands-free.

'Yes, [Sensei Guru] says you're struggling with the complexity of the fight choreography and, because this project is on a tight schedule, we'll have to move on without you.'

'Seriously? Because I throw a left hook with my thumb tucked correctly?'

'He knows what he's doing. He's trained with the Japanese temple and—'

'Yeah, yeah, he told us already,' I said.

I beat most of the LA traffic and got home just as Rebecca was pulling out of the drive to do the school run to get the kids. She wound her car window down as I pulled level with her.

'Home early?' she said.

'Hey, babe!' I smiled. 'So – funny story – about that movie I was doing ...'

On television, I've guest-starred in some great shows like *Twin Peaks*, *MacGyver* and *Magnum PI*. I played the notorious London underground bareknuckle boxer Roy Shaw in a biopic of his archrival Lenny McLean (*My Name Is Lenny*).

Despite the occasional dickhead like Sensei Guru, there are a lot of really genuine, hard-working people in the TV/movie world. Noel Clarke and I met way back in 2010 to talk about me playing an MMA fighter in a movie he was writing and although that movie wasn't made, he cast me in his 2014 sci-fi movie *The Anomaly* and attended some of my biggest UFC fights to support me.

Most of the roles I'm offered are bad guys in the action genre. It's fun to play toy soldiers, running around exotic locations, doing fight scenes and shooting off guns, and it allows me to continue to use the martial arts training I've done for over three decades now. But of course I want to do different types of roles; I'm actually looking to do some more dramatic work, the type which will really challenge my acting skills.

People laughed when I said I was going to get paid as a DJ, they laughed when I said I was going to be an MMA fighter, they laughed at my UFC title ambitions and they're doing it again now I'm trying to make it as an actor.

The biggest role I've gotten so far is playing 'Hawk' in *xXx*, which I filmed after the Anderson Silva fight. It was one of those auditions where I just felt sure I'd done well and given the casting agents what they'd been looking for.

The very next day my dynamite agent Mike Staudt, who now handled much of my career outside the UFC, called me. 'You've got it. They loved you … and you have to leave tomorrow for Toronto. For five to six weeks.'

Vin Diesel is one of the biggest stars in Hollywood – and one of the nicest guys I've met in that world. When I arrived on the set of the franchise he created, Vin stopped what he was doing and made a huge fuss of me. We talked about the UFC, my win over Anderson and fights that he was looking forward to for over an hour. Then he gave me a tour of the set. Any nerves I arrived with were settled right away.

It really was an amazing experience. I'd done nothing even close to this level before. The production was incredible – the movie cost $85million to make. The fight scenes, the stunts, you name it, it was unreal being part of it. Even when I wasn't needed on set or location, the weapons training, going over the choreography, it was like the best get-away ever for someone like me.

There were a few moments on *xXx* when I was having fun, working hard on a big blockbuster movie, where I could have convinced myself that I would be okay if I never fought in the UFC again.

Beating Anderson Silva – the guy I'd measured myself against for a decade – maybe that was enough of a legacy for me to leave behind. It's possible that I could have convinced myself of that.

It's also possible, though, I'd have grown resentful that I never got the chance to fight for the UFC title. It's possible that, on the nights I couldn't sleep, I'd compare my record against some of the fighters who have gotten title shots and feel pissed off. There's only so long you can feel pissed off before you grow bitter.

I don't know how I would have looked back on my career if I'd not fought for the belt. I'll never know, of course, because in the last few days of filming *xXx*, I finally did land my shot.

CHAPTER SEVENTEEN

(ONE) EYE ON THE PRIZE

Eighteen days before I fought for the UFC title, I woke up in a hotel room in Toronto, Canada. I'd been staying in that room at the Soho Metropolitan for nine weeks, filming the movie *xXx: Return of Xander Cage*.

I'd auditioned for the role of Hawk, a badass spy who fights and then teams up with actor Vin Diesel's title character. I felt I'd smashed the audition.

With these casting calls, the best thing you can do is show up prepared, do your best, go home and forget about it. If you get a call back – fantastic, but don't waste energy worrying about it. The very next day my dynamite agent Mike Staudt called me.

'You've got it. They loved you . . . but you have to leave tomorrow for Toronto. For four to six weeks.'

Filming really was amazing. I'd done nothing even close to this level. For one, the cast were amazing. Vin Diesel was just an absolute legend. The production was incredible. The fight scenes, the stunts, you name it. It was just amazing. And on the days off, with all the weapons training, doing all the choreography – it was just a lot of fun, especially for someone like me who is kind of like an adrenaline junkie, if you will.

The four to six weeks had turned into six, and seven and then nine.

I only had one shoot left – on location the following night in the downtown area – and with my mind on finally going home I was looking for gifts for the family. For Lucas, I was after some walkie-talkies. I loved playing with walkie-talkies as a kid, hiding in one part of the house while talking to one of my brothers hiding in another.

After I got a pair, I decided to visit a Starbucks for a coffee and a quick read. It was a Monday and after lunch hour. There were plenty of places to sit. I took a comfy armchair towards the back of the café, fired up Twitter and began to scroll the latest world happenings, 160-character hot-takes at a time.

My thumb froze mid-air.

> *Chris Weidman pulls out of UFC 199 title fight*
> *Middleweight No.1 Weidman injured*
> *Weidman out of UFC 199 title rematch with Rockhold*

Headline after headline confirmed that the rematch between UFC middleweight champion Luke Rockhold and the man he'd beaten for the belt, Chris Weidman, scheduled for 4 June at the Forum in Inglewood, California, was off. The challenger was out. The champion, obviously, needed a new opponent. The fight was only 19 days away. If – and it was an if – Rockhold still wanted to defend his title the UFC would already be frantically searching for a replacement opponent.

If I'd missed the chance to call for a title fight immediately after beating Silva, I wouldn't this time. Shooting upright in the leather armchair, I used both thumbs to bash out a text to Dana White.

Hey Dana if you need someone to step in and fight for the world title on 2 weeks notice you know where I am

The reply came within moments. It was a photograph of Lorenzo sat across an office table. A huge grin was on his face as he gave a thumbs up direct to camera. Underneath, Dana wrote, 'FUCKING LOVE! SO DOES LORENZO!'

From the photo, it looked like the UFC owners were sat at one of the conference tables in their upstairs offices at 2960 West Sahara Avenue.

Then came the follow-up: 'We are talking to Jacaré. Will let you know.'

Ronaldo 'Jacaré' Souza was the No.2 ranked middleweight challenger, one place below Weidman. At *UFC 198* he had hammered Vitor Belfort, ranked No.3, inside of one round. I was ranked at No.4. I figured there was no way Jacaré – who was obviously in fight shape and had seemed to take no damage against Vitor – would turn the fight down. But I wasn't quite ready to move on yet.

My thumbs whirled as I shot off a couple of tweets to stir the pot. My Twitter stream was already flooded with @mentions from fans and even media asking me if I wanted the *UFC 199* title shot. I quickly picked one that also @mentioned Rockhold. My reply was that I wanted the fight – but Rockhold didn't.

You can see what I was doing there: goading Rockhold into a public statement in favour of fighting me.

The fans responded really well to the tweets. A lot of people seemed to be excited to see me get the shot.

I finished my coffee, grabbed the box of walkie-talkies and went back to my hotel. Once there I called the family, had a shower and put the news on while I got dressed to go to my mate Jason Falovitch's house to watch a basketball game. I unplugged my phone from the charger as I left the room. There was still no call or text from Dana or the UFC. There was little doubt in my mind the UFC would be announcing Rockhold vs Jacaré shortly.

Oh well, I thought. *It's probably for the best. Rockhold is a tough bastard and brilliant fighter. I'm not in shape to go five rounds anyway, not at the pace I would need. I'd always said the goal wasn't to fight for the belt, but to win the belt.*

If nothing else that day, I'd reaffirmed to the UFC, to Dana and – most importantly – to myself that I wasn't satisfied yet. The movie had taken my full attention since the Anderson fight, but the day's events had made me realise just how close I was to the UFC championship.

It dawned on me that with Weidman out hurt, Jacaré about to get his shot in a few weeks, and Cheator Belfort about to drop from his No.3 position after getting beaten at *UFC 198*, I would become the next UFC middleweight title challenger after *UFC 199* was done.

This was great. I got dressed and went to my mate's. I didn't go nuts, but I drank a little and indulged in some tasty food. Around 1am I was back in my hotel room and drifted off to sleep with nothing but the following day's shoot on my mind.

My call time for my final day of filming wasn't until the late afternoon. We were going to be shooting on location, outdoors on a closed-off street in downtown Toronto just after dark. With another full day to kill, I took the opportunity to hit the gym and sweat out the previous night's junk food and drink. (And, of course, get a little pump on my biceps and chest. Gotta look buff for the cameras!)

The GoodLife Fitness club I'd been using for over two months was about a ten-minute run away. As I was checking into the gym, my phone started flashing like an office Christmas party. All kinds of notifications were blowing up: Twitter, texts, Instagram, Facebook Messenger. Stepping to one side, I looked at my screen just as Ariel Helwani texted 'Congrats on the fight!'

Not quite believing what was clearly happening, I called Ariel: 'Congrats on what fight? The title fight?' I asked.

'Yeah! Dana just went on ESPN Sport Center and said Jacaré turned it down, he has an injury, and so you are getting the shot.'

Oh, fuck! This was real.

I got off the phone with Ariel quickly and rushed up the stairs and dived into the changing rooms. I leapt onto a set of digital scales, fearing the worst.

It was worse. Displayed right there under my nose in red LED, it read: 215.7lb.

Oh, *fuck*. How on earth am I going to be at 185lb in just 17 days? By two and a half weeks out, I needed to be well under 205lb and, ideally, hovering around 200. This weight cut was going to murder me. It was also going to hurt my chances in the fight.

The fight. *The* UFC title shot I'd always wanted and chased so long after.

Bollocks to all the fancy equipment in the gym, I needed to lose weight and get in shape. Fast! That meant old-school road work – right fucking now! I darted towards the exit in full panic mode, throwing my backpack over my shoulders and apologising for knocking a few gym members flying as I hurried down the stairs.

I exploded out of the gym doors and into the streets like an escaped lunatic. I can't even imagine how crazy I must have seemed to people I was blowing past. I went from nought to nuclear in three seconds flat. My hands snatched at the air, trying to reach top speed.

Fucking hell, Mike. Thirty pounds! In two fucking weeks!

Within a couple of blocks, the city became very built up and there were hundreds of people on the street, shopping, grabbing lunch, climbing in and out of cabs and delivering parcels. I zigzagged around them, trying to maintain a fat-burning pace, then I hit a traffic light and had to bounce around on my ankles for an eternity.

'Fuck this!' I said out loud and leapt into the traffic. I was almost splattered by a white van with a ladder strapped to its roof before I finally started getting room to go through the gears. I ran out of the business district and into a residential area. My body settled into an autopilot rhythm. My mind settled down as well. I began to process the enormity of what was happening.

I was running through a park – I've no idea of the name – that had a winding path through trees when the music in my headphones was replaced by a ringtone. Without slowing my pace, I answered. A familiar voice congratulated me.

'Hey, thanks for the heads up, Dana,' I said with no small amount of sarcasm.

We spoke briefly about the fight, the PR plan and my purse. I kept running the whole time. I ran a few more miles and my phone went again. It was Jason Parillo. I kept up my pace while I downloaded to my coach where my head was at.

'I've not trained for four months,' I pointed out.

Jason let me hear his amusement in his voice. 'You've been training for this your whole life. What would one more month do for you? You're in shape – how's your run going?'

I slowed down to a jog, a walk and then a full stop. I wiped wet from my hairline and checked the tracker app on my phone.

'Jason, I'm not in bad shape. I just ran over five miles at a good pace and I feel great..'

'No, you ran five miles at a good pace dodging through traffic and pedestrians. And talking on the phone the whole time.'

I was already breathing normally, I noted.

'You've been training for this your entire life,' Jason repeated.

I turned around and headed back in the general direction of my hotel. I'd run so far I didn't quite know the way back to where I was staying. But I knew the direction I was heading in – I was on the final mile before reaching the UFC world title.

It was bittersweet being home. I'd missed my family like crazy while in Toronto and even though I was back, I knew I had to begin to fully focus on *UFC 199* almost immediately. I was so happy to be back with them, though.

Lucas was baffled by my gift of walkie-talkies. He stared at the box as if it was a long-division maths problem, so I explained how much fun we'd be having, talking to each other from other parts of the house.

'Thanks, Dad,' he said. 'But we've got cell phones, so …'

Later that evening, once the kids were upstairs, Rebecca and I continued a conversation we'd been having off and on since my first eye operation.

'You've done it now, Michael,' she said. 'You've got the world title fight you always said you'd earn. Win or lose, I think it is time for you to retire. You've been pushing your luck with the eye injury long enough. I don't want to see you go through any more. I think you'll beat Rockhold and that would be a great way to leave. And if you don't win, finally fighting for the title is a good way to sign off, too.'

Despite agreeing with every word, I found I could only meet her halfway.

'If I lose, I'll retire there and then in the Octagon,' I promised. 'Right after the fight, I'll tell Joe Rogan and everyone watching that I'm done. I'll probably make an arse of myself, crying my eyes out. I'll spend eternity as a Twitter meme but, I promise, if I lose this is my last fight ever. Promise.'

'But, if and when you win . . .'

'If and when I win, I'll defend that goddamn belt as long as I can.'

Real fighting isn't like *Rocky*. One pep talk from a Mickey figure doesn't infuse a fighter with the confidence of reinforced concrete. As much sureness as I'd gotten from Jason and that run in Toronto, some of it had evaporated by the third day of training back at the RVCA gym at Costa Mesa.

The bookies made me a 6 – 1 against underdog. I became irritable. Brady caught the worse of it. While I was packing up to go home, I was deep inside my head and didn't notice Jason was stood in front of me until he spoke.

'Mike. Let's talk after the guys leave.'

Twenty minutes later Jason locked the gym door and sat next to me on the apron of the boxing ring. I felt like a dog in a vet's waiting room.

'You're fighting for the middleweight title of the world in two weeks. You are the official top contender to the entire division. This is what you've worked for. This is *it* – the top of the mountain.

'I think you're gonna win. Brady thinks you are gonna win. We all think you will win. But – there's a chance it doesn't go our way. There's always a chance it doesn't go our way. This could be the only two weeks we get as the No.1 contender. Why not go through it with a smile on our faces and enjoy the moment?'

I nodded away but Jason knew I needed to hear a little more.

'No one thought we'd get here and we did,' he added. 'This is a great moment for us – a great moment for *you*. It is everything you have worked for and everything you deserve. This should be a great time in your life. You will look back on these few days for the rest of your life. Mike – fucking smile! You are fighting for the championship of the world!'

Now you see why Jason Parillo is the best coach I've ever had. He's the best coach in the sport, bar none.

I stood up and shook Jason's hand.

'You're right, Jason,' I said. 'You're one hundred per cent right.'

From that moment on, everything went right in camp. It was like destiny. Don't ask me to explain it, but the weight fell off me. On the fourth day in the gym, I was flying. My long-time strength and conditioning coach, Scot Prohaska, did wonders in the short time we had. My wrestling was razor-blade sharp. Brady wasn't able to tap me again for the entire camp.

Most importantly, Jason and I both felt I'd found another 15 per cent in punching power. I'd dropped Anderson Silva twice with my left hook and we all felt that punch would be a key weapon against Rockhold. Not only was the defending champion a southpaw (considered to be predominantly vulnerable to the left hook thrown from an orthodox stance) but Rockhold's style contained several fault lines we fully intended to exploit.

Watching the wins Rockhold had after our last fight closely, we confirmed that he still stood with his feet a little too far apart after missing with punches. This would limit his available escape routes from my counter-punches.

'When he winds up like that he can only pull back in a straight line,' Jason pointed out on a laptop. 'He even does that with his hands by his sides.'

'He's overconfident,' Brady said.

Jason agreed: 'Rockhold is going to be real overconfident now he's the champ. Mike's going to get him all steamed up in the build-up. Rockhold will be overconfident and also pissed off. He usually likes to start slow and find his range before committing in a fight – this fight he'll be rushing. He will make mistakes and we are going to take advantage of every one.'

Fight week arrived and before I knew it the UFC camera crew were following me around everywhere for the fly-on-the-wall series *Embedded*. The crew was positively thrilled when I told them I was going to drive with Rebecca to pick Lucas up from school and, of course, the little terror didn't waste his chance to troll his old man again.

'I think he may be stronger,' my offspring said of Rockhold.

'Who's going to win though?' I pressed, expecting exactly what I got.

'I think ... him!'

While I was volunteering to be clowned by my own son for the cameras, Rockhold had the *Embedded* crew follow him to his regular pedicure spot.

'Bisping thinks this is going to be his fairy tale,' the champion said while soaking his nails. 'I will have none of that. This will be his swan song. I will prove there's no such thing as destiny. I cannot wait to shut his mouth.'

Myself, Jason and Brady all lived driving distance away from the host hotel, the Manhattan Beach Marriott, but on the Tuesday of fight week we were all in the lobby checking in. The traffic in LA is so unpredictable it just made sense to stay at the host hotel. It was only 45 minutes from my house (traffic allowing) so I packed lightly.

Just before I left, I went back upstairs to our bedroom. It took a minute of rummaging through drawers to find, but I put the Breitling Avenger Seawolf watch on again. Its long wait to be passed on to Callum was only a few years from being over, but I wanted to wear it again that week.

And Callum was also with me the whole week, too. He was off school, so it was perfect. He was understanding when I explained he couldn't be in my corner, that the emotional distraction in Scotland the year before had been too much for me. But being with me for all the TV, radio and PR hits, the press conference and weigh-ins plus staying in the hotel was an amazing shared experience for me and my first baby. Callum was one of the boys all fight week. Me, Callum, Jason and Brady laughed and joked our way to challenging for the world title.

In 25 UFC fights, I'd never struck the exact balance between focus and fun like I did in June 2016. One night, when we got back to the hotel after doing a late-night talk show, we were met by a Vicky Coghlan, who was now the UFC head of PR in the UK. She presented me with a British flag with literally hundreds of good-luck messages inscribed on the cloth.

'These messages are from actual fans,' she said. 'We put it out on social media and we took hundreds of them and printed them onto the flag.'

The messages were in tiny print, but were powerful motivation. These were the people who'd been behind me for a decade, and they were with me again before the biggest fight of my life. My throat clicked a little from the inside. I was going to carry that flag – and the dreams of the people who'd supported me the longest – with me come Saturday.

By this stage in my career I'd headlined ten UFC events in eight different countries. I'd fought on massive cards like *UFC 66* and *UFC 100*. None of them compared to headlining as the challenger for the world UFC title. There was a buzz about the event. I got the sense a lot of people who followed the sport were happy I'd finally got my shot.

'This isn't an accident,' I told several interviewers as they pointed cameras and recorders at me at the media day. 'I'm not here because Jacaré turned down a shot – I'm here because of a lifetime's worth of hard work. From the age of eight when I first put on a pair of gloves I knew I could become world champion one day. I've worked tirelessly – you've no idea how hard I've worked for years – I've had twenty-six fights in the UFC, almost forty professional fights and God knows how many kickboxing fights and jiu-jitsu tournaments before that. I have worked for this my entire life.'

On my opponent, I was honest about the task in front of me. 'I know Rockhold. I know what he is capable of. He is a very, very good fighter – but the opponent doesn't matter. This is about me. Me getting the chance to fulfil my destiny and becoming world champion is what I am focusing on. It doesn't matter if it is Rockhold or Godzilla on the other side of the Octagon – it is going to take a bullet to the brain to stop me Saturday night.'

The press conference was held at the Forum itself on the Thursday. Opened in 1967 and located directly under the eastern approach route for planes landing at LAX, at 3900 West Manchester

Blvd, Inglewood, the Forum is about as historic as American arenas get outside New York's Madison Square Garden.

The Forum had served as the home ground for the Lakers basketball and Kings hockey teams as well as hosting virtually every major music act you could think of. As we made our way to the arena floor we passed a huge wall where hundreds of the biggest names in sports and entertainment were listed in painted block letters as previous headliners. I stopped for just a second to see that Elvis had sold the place out, Bob Dylan had recorded his famous *Before the Flood* live album there and Muhammad Ali had fought there.

The press conference was set up on the arena floor. A lot of press and perhaps 500 fans were in attendance. There was a real buzz about *UFC 199*. The co-main was another grudge match, the third (and final) clash between Dominick Cruz and Urijah Faber, and both the bantamweight greats were sat with Rockhold and me as Dana White introduced the two pay-per-view title fights.

With the presser under way I wasted no time needling Rockhold, who had shown up dressed like a daytime talk-show host.

'Luke says he's on a different level, that he can destroy everybody and this, that and the other. I don't turn down fights. Two weeks, two days, two hours – I'll fight anyone, any time, any place, and certainly against this arsehole.'

It was a jab, intended to sting. I wanted to draw a response from the media and fans in the audience – and from Luke. And that's what happened. The fans giggled and Luke started his first pre-fight press conference as champion on the defensive.

'I chose you, I said I wanted—' Rockhold began, but I cut him off.

'You chose WRONG!'

Rockhold takes himself extremely seriously. I know how thin his skin is from mutual friends who delight in ribbing him. Luke had come to the press conference intending to project himself as a professional, a well-spoken and well-respected sports champion. My job that day was to ruin all that for him and send him away off-balance and angry.

Cruz and Faber were two old rivals and they went at it too, making for a lively opening few minutes of a press conference. Then Rockhold answered a question from my regular broadcast partner on Fox Sport (and now ESPN) Karyn Bryant about people confusing his confidence with arrogance. And MMA's answer to a Ken doll launched into this homily about putting positive energy out into the cosmos.

'Some people strive to hate but some people strive to achieve things.' Rockhold spoke as if he were revealing the secrets of the universe. 'If you think something, the likelihood of it happening is very slim. But if you *believe* something, if you *know* something is going to happen and have *confidence* ... you will *achieve* things in life.'

A vague embarrassment blew across the room, but guru Luke had more pretentious nonsense to drop.

Mic in his right hand, he leaned forward and started hitting the table, televangelist style, with his left. 'That's how you *overcome*. That's how you put yourself *out there*. That's what I do. I *believe*—'

I'd had enough: 'Sounds like the worst self-help book you've ever read: conceive, believe, achieve ... Shut the fuck up!'

Half the room, including Dana White at the podium, laughed out loud. More than just uncomfortable, Rockhold was now embarrassed. I pressed home the advantage.

'You're talking as if you are this dominant champion,' I said, turning to look in his direction. 'You just won the belt. This is your first defence. It's not like you are Anderson Silva – who I just beat, by the way.'

Rockhold did his best to come back. 'You're just an average bloke … I AM A SAMURAI!'

'Samurai? What is this? "Conceive, believe, achieve – I am a samurai!" Stop it. You are making a fool of yourself.'

I turned to the crowd. 'I get to come in on two weeks' notice, punch him in the face, and become world champion. I am a happy man. This is my destiny. I *believe* it, Luke! I *bee-lee-ve*!'

Uproarious laughter rained down on the champion and his fresh pedicure. This press conference was already a 10–8 round.

Then Ariel Helwani asked Rockhold about the infamous sparring session and I jumped in again. 'Here come the excuses! Don't worry, Luke, I got them: he was drinking red wine, he'd had a late night, he hadn't sparred for a while and he was hanging out with chicks. Did I miss any, Luke? It's okay, mate. I know it's sparring and you shouldn't talk about it – but I did. It is out there. I whupped your arse!'

It was all too much for the housewives' favourite. He was now stripped of his zen yoga master affectations and the real him started to leak out.

In response to Anderson Silva's name, he spat, 'I'll show you the greatest!' Trying to change the narrative that he had all the advantages in the fight, he stupidly volunteered that he had a knee injury. Finally, as if to show me how clowned and humiliated he felt, he went below the belt and made several nasty remarks about my eye injury.

It was like getting an FBI psychological profile on my opponent. His mindset was reckless, angry and easily manipulated. That's exactly how I wanted him in the fight.

CHAPTER EIGHTEEN

CONCEIVED, BELIEVED, ACHIEVED

After the fun and games of the press conference came the serious matter of making 185lb the following day. *UFC 199* was the first event where the weigh-ins were held from 9am to 11am the day before the fight. Until then, the practice had been for fighters to step on the scale at 4pm, but the California Athletic Commission had come out with a new procedure to give fighters additional time to recover from squeezing their bodies into their chosen weight division. So, for the very first time, the weigh-in would be held in a small function room at the hotel. That was when I needed to hit 185lb.

But UFC weigh-ins were a tried and tested part of promoting a big fight and so in addition to the official weigh-in a 'ceremonial' one was scheduled for 5pm at the Forum arena. The ceremonial weigh-in would be identical to the usual big production weigh-ins – big stage, music, Dana, Rogan, Octagon girls and thousands of fans – except just for show.

'The early morning weigh-in is the one you hit weight on,' we were all told a million times. 'The 5pm weigh-in doesn't count.'

Me and Rockhold would be fighting at around 9:15pm the following evening – that was 36 hours after weighing in. Looking back, it was very possible that those additional six hours could have handed the naturally bigger Rockhold yet another advantage. However, I was focused on myself. I welcomed the early weigh-in because I knew it would do me good.

A 9am weigh-in meant that if I woke up overweight at a normal time, say 8am, there would be little or no time to correct course. That gave us three choices. 1) Cutting all the weight before I went to bed and trying to sleep weighing 185lb – a total non-starter. 2) Waking up at 5am and cutting weight then – I didn't fancy that either. So we split the difference and went for 3) I cut weight until midnight and then woke again at 7am to cut the rest.

Just before 9:15am we made our way down to the second-floor function room that had been set up for the weigh-in. I was surprised how much media were there, sat to one side in rows. There was a step-and-repeat banner and a stage with the scale on. Behind the step-and-repeat – and out of view of the media – the UFC and Commission had an area to complete the official particulars. I took care of that, selected the gloves I would fight for the world title in, got undressed and went out to step on the scale.

185lb!

Job done, I started rehydrating immediately.

Seven hours and about 14lb later, there was a crowd of thousands at the ceremonial weigh-in at the Forum. They knew the real weight-making had come and gone, but the ceremonial weigh-in was free to get in and had become part of the anticipation for a big fight.

With the heavy towels and salt baths a distant memory, I felt amazing. Sat backstage, all the fighters looked to have more energy. Instead of slumping lethargically in chairs like we usually would be, we were all up and about chatting to each other and staff.

Callum, the expert in MMA that he'd become, was loving it. But he was nervous and excited when it came time to walk through the curtain and climb the stairs to the stage in front of 3,000 people. While Dana, the matchmakers, Joe Rogan and the rest waited I began stripping off. I'd gotten my shirt and a shoe off before there was an awkward moment as a floor manager leaned in to explain stripping off wasn't actually necessary.

Kinda like *UFC 66*, I thought, another echo from a decade ago. Everything is coming full circle. I stepped on the scale and hammed it up for the fans.

'THE CHALLENGER – MICHAEL BISPING!' Rogan boomed into the microphone, drowning out cheers and piped-in rock music.

Now Rockhold came out, skipping from behind the curtains towards the stage. I didn't notice he wasn't cheered as much as I was. The fact he appeared fully recovered from the weigh-in had my entire focus. Reaching the stage, the champion threw off his white T-shirt and stepped on the scale. As Rogan bellowed out his name, Rockhold raised closed eyes to the heavens and stretched his arms out in a Jesus Christ pose.

Every single time you see Rockhold you can't help but notice he's fucking big. No beanpole, either. His long limbs are wrapped in the kind of tight, cabled muscle that generate power. He was impossibly huge for a middleweight. He got off the scales and walked towards me. Dana stepped between Rockhold and me, on high alert.

'Let's see what you got, big boy!' I said. Luke got into it, too, and we smirked and gestured aggressively at each other while lobbing insults. The crowd was loving it, which was why I was doing it. I was now a hugely experienced UFC veteran and had learned to manage my temperament. Fighting under a red haze of anger was not going to help me win the UFC title. The banter on the stage was only for fun.

Dana wasn't so sure. 'Don't touch! Don't touch!' he yelled as he gestured me towards Rogan, who was waiting mic in hand to do a quick interview.

Joe asked me what it meant to be fighting for the belt. 'I've been in the UFC for over ten years,' I said. 'I've fought the best in the world. I've had my ups and downs but you can't keep a good man down. I'm here now and I do believe this is my destiny.'

Then I played to the audience, adding, 'There's not a single person in the world I'd rather take the belt off than this smug arsehole!'

The crowd cheered and laughed. I'd given them what they wanted from a Bisping weigh-in. They were very welcome.

After about ten hours of deep sleep I woke up. Here it was. Saturday, 4 June 2016. In 12 hours I'd finally challenge for the UFC championship of the whole world. This was the end of the road I'd been on since I set off for Nottingham. Before that, even. Since the age of six when I wanted to be the best kid in the jiu-jitsu class.

After a good breakfast downstairs and a little rest, I tried something new for a fight day. I went to work out.

While attending an event as a commentator, I'd been stunned to see Jon Jones sweating in the hotel gym just hours before one of his fights. I'd gone my whole career hoarding every drop of energy from the moment I made weight to the second I stepped into the Octagon. But here 'Bones' was pounding a treadmill with his size 15s.

Jones explained that, after putting our bodies through the horrors of a weight-cut, the first time we asked them to perform athletically should not be under the win/lose circumstances of the fight. This idea had sort of occurred to me before, but having one of the best ever swear by it convinced me. So, about 1pm on fight day, Brady, Mario, Jason and I went to the fighter workout room. The blue mats the UFC provide all week had already been packed away and the standalone, UFC-branded punching bags were gone too. The room was now just a room, but it was all good.

'Let's get some music on,' I said, and Brady set up his phone and a speaker on the windowsill. I'd previously introduced Brady to some old-school British music and, as chance would have it, Stereo MCs' 'Connected' was the first song on his playlist.

As I shadow-boxed, hit pads and drilled takedown defences for the next 50 minutes I absorbed the soundtrack of my carefree teens and early twenties. I wanted to carry some of who I was back then into the Octagon. Not the recklessness and anger but the feeling of having nothing to lose. That every chance was one worth taking.

The 90s-infused workout helped me cast away into a restful sleep for a few hours. I woke up feeling good. At the pre-arranged time, Jason and Brady came to my room and we packed our gear for the fight. Callum had now joined Rebecca and Ellie. I'd see them all Octagonside later.

'Feeling good?' Jason asked.

'Great,' I said. The confidence was still there but the fight nerves had now made their appearance too.

We went through our checklist. Fight gloves, check. Cup, check. Mouthpiece, check. Something to play music on, check. Shin pads just in case I wanted a light spar, check. Boxing gloves just in case, check. Bucket, check. Stopwatch, check. Separate bucket for ice, check.

And I was already wearing the watch I'd first put on the evening of 24 June 2006.

'Full circle,' I said as we made our way downstairs to be transported to the arena.

The early prelims were well under way when I arrived at my dressing room at the Forum. The ceiling was lower than in more modern arenas, but there was a lot of space. My Reebok fight gear was waiting for me, neatly arranged in an open locker. Several BJJ mats were taped down to the floor. As usual, there was a monitor showing the prelim fights. I turned the sound up a little and sat down to watch as my team began unpacking our gear.

Sitting there like any other fan watching on any other TV screen, I let myself become absorbed by the fights. The idea was to delay getting into 'fight mode' for as long as possible. That was easier said than done with people constantly coming in and out of the locker room. First the California Commission needed to see us. Then my assigned cutman came in. Then the UFC needed to shoot some inserts. Then the referee of my main-event fight, Big John McCarthy, stepped through the door for his pre-fight instructions.

I listened intently, as I always did whenever McCarthy spoke. Then, respectfully, I said to Big John, 'Don't stop this fight. If I am in trouble, I'll let you know. I'm going to turn this fight into a war. That's the plan to win. Don't you stop it just because I'm in trouble.'

McCarthy had heard this before in his quarter-century of serving as the third man in the cage. He said simply, 'I'll do my job. Nothing more, nothing less.'

After Big John left, I got back to watching the fights. The pay-per-view portion of the card was starting. I began to get changed into my fight gear. I let the reality of the evening begin to build. My hands were taped and the fight gloves wrenched over that tape.

My fists felt strong. I stretched my leg, back and shoulder muscles out, all the better to squeeze them tighter in the fight.

Brady and I drilled on the mat. We moved in circles, sliding arms and legs in and out of jiu-jitsu holds.

On the monitor, the second PPV fight was about to begin: Henderson vs Hector Lombard. A horrible and overhyped little man, Lombard was someone I'd had several run-ins with at UFC events over the years. I thudded punches into Jason's target pads. I raised my heartrate up, then paced the room and let it drop. Hendo got a massive win with an elbow strike. I was happy Hendo had scored another one of his big knockouts, especially against that Unhappy Halfling. I smiled and pointed, but didn't focus on it for longer than a moment.

I went back to the drills. I felt amazing. I was enjoying the moment. I'd earned this.

'Two more fights and then we walk, Bisping!' came a voice as the door shut again.

(The only sour moment came when I was told I wouldn't be able to walk out with the British flag with the messages from the UK fans. Even though it was, y'know, the flag of my nation and it had been given to me by literally the UFC PR department, the people in charge of enforcing the Reebok policy told me they'd fine me $20,000 if I walked out with it. Despite this nonsense, that flag is one of my most prized pieces of memorabilia from my entire career. It's folded into a triangle and in my office as I type this.)

It was now time to fully focus on the battle ahead. I hit the striking pads with 85 per cent power. I felt *amazing*. My weapons were ready. My confidence was sky-high. Thirty, forty minutes melted.

'Bisping – time to walk!' came the call.

And so we walked. But this time was different. It was unlike every other fight I had in my career. This was usually the time when the fight became real. Physiologically, my autonomic nervous system would recognise the 'fight or flight' situation and shut down non-essential functions, diverting their energy into my muscles. (One of the non-essential functions is the digestive system – hence the feeling of butterflies in the belly.)

By now, just minutes before the start of the fight, I knew the butterflies and nerves wouldn't be making an appearance this fight. I felt focused, not fixated; energised, not hyper.

We arrived at the tunnel from backstage to the arena floor. The pre-fight promo was running in the arena and the lights were dark. The only illumination was coming from the camera in front of me, which would beam our short walk to the Octagon to the world.

'Man,' Scot said, 'I've never seen you move as well as you have this camp. I've never seen you as calm as you are tonight.'

'Destiny,' Jason said.

The air inside the arena was warm. Because of the body heat of the crowd, it always was come main-event time. 'Song 2' blasted out. The lights blazed colours. The cameras sped towards me. Fans outstretched arms. I got close to the Octagon and looked for Rebecca, Callum and Ellie. There they were, front row. I went over and hugged them for a second. Their expression told me everything I needed to hear.

'YEAH!' I yelled.

My team took my walkout shirt off. I was checked over at the prep point. Vaseline was applied to my face so Rockhold's punches wouldn't tear at my skin. The roar of the crowd registered for the first time as I ascended the Octagon steps. On the top step I turned around and flexed my biceps to cheers. The fans – these American fans – were for me. And not just Americans – I saw several British flags wiggling excitedly in the stands. More than just enjoying it all, I took the best of each moment – the support, the love, the thrill of what I was about to do – without allowing anything to weigh down my concentration.

Rockhold walked through the Octagon gates minutes later. He looked even bigger than the day before and had regained that look of can't-be-bothered confidence. He was prancing around, running backwards and doing weird dance steps. Like all samurais do, I guess. He pretended to yawn several times. What a bell-end.

Bruce Buffer did his thing. While he was introducing me, I took out my mouthpiece and made sure the British fans watching at home saw I had our flag on it.

Jason and Brady were on the other side of the fence now, leaning in. 'I feel fucking great,' I told Jason. 'You fucking look great!' he said. 'Best I've ever seen you!'

Rockhold was announced. He did some Bikram Yoga bullshit for the camera. Buffer left the Octagon. All but one of the camera crew followed. Very near now. Referee McCarthy waved Rockhold and me towards the centre. The crowd noise rolled up into a roar. Big John gave his final instructions but Rockhold and I were more interested in a final few verbals.

Rockhold mumbled something and shook a hand side to side.

'What's that, buddy?' I smiled.

'No touch,' said Rockhold, announcing he wouldn't partake in the traditional show of respect.

I smiled wider. 'No touch?'

Rockhold shook his head again. 'No touch!'

'I'll touch ya in a second, mother-fucker!' I laughed, backing up into my corner.

The cameraman retreated to the safe side of the fence. The Octagon door locked. We waited for McCarthy to signal us to fight. The final few moments were ticking away and I was still as relaxed as I'd ever been. Measured in years, sweat or tears, it had taken an eternity to get here. Now the UFC champion was 20 feet away; the title 25 minutes of everything I had away. Rockhold looked bigger still. I didn't care. He was a great athlete. I was a great *fighter*. And we were about to have a *fight*!

I barely heard Big John's catchphrase: 'Are you ready? Are you ready? Let's get it on!'

Rockhold came forward to meet me, smiling. I kicked him in his lead right leg and the smile disappeared. I tried a little pressure, but while searching for my range Rockhold whipped my lead leg with a kick. That stupid ho-hum expression expanded across his face. I landed a right cross. Then a jab came close. My arms, shoulders and back felt loose. Rockhold looked annoyed.

One minute in, my scouting report read that 1) Rockhold was indeed predisposed to moving his head to his left every time I threw a straight punch; 2) while he'd added a much heavier jab to his game, he overcommitted to it and became off balance when it missed; and 3) he was again looking to take my head off with the left head kick.

I put 1) to good use immediately. I threw a jab which was never intended to land, tricking the champion into moving his head to the left – and into a nice right cross. Then I continued to batter Luke's right knee. I didn't know whether this was the one he'd hurt in training but, for sure, it was the one that needed planting in order for 3) to happen.

The war began at the 3:15 mark. I stepped in and missed with a left hook but had time enough to throw a straight right behind it. Luke slipped the cross exactly as I expected him to – and my second left hook landed with a thud. Rockhold retaliated with his best punch – the right hook – and came after me.

In most other fights, I'd have moved away at angles only to return a second later to take the initiative back. Not on this night. I planted my feet and fired my fists. Another left hook bounced off Rockhold's head. There was no poker face about him. Luke Rockhold was very pissed off and overconfident. The smack-talking, the disrespect I'd made him chew on in the build-up and his own condescending superiority was working against him. So was his lack of fighting IQ; I knew from that sparring session that when it came to reading a fight in real time, Rockhold was a functional illiterate at best.

My last left hook had clipped Rockhold but didn't land with full authority. I could have felt a little anxious that I'd given the game away – but I didn't think that one technique was going to win me the fight all by itself. In our game-plan the 'draw his right hook/side-step/left hook counter' was one of a dozen micro-strategies in place to bring Rockhold to a place where he'd begin the championship rounds tired, hurt and discouraged.

And once we were inside that inferno where our lungs were choked and our arms were filled with lactic acid, I knew – *I knew* – that I could remain in that place longer than Luke Rockhold could ever believe possible. I knew that I would emerge from that kind of firestorm as the UFC middleweight world champion.

He landed a solid left shin to my stomach. I snapped my heel into his right knee. Maybe recognising that I was laying foundations for the later rounds, Rockhold's aggression sky-rocketed. He landed four kicks – to my body and leg – in a row. Then he landed a left cross. That look was back on his face as he swaggered towards me with his hands by his side.

Whether it was anger or arrogance, Rockhold was now intent on a first-round KO. Rockhold's corner were not happy with what they were seeing. 'Tighter!' 'Not so hard!' 'Don't rush!' 'Quit chasing him!' they shouted.

On the PPV broadcast, Joe Rogan noted at this point: 'Rockhold's chin is straight up in the air.'

I'd noticed that, too, as I bit down harder on my mouthpiece. *You arrogant dickhead*, I thought. *I can't wait to see the look on your face in round three, round four, round five, as it dawns on you – way too late – that you had no idea what you were in for tonight.*

He landed a hard inside leg kick before whipping another towards my face. I used both hands to parry it and even through my gloves my palms stung for a second.

Rockhold then skipped forward and threw his jab. It was a good shot but instinctively, I'd placed my left foot on the outside of Luke's right. I fired a right hook to his body and the left hook that Jason and I had drilled. The telemetry from my fist reached my brain immediately. I'd landed a massive shot direct to the champion's jaw.

He dropped to the canvas. He was hurt.

YES! I thought. The crowd's roars faded into static. Time slowed down. Rockhold scrambled to his feet.

No you don't!

BOOM!

Another hook detonated on his chin. The impact sent him spinning backward. He crashed on the canvas again.

Instead of his expected day at the beach, I'd now swept Rockhold far out to sea. He was out of his depth, broadcasting panicked distress signals with every short-circuited movement. I went in for the finish like a Great White.

Rockhold was slumped, arse on the canvas and his back against the cage. The angle was awkward. I was conscious to avoid getting pulled into his guard. I side-stepped his prone legs and torqued every bit of power I could into my punches. Rockhold's head snapped right. Then left. Then right again. The lights cut out behind his eyes.

Suddenly Big John's oak-tree forearm swung against my lower neck so fast the impact hurt. It was the best feeling in the world because it meant the referee had waved the fight off. It was over.

A second of time snapped and I heard my own voice inside my head say, *I've won!*

'MICHAEL BISPING! IS THE NEW! UFC MIDDLEWEIGHT CHAMPION OF THE WORLD!' Mike Goldberg screamed on the broadcast.

The moment overloaded my senses. A thousand different thoughts flooded my brain all at once. There would be no need for a war. I wouldn't need to take this fight into the trenches. I wouldn't have to fight my way out of any tough spots. I wouldn't need to ignore painful cuts around my eyes or climb off the canvas. My heart and will to win would not even be needed. Because it was over, already. Done! I was already the UFC Middleweight Champion of the Whole World!

I screamed in victory and vaulted to the top of the cage. My arms shot into the air as the fans roared noise down at me. As I celebrated the Octagon was rapidly filling up with security, commissioners and whoever the hell these people are who materialise the moment a big fight is over. My eyes found Rockhold. He was still sat against the fence; now surrounded by methodical medical people and concerned teammates.

I understood immediately what was beneath the bewildered look on Rockhold's face – an offline human brain sprawling to reboot. Then his expression changed and I knew he could now see me again, too.

'FUCK YOU!'

He couldn't possibly have heard me yelling, not over the racket of the 15,587 fans who were cheering and yelling after witnessing what to them was one of the biggest upsets in recent UFC history. But it wasn't necessarily a *fuck you* to Rockhold. It was a *fuck you* to everyone who'd doubted me, underestimated me and tried to stop me from becoming the man and father I wanted to become. Sat on that Octagon fence, at the summit of the MMA world, it was a *fuck you* to anyone who'd ever written me off, and a *fuck you* on behalf of everyone and anyone who'd ever believed in me.

Nothing I say can do justice to what I felt in those few seconds. That left hook had whacked the top off a fire hydrant and I could feel emotions I'd kept shrink-wrapped inside since school gushing out.

I dropped off the fence and my bare feet hit the canvas. 'Easiest fight of my life!' I told the camera.

This was the moment I'd chased for long years – I was now living it! UFC world middleweight champion! Won it forever. No one could ever take what I had done away from me! First round! No one gave me a chance! No one! No one except ...

My family. Where's my family?

I saw Audie Attar had already managed to get Rebecca, Ellie and Callum to the top of the steps. I waved the security guy to let them through the Octagon door and hurried towards them.

Rebecca and I sank into a massive hug in the centre of the Octagon. 'We did it! We did it! We did it! Babe – we did it!' I repeated it over and over into her ear.

We did it – as a team. I wouldn't have got as far as Eldon Square Leisure Centre without Rebecca. She is the only woman in the world who would have supported such a crazy idea in the first place. She'd put a roof over our family, then put her own ambitions aside so I could pursue my dream. She'd put me back together so many times; after the army rejection letter, the visa issue, *UFC 100* and other defeats, the manager issues, nearly losing my eyesight. When sections of the media painted me as a villain, she reminded me who I was to the people who knew me the best. She was my wife, my motivation, my sports psychologist and my best friend.

For a second, it was a decade before and I was running up to her at the MGM Grand with that first bonus cheque at *UFC 66*. I snapped back into the present and I hugged my two eldest kids.

Only dads of daughters know the special pride when his little girl looks up to him as her protector. Ellie was looking with tears of pride in her eyes at her dad – me – the UFC champion of the world. I choke up even thinking about it. And Callum – my first-born's face said it all. He understood what we'd all achieved together. He was crying and cheering both at once.

We all held each other in the centre of the Octagon. We'd all sacrificed time together in order for this to happen. Spending the first minutes of my reign as world champion in a group hug with my family was my proudest moment on earth.

I celebrated with Jason, Brady and Scot. Lorenzo Fertitta, on the verge of selling the UFC for over $4 billion, was in the Octagon and looked thrilled for me. Back in the locker room my phone was blowing up with texts that would take me days to return 'thank yous' to.

The UFC title belt – identical but much heavier than the replicas I'd allowed myself to hold once or twice – was wrapped around my waist by Dana as I heard Bruce Buffer, the man who'd MC'd the other happiest day of my life, announce the greatest moment of my career.

'Ladies and gentlemen, referee John McCarthy calls a stop to this contest at three minutes, thirty-six seconds of the very first round ... Declaring the winner ... BY KNOCKOUT! AND NEW! UNDISPUTED! U-F-C MIDDLE-WEIGHT CHAMP-I-ON OF! THE! WORLD! ... MIKE-AL! THE COUNT! BIS-PING!'

Rogan asked me to describe what I was feeling. I did my best.

'Listen, I want to be humble here even though I want to be an arsehole. First of all, thank you all for being here. I am so happy right now. I started fighting when I came out of my mother. [Ugh, what I meant to say was "I was born a fighter".] I have always been a fighter. It always got me in trouble. But there's nothing I do in this life better than fighting. This woman here [Rebecca] supported me every step of the way. If it wasn't for her, my family, my dad, my mother, the support of the UK, everybody here, I could not have done this. I'm an average guy. This was my dream. Nobody was taking this away from me!

'People say I've got no punching power. I knew I could punch. This guy [Rockhold] demolishes everybody – finishes them in the first round. Check this out: first-round knockout. Left hook! Thank you, Jason Parillo. Everyone in the UK – thank you so much! Apart from my children and my wife, this is the greatest moment in my life.'

CHAPTER NINETEEN

FIVE O'CLOCK IN THE MORNING

The UFC's UK office arranged for me to fly over for a 'victory tour' after I became Britain's first ever UFC world champion.

We did a bunch of interviews and TV appearances in London then moved on to Manchester. Vicky from UFC PR picked me up from the hotel lobby for an early start on 17 June. I climbed into the 'executive class' people carrier that would be driving us around Manchester and she handed me the schedule for the day. The last item on the list was the one I was looking forward to:

FAN MEET & GREET – TRAFFORD CENTRE, STRETFORD   (6pm – 7:30pm)

It was the highlight of the tour. Actually, it was one of the highlights of my career – and I'm a veteran of these things. I've always enjoyed meeting the UFC fans, especially those in the UK. In 2009, me and Ross Pearson did an appearance at a video-game store in Glasgow which drew so many people other store managers called the police, complaining their store fronts were blocked with UFC fans. At the Oxford Street HMV in London two months before *UFC 120*, the line went out the door and around the building into a back alleyway.

The crowd at the Trafford Centre, though, was easily three times the size of the one at HMV. I was set up on a raised stage/bandstand area in the middle of the shopping centre. As I walked out onto the polished faux-wood floor I could see only a sea of faces in front of me all the way past the fountain-pool features, above on the upper levels and all the way to the lifts in front of me. It was humbling. There were over 2,000 people in line already. The ones at the front would have been waiting in place for hours; the ones at the back of the line had hours of waiting in front of them.

I was handed a mic. I managed to thank the fans for coming. I added, 'I'll see you soon.'

'We better get this going,' I said to Vicky as I handed her the mic back.

The fans were allowed up in ones, twos and threes into the small stage arena for pictures and, if they were old-fashioned, they could also get a signed 10x8 autographed picture of me with the UFC belt.

One of the first guys up was a bear of a bloke in a grey T-shirt, jeans and biker boots. He was crying. Tears streaked from his brown eyes and into his black bush of a beard.

'Mate – thank you,' he said. 'Never thought I'd see a British UFC champion ...'

I stood up and we clasped hands. This guy was enormous and here he was in tears because of something I'd done. One of the UFC staff had the big guy's phone all ready and we did a picture together.

'I'll be at your first defence,' he said. 'It'll be here in Manchester, yeah?'

'Thank you,' I said. 'And, yeah, if I've got any say in it, yes, I'll defend the belt here.'

Twenty minutes and forty selfies later, I met a dad and his two lads, both blond and about aged ten. They'd driven up from Exeter, the dad told me. Up the M5 and M6 ... on a Friday afternoon?

'Yeah, they both really wanted to see you,' the dad said. 'We all stayed up to see you win. The big 'un 'ere lost his voice shouting for you.'

The lad in question, his larynx apparently recovered, asked quickly, 'Will you fight in England again?'

'I think so, mate, the UFC are working on it,' I said. 'If it is in the UK, will you and your brother come see me and cheer for me?'

They both nodded excitedly. Then they held either end of the UFC world title belt, the big gold plate between them, and posed with their dad and me.

These were the stories I heard – or saw in teared eyes – for over three hours. I knew the British fans supported me, I knew they'd have been thrilled to finally get a British world champion but, again, the personal connection they'd made with me ... it was almost overwhelming.

When we finally left late into the evening, after every person in line got a picture, or a signature, or even a fist bump if that's what they wanted, there were still hundreds of people there wanting pictures. They swarmed around the entrance to the back-of-house area so tightly the mall's security people were worried someone could lose their footing and get trampled on. Before we made a break for it, they asked me not to stop walking for any reason, and they escorted me out of there like I was the US President during an assassination attempt.

The fans followed us to the door and – somehow – were even waiting by the service entrance. They cheered and flashed camera phones as I was bundled into the black people carrier and driven away. It was like being in a boy band for the evening.

I texted my manager, Audie, a picture I'd taken of the crowd.

'We've got to get the UFC to confirm my next fight will be in the UK!' I wrote underneath the image.

I was the oldest first-time UFC champion ever. My wife and manager were hinting that I shouldn't be fighting much longer. My body was delivering the same message, only less ambiguously. I had to use my status as the world champion to open as many doors for my post-fighting life as possible, I knew.

And things were going well. My acting career was gaining traction. My regular work with Fox Sports and presenting the *UFC Tonight* magazine show had seen me develop into a competent television analyst and host. I had several business interests including UFC Gym locations in California and the UK. Plus, I'd launched a regular weekly podcast with comedian and undefeated mixed martial artist Luis J. Gomez.

Luis J. Gomez (I have to write his entire name out – he insists on his middle initial as if he studied eight years at Yale to get it) and I started working together on a weekly show for American talk radio. We had a great chemistry together on the air. About 18 months into our show's run (which I did from home on a DSL, aka broadcast-quality, line) we were both frustrated with our compensation. Luis J. Gomez suggested we strike out by ourselves with a podcast. That's how the *Believe You Me* podcast came out.

Around the same time, I also branched out into commentating, first doing the *Contender Series* on the UFC Fight Pass streaming service and then for televised UFC events.

Whenever it came, I was determined I would be ready for life after active competition. This was completely different to when I thought my career had been ripped away from me due to the eye injury in 2013. I'd won the title now, I'd won respect and my place in history. I wasn't ready to go yet; but I was ready to start getting ready.

Given the heat between me and Rockhold and the fact the score was 1–1 between us (well, 2–1 to me when you include the sparring session – ha!), I thought the UFC could give the ex-champion an immediate rematch. I also expected to hear 'Jacaré' when Dana called with the name of the first challenger to my title. Or, maybe, 'Mousasi', who I was originally scheduled to fight in London. And, around this time, there was the first crazy talk of legend Georges St-Pierre coming out of retirement to fight me.

Instead, when the call came, Dana said a name that had been linked to mine for over eight years: Dan Henderson.

Joe Rogan is the UFC's most respected colour commentator, an arena-packing stand-up comic, a TV host and BJJ black belt. But perhaps his biggest success is turning *The Joe Rogan Experience* on YouTube into the most influential podcast on earth.

If *The JRE* gets behind something, it blows up; on the 16 June episode, Joe was getting behind Michael Bisping vs Dan Henderson, the rematch, for the UFC middleweight title.

'What could be a better, more exciting fight to see than Bisping versus Hendo two?' he enthused. 'How often do you get to do a rematch of the most brutal knockout in history, with both guys just having KO'd two monsters? That's the most exciting fight right now.'

Rogan added that he'd already called Dana with his matchmaking brainstorm. The fans and media ran with it. My Twitter blew up asking if I'd take the fight. Of course, I answered. Henderson was asked and answered in the affirmative, too.

I mean, what did people think we were going to say?

The call from Dana came.

'Yeah, sounds great,' I told the UFC boss. 'But what about it being in the UK? Is that going to happen?'

Manchester Arena or 'a stadium in Cardiff' were both available, he answered.

'It's gotta be Manchester!' I said.

And that was that. The rematch of the worst defeat of my career was on.

There was some bellyaching from the middleweight division over the fight the UFC had put together. Guys like Jacaré (who'd turned down a title shot already), Yoel Romero (forgetting he was suspended for a USADA violation), Vitor Belfort (who'd started a streak of getting knocked out in the USADA era), they all felt very entitled to tell me, the champion, where, when and whom I should fight.

Contrary to what was reported at the time, I didn't ask for Henderson. My only ask was to fight in the UK. But, believe you me, if only I'd known how much it would piss off these self-entitled whiners, I'd have beaten Joe Rogan to it and called Dana White to suggest it myself.

Henderson and I did a press conference together in Las Vegas on Friday, 19 August, and of course I was asked about Henderson's past TRT usage.

In the first fight, I got the weight-cutting wrong in the same way that I got circling into his right cross wrong. While I was holding my body hostage and starving it of nutrients, Dan Henderson was darting needles containing synthetic testosterone into his backside, which boosted his energy levels, bone density, strength and muscle mass.

Would I have liked to have known Henderson was on TRT before I fought him at *UFC 100*? Well, yeah, of course. I'd also have liked to have known there even was such a thing as TRT, too, because back then I had no clue this legal cheating was going on in the sport.

There's a difference between what Henderson was doing with TRT – exploiting a loophole and using a medical therapy that these commissions ignorantly allowed him to use – and what Vitor Belfort was doing. Hendo's physique had barely changed in the post-TRT era, to be truthful, while Belfort now sported moobs like a grandmother.

'After TRT was banned and USADA testing came in, I became UFC world champion,' I said. 'I've never been a big believer in coincidence. Dan Henderson said he needed TRT to compete, that he'd get sick without it, but here he is today alive and well. He's a miracle of modern medicine.'

The MMA community was probably expecting something a little stronger than that but, the truth is, I've never had much animosity towards Henderson.

True, I didn't appreciate the incident with Mark Coleman but, looking at it literally from his perspective, maybe he just saw me and Coleman getting into it and had no idea what Coleman had just said to me. And other than that, Dan's pretty inoffensive. He really doesn't say much. He just sort of mumbles and shrugs his way to fight day.

That doesn't necessarily help the box office, though. Like I said earlier, I always felt responsible for putting arses in seats when I was headliner and especially so in the UK.

Just like with all PPV events the UFC presented outside of North America, *UFC 204: Bisping vs Henderson 2* would be broadcasting live at 7pm US Pacific Time. That meant my fight would begin around 5am in Manchester. I was a bit worried the tickets wouldn't sell well for an event where fans would be filing out the arena at breakfast time. It was a huge ask of the British fans, I felt.

Yet all 16,693 tickets sold out in six minutes. The British public were pumped the UFC championship of the world was coming home.

For two weeks of the camp I was on a movie set in London, playing real-life 70s London hardman Roy 'Pretty Boy' Shaw in *My Name Is Lenny*, the biopic of Shaw's underground boxing rival Lenny 'The Guv'nor' McClean.

Again, it wasn't like I'd won the UFC belt aged 28. I had a short window to use my world-champ status to help open up as many doors as possible for my post-fighting career.

Jason Parillo, as you can well imagine, was positively thrilled when I told him I'd be on a British movie set for a fortnight, then would come back to California for a month, and then we'd head back to the UK for the fight.

My call time for the movie was typically before 7am and I'd leave the set about 6pm, but I still trained twice a day. My friend Daz Morris was with me the whole time; we'd run in the mornings (well, Daz came with me once) and he'd take me on the Thai pads after filming was done for the day.

Playing a character like Roy Shaw was a lot of fun and a new challenge. I researched the real-life 'Pretty Boy' extensively. I watched his old fights so I could mimic his wild, aggressive style and read his autobiography to get a handle on who he was. I studied his old interviews, and noted he licked his lips as he spoke, almost like a nervous tick. I incorporated this odd habit into my portrayal.

Josh Helman and John Hurt were the movie's leads but, for me, the real star was this beautiful woman, Rebecca something her name was, who had a small part in the film.

As a team, we made the decision to remain on Pacific Time once we landed in Manchester the week before the fight. We were going to sleep during the day and be awake during the night. The fight was taking place to suit Pacific Time, after all, and we wanted to confuse my body clock as little as possible.

Team Bisping – Jason, Brady, Daz and Lorenz Larkin and me – stayed in the Lowry. The last night I'd stayed in Madchester's only five-star hotel was hours after I'd beaten Elvis Sinosic at *UFC 70*.

It felt like a lifetime and five minutes ago. As I walked into the hotel's plush bar/café area on the first floor with its deep cushioned armchairs and sky-blue mood lighting, a flash-flood of memories came back to me of the *UFC 70* after-party. This same empty bar had been packed as tight as a nightclub in the small hours of 22 April 2007. Everyone had congratulated me on winning the Fight of the Night and, by the time I'd made my way over to order food, the kitchen had closed.

'Aww, really? I'm starving,' I'd said. 'I've not ate anything since before the fight.'

There had been a tap on my shoulder. I turned to see Jean-Claude Van Damme, my childhood action hero large as life, offering me half of his prawn sandwich. It had been a surreal moment for a guy only three years removed from working in an upholstery factory.

Now I was back in the same place a decade later. I was no longer young or wide-eyed, but a grizzled, seen-it-all champion.

Even though jetlag wasn't a factor, preparing for a 5am fight had its own challenges. I trained Monday and Tuesday night around 2am, getting my body used to working out hours after the sun went down. The Lowry staff were fantastic in accommodating our sleeping patterns during fight week, even serving us all breakfast from 3pm to 6pm, but, mostly, we were bored.

It is pitch dark by 5:30pm in Manchester in October and we were waking up around 4pm. It's not like we could pass the time going sight-seeing or take a wander around the shops in the middle of the night. So, we spent a lot of time in my suite at the Lowry, just bullshitting and enjoying each other's company. The highlight of the week was listening to Brady's lunatic-fringe conspiracy theories.

During the media interviews and press conference, I talked a great game about getting my revenge on Henderson, and I meant it. Even at the weigh-in, I felt confident in every word I said to my challenger on the stage, including that I would knock him out.

Confidence ebbs and flows, though. Yes, I was a completely different fighter to the over-trained, undernourished and over-thinking lad who showed up to *UFC 100*. That was a fact.

But ... it was also a fact that the last time I got hit by this guy, I came to in a shower not knowing what month it was.

There was a jagged energy about me on fight day. I was fidgety at breakfast and irritable at lunch. My afternoon workout rounded some of the sharp edges away but I still struggled to fall asleep for my usual pre-fight nap. I must have lain there for an hour in my blacked-out bedroom, listening as the people and cars outside the hotel went about their Saturday evening.

The UFC bus to the arena wouldn't leave until 2:30am. It was a ten-minute drive in the day; in the middle of the night the trip would be five minutes, door to door. Then there would be the two-hour wait in the dressing room. That was all ten hours away. So, I needed to sleep. I couldn't sleep. All I could think about – the only thought that took form between my ears for over an hour – was *UFC 100*.

When I eventually nodded off, I flinched from right crosses in my dreams.

Around midnight my mate Jason Falovitch, who'd flown from Toronto, Canada to support me, stopped by my suite to say hi. Jason Parillo and the team were already with me, checking and double-checking all our fight gear was packed. I was sat on a cappuccino-coloured couch, putting on the mental armour I needed to wear into battle. On the wall behind me was a framed, oversized photograph of a tree leaf.

Falovitch is a really trusted friend – we're now partners in a fantasy sports business called PlayLine.com – but I was still unusually tense. It wasn't the time or place for me to hear about his adventures in Prague earlier that week.

'Jason, you've gotta go, mate,' I said abruptly. 'I love you and thank you for coming to support me but I need to get into fight mode now. Please, I need to be left alone with my team.'

He understood, and I'd managed to say all that to Jason in a friendly, even tone. My mood continued to blacken after he left, though, and Brady wasn't so lucky. We began warming up, using some of the carpeted floor space to drill a few techniques. The little errors in communication that always happen when you are rolling were somehow all unacceptable – and all Brady's fault.

'Ferfuckssake!' I said more than once.

My temperament darkened the energy in the room. I was the same in the van as it looped its way through Deansgate's deserted streets. We pulled up alongside the service entrance to the venue. The van door swung open and we climbed out into the cold autumn air. There was a noticeable difference between the cold and quiet air outside, and the warm humidity and noise inside the packed Manchester Arena.

If I warmed up in the same dressing room I'd been in at *UFC 70* or *UFC 105*, I couldn't tell. I barked at Brady again; more than once.

Then, about an hour before the fight, something levelled out inside my mind.

Brady was sat in front of me, thrusting fight gloves over my already-wrapped hands. He was fully focused on his task, sure, but I knew his eyes were locked in a downwards position because they didn't want to catch mine.

Brady pushed my left glove on. Then the right.

'Feel good?' he asked.

'Yeah,' I said, knowing I needed to say a lot more.

Brady Fink is a great guy who takes shit from exactly no one. But all night he'd been doing just that – because he understood his friend was going through a motherload of pre-fight anxiety.

Some friend, I thought. I felt horrible.

Like I had on the phone with Callum in another dressing room years before, I took off the mental armour and became a fully functional person again.

'Brady, I'm sorry for being such a twat all day,' I said, breaking the silence in the room. He looked up for the first time all night. 'Mate, really, I'm sorry.'

He shrugged. We looked at each other for a second longer. Then he enjoyed a silent chuckle in front of me while shaking his head.

Yeah, Brady knew me. He knew the whole stupid process. He knew I could be a right arsehole fight week. He knew I didn't mean to be. He also knew that after the fight was over I'd be mortified by my behaviour and apologise profusely.

And then – we both knew – the process would be completed by everyone taking the piss out of me without mercy for days afterwards. That's when everyone got their own back. There would be impressions of my mood swings, which would draw howls of laughter at my expense. I'd have my own words twisted into darts and thrown back at me in bars and restaurants. Then, it would be my turn to sit there and take my medicine.

Yes, Brady was familiar with how it was going to go.

Or ... maybe not this time. Because then I started to laugh along with Brady. Not silently, though. Loudly! It felt *good*!

Brady looked at me with a 'Why are you laughing?' expression.

'All of you – guys, guys – listen. I'm sorry. I'm sorry I've been a miserable arsehole all night. I don't know why I'm stressing like this and putting us all through this. I mean, what's the worst that can happen tonight? I lose a fight? I've lost before and it wasn't the end of the world.'

A weight lifted off my shoulders as I spoke and I added: 'I do *really* appreciate all of you being here for me, away from your families all week. I'm sorry I've been a dick ...'

Without turning his body, Jason's head spun round from watching the undercard fights: 'You are the biggest wanker, Bisping!'

The sound of a British-English curse-word deadpan delivered in Jason's hybrid New York/California accent was too much. Daz and Lorenz cracked up. So did Brady and Jason. The vicelike tension I'd felt all night just melted as we all fell about pissing ourselves.

We all started talking. The music was cranked up. I began to hit pads with Jason. The energy built and built. I felt better. I felt like myself. I felt like the champion of the world.

I didn't go through the process of putting back on the mental armour. I never put it on again; didn't need it. I was a different fighter, a different man now.

There was a knock on the dressing-room door. It was fight time.

'This isn't *UFC 100*,' I told Jason as we left the dressing room.

It had been seven years since Manchester had given me that amazing, inspiring welcome at *UFC 105*. They were there for me when I needed to put *UFC 100* and the knockout to Dan Henderson behind me. We were here together again for the rematch.

The entire camp – the entire plan – was based around avoiding Henderson's arched right cross. Of course, I knew better than most the 'H-Bomb' was his primary weapon.

In the later stages of his two-decade MMA career, Hendo was content to spend long moments doing next to nothing offensively. The threat level he eradiated out, though, was constant. He always had enough energy to throw one of those big right hands. And – bless him – one was usually all he needed. Henderson's punching style would horrify boxing purists; but, in MMA, when opponents had to worry about the two-time Olympian's takedowns, kicks and back fists, torque was more important than technique.

The opening minute was rigidly tense, all feints and range-finding. Then a right cross swiped the bridge of my nose, tearing open the scar tissue that had grown over the cut caused by Anderson Silva's knee.

Henderson ducked very low and to his right whenever I threw my cross. He was intelligent and experienced, of course, in using his 5ft 11in stature as a defensive advantage.

He landed a solid right, and I gave him a nod and a smile. I planted my left shin into his guts. It stung him into surging forward and he almost threw himself to the canvas trying to land an axe of a right hand. He missed another a few moments later. He *badly* wanted to land that H-Bomb.

Meanwhile, I was almost as anxious to land my left hook. Several got through; most were blocked. Henderson carried his right fist very high near the ear, almost like he was clutching an invisible satellite phone. I tried the lead left hook once too often – BANG!

With 42 seconds remaining of the first round, *UFC 100* exploded into the present as Henderson landed the H-Bomb dead on my chin; my legs went stiff and I was sent sprawling to the canvas.

No! No way! This isn't happening again! No!

This was different to *UFC 100*. It had to be. I wasn't knocked unconscious. I had enough about me to try the up kick that Anderson had got me with. It didn't land. But – it changed Henderson's trajectory through the air. He missed his patented leaping hammer fist that he'd aimed at my jaw.

The challenger landed in side control, kneeing to my right side. I dodged an elbow strike + righthand + another elbow. With everyone in the area thinking I was one shot away from going out,

I spun on my back. I need to get my legs between me and his fists. I raked his face with my heel.

He was now on the left of me, though, and his right hand that much closer to his target. A hammer fist landed on my temple. A fist to my ear. His fingers pressed down on my eyes so I couldn't see – STAB! – an elbow spiked into my orbital bone. The pain was startling.

Fight! Fight! He's not taking my belt! Fight of my life! Now! NOW!

He drew his arm up for another strike. It landed. He drew up again – and I sprung off the canvas. We were back on our feet. He was swinging, hacking away with his fists like a madman. I was calm, giving myself every chance to weather the storm. I was able to deflect almost everything but the force of his blows threw us both off-balance. With my back against the cage I threw a right cross – it bounced off Henderson's shoulder and knocked him backwards two steps.

Henderson smiled at me – but didn't advance. Whether he saw I wasn't close to being finished or made the decision he'd used up enough energy for the first round already, Henderson called off the assault.

With the fans in a frenzy, we glared at each other for several moments. We were ten feet apart, far out of range. I had time for an inventory. My left eye – my *good* eye – was a mess. Blood was gushing into it and my fingertips felt a bruise the size of a slice of orange swelling up. It was a bad contusion that, I was sure, would get worse and limit my vision. My legs felt solid, though. My equilibrium was there. There had been no white flash behind my eyes when I got dropped. I was okay. The crowd kept the noise at a deafening level as I skipped forward and threw a head kick. He blocked it and the round ended.

'Your conditioning is there, man, his mouth is open already,' Jason said in the corner. 'You were winning that round and he caught you at the end.'

'What was it?' I asked.

'The right hand,' Jason said. 'The big right hand. Stay focused.'

'I'm alright,' I said.

At the start of round two I went back to the game-plan: intelligent pressure. I threw my left hook, kicked his thigh and his calf and jabbed. I tried to keep him guessing. I began to time his footwork – as he stepped to his left, I beat him to where he was going by skipping to my right and landing lead right crosses.

'Bisping is finding his rhythm,' my former opponent turned colour commentator Brian Stann told the broadcast audience.

Another combination – an inside leg kick followed by a right cross followed by a jab – pushed Henderson backwards. He smiled at me. I landed a harder inside leg kick, a harder right hand and, this time, a left kick to the head that the American only partially blocked. The crowd went nuts. I'd taken over the fight. Hendo threw a leg kick of his own – but I knew what was next – I stepped back before the H-Bomb was off the launch pad. I threw a right cross to distract him and whipped up another left kick to the head. It landed. The stutter-step confused him. I was able to land another lead left leg to his jaw. He disengaged for a few moments. A right cross found a home. I was in control.

Another lead left shin to the head rocked him. Another right cross thudded into his cheek. Henderson now covered up in the 'peek-a-boo' defence made famous by Floyd Patterson in the 1950s and again by Mike Tyson in the 1980s, so my one-two punch combo follow-up was partially blocked. A kick to the beltline sent him scuttling around the circumference of the cage. I chased and landed another right cross. The fans were going crazy.

BANG!

I was down! That fucking right hand again! But, no, it wasn't as bad as in round one. My legs felt fine and I managed to wrap them around Henderson's waist as he threw himself down on top of me. I held the challenger tight in my BJJ guard for the final minute of the round. Henderson smothered me with his hands but, more importantly, I smothered his ground and pound. Unlike the previous round, I took no damage.

'The whole world knows it's coming,' play-by-play commentator Mike Goldberg said during the replay of the second knockdown, 'but Henderson still connects with the H-Bomb!'

Despite the knockdown, I felt like I'd won the round. I'd probably pulled level on the cards *if* the three official judges had scored the first round 10–9 for Henderson rather than a 10–8.

Whatever, there were three rounds to go and I felt coldly confident.

'You've started to take control,' Jason confirmed to me. 'Push him back with the kicks, fire the right hand.'

Another stutter-step + left kick landed in the first 20 seconds of the third round. Henderson was going backwards, conserving his energy and, I knew, trying to get me to chase him into a trap.

'That's the thing with Hendo,' Stann said. 'He can be throwing no punches into the last thirty seconds – but if he just lands one he can end the fight. This is a really smart plan by Dan Henderson. He knows he's not going to outpace Michael Bisping over twenty-five minutes so he's staying patient and waiting for what he knows best – the knockout.'

Henderson was backing up in a crouch, his chin tucked down so far it was swallowed into his chest. The beef of his shoulders seemed to surround his temples. There was barely a square inch to aim a punch at. And all the while he ambled backwards, I knew, he was carrying that H-Bomb in one glove and the detonation device in the other. He wasn't throwing much but what he did was aimed directly into my swollen left eye. He knew exactly what he was doing.

In order to not give Henderson an opportunity he couldn't create without a mistake from me, I used constant movement. In and out, side to side, and different attack from a different angle every time. It's absolutely the correct strategy to use with an opponent like Hendo. The problem by the third round, though, was that I had to keep Henderson within an increasingly narrow field of vision. Put simply, I had to remain in front of him because my peripheral version was becoming nonexistent.

The level of concentration I needed to maintain – at 5:20am – was inhuman. But I landed combinations, kicks, jabs, left hooks and lead rights. I noted Henderson would sometimes come to a complete stop and I timed that to land a huge kick to the back of his legs. That clearly hurt him.

'LET'S GO, BIS-PING! LET'S GO, BIS-PING! LET'S GO, BIS-PING!!' reverberated around the stands.

The challenger threw a fastball right at the two-minute mark. It missed. A full minute later he threw the next one – directly into my rapidly closing left eye. Within moments my eye was almost swollen shut. He became a blur under the bright lights.

Now Henderson was looking for a breather. I gave him a left-hook/right-hook combination. He steadied himself on the fence after the right thudded into his cheek.

'Bisping has made the adjustments,' Stann said.

'Just like against Anderson Silva,' Goldberg added.

'He did it against Anderson Silva, he did it against me – he's done it to a lot of fighters,' Stann continued. 'He gets rocked early, makes adjustments and goes on to win the fight.'

But Henderson still had his moments – targeting my swollen eyes over and ever. My eyes were slits in blood-drenched curtains. One reporter, Chuck Mindenhall, wrote my face wouldn't have looked out of place on the cover of *Fangoria*, the magazine dedicated to horror movies.

Another one of those bastard right hands struck directly on the left eye. Nevertheless, I'd dominated the round – landing triple the amount of strikes and easily stuffing Hendo's two takedown attempts.

The fans knew it, too. They roared at the end of the third round. I gave them a thumbs up, took my mouthpiece out and showed them I had the Union flag on it.

We're going to do this. I got it.

An accidental kick to Henderson's family jewels gave the American a much-needed time-out at the start of the fourth. The fans clearly didn't buy he needed 85 seconds to recover and booed lustily. I didn't buy it either; he was wearing a protective cup and had taken a kick to the balls, not undergone a fucking sex change.

Henderson was much more aggressive after his second minute's rest. He threw combinations, his leg kicks came back into the fight and he caught me with a solid knee to the jaw. My 'good' eye had now become my 'other bad eye'. I was relying on stolen glimpses here and there, like when you are driving a car uphill into blazing sunlight.

But if I couldn't see, I could *sense*. My right hand thudded home once, twice, three times. Henderson still had no counter to my high kicks. I worked his body and his legs. Henderson continued to throw giant, oval punches on the assumption he only needed to land one. But, I allowed myself to think, I'd already taken his best shot while he was fresh. He wasn't going to hit me any harder now.

'We got this,' Jason said before the final round.

Although the fifth and final round began at 5:32am local time, the British fans showed no sign of fatigue. They screamed encouragement at me as I prepared for the last five minutes of another fight that, perhaps, would be decided in the final round.

'Hendo is starting to go hunting now,' Stann said.

In the last round of a career that began in 1997, Henderson went for broke to win a UFC world title on his third attempt. He threw more strikes in the first minute than in any of the previous three rounds. His best was a right hand to the left side of my head that, quite honestly, I didn't see until I watched the fight back days later. I adjusted my stance so I could peer out of the cracks of my eyes. Hendo threw another big right, I saw it, side-stepped, and landed a big hook and then a kick to the ribs that made him exhale hard. I kicked his guts again. I stuck an arrow of a right cross in him. Then a left hook.

Henderson looked up at the clock on the giant screens, calculating, no doubt, when to throw what he had left into the fight. I landed a right uppercut. Henderson caught me again on the eye with a solid punch. With 1:45 left on the clock, Henderson shot for a takedown. We scrambled and he ended up with a half-nelson, pressing me against the cage. I popped out and, by the way his outline swayed and staggered, I could tell Henderson's reserves were gone. With my opponent virtually stationary, I threw and landed a flying knee strike that struck the chin. The fight ended seconds later.

I was confident I'd won. I'd been the aggressor for 23 minutes of the 25-minute fight; I'd landed over 40 more significant strikes. The scores were read out: '49–46 ... 49–48 ... and 49–48 ... declaring the winner ... AND STILL ... !'

During the walk-outs half an hour before, the British fans had done what they felt they had a duty to do – boo Dan Henderson. Afterwards, though, with Henderson confirming his all-time-great career was over, the Brits saluted him.

'Give it up for Dan Henderson,' I encouraged them. 'He just kicked my ass, man. Dan, good job. He's tough as old boots. You've gotta respect a legend.'

The fans responded with a resounding chant of 'Hendo! Hendo! Hendo!'

Fight-day nerves aside, I'd long since gotten over *UFC 100*. In fact, without that 2009 result, I might not have developed into the fighter that beat Anderson Silva and won the world title. I wouldn't change a thing about that first Dan Henderson fight but, when fans in the future look at my record, they'll see I won the rematch.

Backstage, the UFC medical staff only approached me once about going to the hospital before calling in reinforcements. This time they went to get the big guns, my manager Audie and Dana. They were both waiting for me in my dressing room after I'd showered and put on my clothes. I don't think they saw that I needed Daz to help me in and out of the shower due to my entombed eyeballs, but they could have been right there the whole time for all I could see.

'You need to go to the hospital, Mike,' Dana said.

'Nah, I'm good. I'm good, Dana.'

'You don't fucking look good,' Dana shot back. 'You need to go to the hospital to get that eye checked out.'

My eye getting checked is exactly why I'm not going to the hospital, I thought.

'Nah, I'm fine,' I said.

'You know, I fucking care about you,' Dana said. 'You need to get the eye looked at and an MRI done. That was a crazy fight. You took a lot of big shots. You are going to the hospital.'

It wasn't a suggestion.

Then Audie tagged in, 'You need to go to the hospital tonight, Mike. You aren't going to the post-fight, you are going to get looked at now.'

So, I climbed into the waiting ambulance and was driven to Manchester Royal Infirmary for an MRI. I was as abrupt and uncommunicative as possible ('No pain', 'No headache', 'I'm fine', 'Are we done?') and left as soon as the MRI scan came back clear.

My after-party began in my suite as the first rays of sunlight slithered through Manchester's grey clouds. My team was there, I had my friends from the US and the UK there and, extra special to me, my big brother Konrad had come to the fight and stayed with me all night.

We were buzzing with energy and we had a great time all day. In the early evening we went out for something to eat at a nice restaurant. I apologised and explained to everyone in there – the waitress, the staff and the other guests – that despite my appearance I wasn't on the run from a rival street gang.

We had a great day. I finally went to sleep around midnight.

I was still peering over and under black bruises on Monday morning. I knocked my aftershave over when I reached to turn the light on in the bathroom. My face had a shade of black-purple I'd never seen before. I moved closer to the mirror. I was swollen and technicoloured. I grabbed a bottle of water and got back into bed.

Outside, it was around 9:30am. Already, I knew, middleweight contenders had tweeted challenges at me, and their managers were machine-gunning texts to new UFC middleweight matchmaker Mick Maynard. Before I wrestled myself back to sleep I ran the tips of my fingers around my head, ribs and forearms. Every inch felt like Braille, telling me a story I already knew: my time as a UFC fighter was almost over.

The Dan Henderson win wasn't supposed to be the last time I competed in Great Britain. I always wanted my final fight to be in the UK. That was the plan for years and years. In my mind's eye I saw myself – sweaty but hopefully not too bloody and having spent every last effort to win – taking the microphone after the fight. I would say thank you to the British fans. I'd try and articulate how grateful I was.

But I didn't get to do that, and so I'll write down here what I would have tried to have said in the arena *if* I could have got through it without choking up.

Believe me – I never, ever, took your support for granted.

More than anyone outside my family, there's no one I wanted to make proud more than the British fans. Early on in my career there were times I experienced this as pressure. Pressure to perform, pressure to win, pressure to send you home happy. Quickly, though, it wasn't pressure, it was support.

There's no doubt in my mind I achieved more because I had that support. At the elite level of MMA, every extra percentage of energy, confidence and will makes a difference. When I walked out in Manchester following *UFC 100*, when my toe was hanging off in Scotland, at the start of the fourth round against Anderson Silva in London, during the fight with Dan Henderson in Manchester, you made a difference.

When I climbed into the Octagon on British soil, I was invincible.

Bringing the UFC world championship home to Great Britain was the honour of my life. I'll never forget the support you gave me as long as I live.

Now, there's a new generation of British mixed martial artists coming through. Support them like you supported me and – believe you me – there will be more British UFC title challengers. There will be more British UFC *champions*.

From the bottom of my heart, thank you.

CHAPTER TWENTY

THE FINAL COUNTDOWN

The surgeon wanted to weld a metal rivet into my face.

I was back in California, getting the bruise under my left eye checked out. Turned out Henderson's big punch (or maybe big elbow) in the first round had separated the zygomatic arch and maxillary, the two bones that join together to form the underside of the orbital socket. That's why my left eye had swelled up so nastily, the doctor told me.

The bones had already knitted back together, and a metal plate under my good eye sounded like another athletic commission licensing nightmare. So, after getting assurances the fracture would quickly heal on its own, I demurred.

Besides, my most pressing medical concern wasn't my fractured face ... it wasn't the stinger I'd first suffered training for Brian Stann years before (which had gotten so bad my right shoulder, biceps and triceps were atrophying) ... it wasn't even my right eye.

No, my biggest concern was always with injuries that could physically stop me from training and fighting and, at that moment, my left knee was pretty close to doing just that. The same kind of calcified floaters that had caused my elbow to lock out were causing my knee to lock in place periodically.

If I was going to have any operation done, it was to fix my knee. I was looking at getting the procedure done in November 2016. I was done fighting for the year – or was I?

My flight to Dubai had reached the halfway point over the Atlantic. The cabin had been blacked out for the night and I'd just finished watching a movie. The main source of light in the business-class cabin was the white glow from the dozens of television screens which hung silently in front of my fellow passengers' sleeping faces. I couldn't rest, though. My left knee had locked up in exactly the same way my elbow had two years before. Twice on the flight, I had to dig my fingertips into the joint and root out the calcified shards. It bloody hurt.

I ordered another glass of wine and began searching for a second movie to watch when my phone buzzed with an SMS.

It was Dana and the text conversation went like this:

> Dana: Call me.
> Me: I'm on a flight to Dubai. What's up?
> Dana: U healthy?
> Me: Problem?
> Dana: Are you healthy/healed up?
> Me: Yeah, healthy as fuck. All healed and pretty. Why?
> Dana: Keep between u and me and don't EVER say I don't love u!! I don't have deal done yet but U vs GSP in Toronto Main Event!!! If I can get this done are u in?

A fight with Georges St-Pierre! I'd paid little attention to the rumours that 'GSP' – who for years was neck and neck on the pound-for-pound list with Anderson Silva but a much bigger box-office draw – was close to breaking his three-year sabbatical from the sport he'd once dominated. The two-time welterweight champion had vacated his crown in November 2013, saying he needed time away from the grind of defending his title. He'd remained a martial arts fanatic, though, and never stopped training. Now he wanted to come back and become one of the very few fighters to win UFC titles in two separate divisions.

Beating Anderson Silva and GSP would be like having wins over both Floyd Mayweather and Manny Pacquiao on your record. Plus, I understood immediately my cut of pay-per-view revenue would be double, no, triple the biggest payday of my career.

It took me a moment of just sitting there in my half-reclined seat before I could take it all in.

I texted back:

I'm healthy enough to beat Georges. I'm in!

My trip to Dubai was in and out, very short, to open a UFC Gym there. My mobile phone couldn't dial out while I was there but, as you can imagine, I was texting Dana every day for updates. There weren't any, nor when I called the day after I returned from the Middle East.

Whatever the hold-up was, I had to move forward as if the fight was happening. There were barely seven weeks until the mooted Toronto date, so I worked with Jason and Brady to put together a tight, intense camp heavily focused on countering GSP's formidable takedowns. I continued to either speak or text with Dana every day – until the day he texted me: 'IT'S OFF'.

Apparently, the UFC and the former champion had not reached an agreement. GSP was remaining retired and I'd got excited for nothing.

It would have been for the best if I'd had the knee surgery as soon as I got the news St-Pierre wasn't coming back, but there was a constant stream of rumours and chatter from people close to the former pound-for-pounder, so I held off over Christmas, just in case the GSP fight suddenly reappeared. It didn't, so I had the surgery in January.

In February, Dana contacted me saying the UFC and St-Pierre were having productive talks again.

'He's in on fighting you,' the UFC president told me. 'We got some stuff to figure out, but you are the fight he wants.'

St-Pierre, I was sure, had hand-picked me as his comeback opponent for two reasons. First, I had the middleweight belt. Second, he'd outwrestled me when we'd trained together all those years ago, before I'd won *TUF 3*.

I was confident for the opposite reason. I knew there was a world of difference between the wide-eyed kid he'd out-grappled at that UFC HQ basement gym in Las Vegas and the fighter I had become. A career of difference. A world *championship* of difference.

I still laugh at how dismayed poor Georges was when I showed up late to our mid-morning press conference in Las Vegas, 3 March 2017, hoarse and a little worse for wear.

'My God, Biz-ping! My God!' he gasped with that accent that literally everyone on earth can do a spot-on impression of. 'What haz 'appened to you? Biz-ping – what haz 'appened? Are you en-tock-zeek-ated?'

'I am en-tock-zeek-ated,' I admitted with zero shame. 'I'm English; I'm in Las Vegas so I went out and had a good time last night. It's not like I have a date to train for … when is the fight, Georges?'

Georges didn't say. In what I think was a first for the UFC, we were there to announce a fight would happen – but couldn't inform the public as to where or when. I heard rumours as to what the delay was – everything from GSP having an issue with his eyes (which, obviously, I didn't have much sympathy with) to disagreements between the UFC and Georges over everything from money to where and when the fight would take place.

It could well have been a combination of all those things – I didn't care. I just needed a date to aim for. If it was going to be in the next three/four months, I needed to begin organising a training camp and sparring partners. If the fight was five months or more away, I wanted to know now.

But – even after we'd announced the fight, done a press conference and squared up in front of the MMA media's cameras – no confirmation of any date came.

It was frustrating for me and the UFC. A couple of months after the face-to-face press conference in Vegas, Dana announced that whenever St-Pierre felt ready to commit to an actual date for his big return, he would be fighting for his old welterweight title, held by Tyron Woodley.

'The shot at the middleweight title has sailed,' he informed the media.

Obviously, I was pissed off. Twice now I'd had this massive, career-best-and-then-some payday dangled in front of me only for it not to happen. And yet, St-Pierre himself continued to indicate it was me he wanted to fight and no one else. I remained quietly confident the fight would happen eventually.

I underwent a second knee operation in early summer. Dr Steve A. Mora, who'd done all my orthopaedic surgeries, told me the prognosis wasn't terrible. The floating bodies had done a little damage before he'd removed them in January. In layman's terms, my knee was no longer able to lubricate itself and friction within the joint was causing the swelling. The treatment was to inject fatty tissue, removed from my mid-section, into the knee to prevent further friction.

It was a relatively minor procedure and the recovery time was only a few weeks. Only, I left for Thailand to film the movie *Triple Threat* two days later. As you can imagine with a film featuring martial arts movie heroes like Scott Adkins and Michael Jai White, *Triple Threat* called for a lot of fighting, jumping off things and running. Every evening I'd get back to my hotel room with my left knee twice the size of my right.

One evening I was sat in my room icing the knee when Dana called. He wanted me to defend the belt in early July at *UFC 213* at the big annual International Fight Week event.

'I'll text you a picture why I can't,' I said, 'I'm sorry.'

Dana saw what I meant. He called back a few days later and said he planned on moving ahead with the two leading 185lb contenders, Yoel Romero and Robert Whittaker, fighting each other at *UFC 213*. He told me the plan included awarding the winner an 'interim UFC middleweight title' and asked me if I was okay with that.

'It seems a little unnecessary to me, I defended the title six months ago,' I shrugged, 'but I appreciate you asking. I don't care either way, to be honest. Neither of them has headlined a big card before so if we can bill my fight with the winner as a "champion versus champion" fight, and maybe sell a few more pay-per-views as a result, fuck it, I'm good with it.'

Dana told me he wanted me there for the fight and to keep him posted with how my knee was doing.

The plan for the middleweight title for the rest of the year was for me and the winner of the 8 July Whittaker/Romero fight to coach *The Ultimate Fighter*, season 26, opposite each other and then fight in November or December.

In Dana's dressing room before the fights began at *UFC 213: Whittaker vs Romero* I sat down with him and Hunter Campbell, the UFC's chief legal officer, and Craig Piligian to negotiate my fee for doing *TUF*. I wasn't unreasonable, but I pointed out this would be the third time I'd coached the series, that I was now the world champion and, most importantly, I'd developed my television and film career to the point where me filming for two consecutive months for any show had to require compensation.

We hashed out a deal and, with that done, I took my Octagonside seat next to Dana for Whittaker vs Romero. The lights went out inside the brand-new T-Mobile Arena and the giant screens began blaring the pre-fight promo.

Dana leaned in. 'Who you got?' he said.

'Probably Romero early or Whittaker late,' I shouted over the in-arena music. 'Romero would be better for me, though. He gases. Plus, there's some needle there for *TUF*.'

The fight was one of the best of 2017, with Whittaker sweeping the last three rounds to win on points. I knew the Australian had a quieter personality so I went into the Octagon to ignite Bisping vs Whittaker in the fans' imaginations. I took a replica UFC title belt with me and threw it down at Whittaker's feet, telling him to pick that one up, too. My point was there were plenty of belts with 'U-F-C' written on them – but no matter how many he had, he still wouldn't be the champion.

'See you in a few days,' I told Dana. I went home and spent some time with the family, waiting for the call that my return flight to the Fight Capital of the World had been booked.

Monday came. Then it went.

Tuesday, came. Then it went, too.

On Wednesday afternoon, I called Dana.

'*TUF*'s not happening,' he said. 'We had to go with two other coaches.'

Dana explained the new 'interim' champion had torn the medial ligament in his knee fighting Romero. I'd flown to Vegas the week before to see if I'd be fighting Romero or Whittaker; with one beaten and the winner injured, I'd be fighting neither.

With the 'interim champion', aka No.1 contender, Whittaker out, there didn't seem to be a natural match for me for my second title defence. There certainly wasn't one that would do even one quarter of the PPV buys that the GSP fight would generate nor, with respect to the available opposition, mean half as much on my record as the former two-time UFC champion.

The rest of the middleweight Top 5 were all coming off losses; No.2 Romero of course had lost to one-legged Whittaker, No.3 Rockhold hadn't fought since I'd KO'd him, No.4 Souza had been KO'd by Whittaker and Weidman had been stopped in his last three fights in a row.

These were the fighters – along with their financial dependants – who fertilised Twitter with a blizzard of bullshit. 'Bisping's ducking me,' they blarted; 'Bisping's hand-picking challengers,' they moaned.

Well, I'd fought Rashad Evans on six weeks notice, and Vitor Belfort on super-unleaded in his home town. I'd faced Dan Henderson in America during the 4th of July weekend, I fought Chael Sonnen on one week's notice and I beat Anderson Silva. I did all of this – just to earn a last-minute title shot.

So, forgive me if I was indifferent to these entitled demands from contenders who couldn't string two wins together.

I had to fight someone, though, and of the possible challengers I figured I'd get either Romero, the rubber match with Rockhold or maybe the rematch with Anderson (who was at least coming off a win). I was wrong on all three.

The call from Dana came just before 11pm on 29 July. That night's *UFC 214* hadn't been off the air for even an hour. Dana was still in his dressing room/office at the Honda Center in Anaheim, California.

'You and GSP, one hundred per cent, November four, Madison Square Garden,' he said. 'You in?'

I knew what had happened. Tyson Woodley's successful defence of the UFC welterweight title vs Demian Maia earlier that night, while one-sided, had been far from a classic. It was the second straight fight where the UFC president had been displeased with Tyron's performance as champion.

'You in?' Dana repeated.

There was no point playing hard to get – of course I still wanted the fight. And competing at the iconic Madison Square Garden on New York's 7th Avenue, where so many legendary boxing matches had taken place, was appealing as well.

But I still turned the fight down.

Booking a fight under the administration of the New York State Athletic Commission would be the end of my career. I was sure of it.

The NYSAC had a reputation for applying its own rules unevenly. During *UFC 205* the previous year, the regulator refused Rashad Evans a licence due to an 'irregularity' that no other commission – before or since – had found.

It also refused to license a female fighter the same day, waiting until the actual weigh-in to inform her that, due to her breast implants of all things, it was too dangerous for her to compete. All this was made public, needlessly embarrassing the athlete, only for the NYSAC to change its mind and allow her to fight anyway.

If the NYSAC thought boobs too dangerous, I could only imagine what it would make of my right eye – especially as it was about to settle a lawsuit for gross negligence to a boxer named Magomed Abdusalamov for $22million.

'I don't want to fight in New York,' I told Dana plainly. 'Can't we do it in December in Vegas?'

'No,' Dana said. 'I need GSP for Madison Square Garden.'

'Can't do it,' I said.

Dana asked if I was sure. I went radio silent on him for a second.

I've rolled the dice on my eye situation this long, I said to myself. *This fight is the biggest purse of my career. It's worth rolling the dice for again, isn't it?*

'This GSP fight will definitely happen this time?' I asked.

'If you are in, I'm going to walk into the press conference here at the arena in five minutes and announce it,' came the answer.

Five minutes later, Dana did just that.

'I know Michael Bisping will fight,' the promoter told the assembled media. 'I know Bisping will show up, and he will fight. No doubt about it.'

'You told us that ship had sailed,' a reporter pointed out.

'It sailed right back.'

Now we had a location and a date – MSG in New York City, 4 November 2017 – it was time to promote the fight with a series of interviews and appearances across the US and Canada.

Georges St-Pierre was the guy I'd thanked on live TV when I won my very first fight in the UFC, all those years ago in Vegas vs Josh Haynes. If you don't respect GSP as a fighter, you don't like mixed martial arts; if you don't respect him as a person, you don't like people.

But I had a fight to promote, an opponent to unsettle and, to be honest, a lot of talking about the exact same thing that I needed to get through without sounding bored out of my mind. St-Pierre is cerebral and calculating, a difficult man to get an emotional response out of. The Canadian has heard it all during his 15-year career; between them, GSP's former opponents Matt Serra, Dan Hardy, Josh Koscheck and Nick Diaz called him every name under the sun, questioned his manhood, insulted his country, his accent – none of it worked. St-Pierre never seemed to anger; and come the first round he was never emotional.

The only subject that elicited uncontained passion from the man from the Great White North was palaeontology, the study of dinosaurs. What the hell could I do with that? Tell him he has the reach disadvantage of a T-Rex? That brontosauruses aren't real? That a triceratops couldn't hack it during the USADA era?

St-Pierre steadfastly refused to return fire whenever I trolled him at press engagements and laughed with genuine amusement when I ribbed him. Nothing I said particularly fazed him – until mid-October. Following a press conference at the Hockey Hall of Fame in Toronto, Canada, Georges was standing among the exhibits of Wayne Gretzky and, y'know, other people who were good at ice hockey. He had some of his team around him and there were UFC PR staff dotted around. Georges was in the process of signing autographs for a couple of hockey moms – and I spied a camera guy who I knew worked for news website TMZ was filming him.

I turned to Jason and said, 'Let's go sell some pay-per-views.'

One hundred per cent playing the character of 'Michael Bisping, MMA villain', I stormed up to St-Pierre yelling, 'Hey, Georges! Georges! Keep your fucking hands to yourself! If you put your hands on a man – that means you got a fucking problem. I will knock you the fuck out right now!'

Jason played his part, too, halting my momentum exactly in front of the TMZ camera. The alarmed UFC staff also stepped between me and Georges, as I wanted them to.

'Keep your hands to your fucking self!' I continued.

'You put your hands on me,' GSP said as his confusion gave way to anger. 'Fuck off, man! Fuck off!'

I revved it up some more, pointing my finger in his face as I cursed at him.

'Don't touch me!' he said. 'Don't touch me! Fuck off, man!'

Job done, I turned and walked away. As I did, I offered this advice to the most professional and composed athlete in the sport: 'Learn to control yourself, Georges!'

TMZ captured the whole thing – including the aftermath. After I left, Georges turned to the hockey moms – and the young lad who'd stood there during the blitzkrieg of f-bombs – and tried to continue his autograph signing. The kid ran off in tears.

The video was posted on TMZ and got over a million views that day alone. Like I said, job done.

I had to let Georges in on the act later that day. While waiting to appear live on Rogers Sportsnet (kinda like the Sky Sports News of Canada) at their studio, I went to the bathroom and found myself standing next to my opponent while having a slash.

It was a small staff bathroom, with only three stalls and two urinals, side by side, next to the twin sinks. I didn't even know it was GSP I was stood next to until the UFC camera crew came bursting in the door.

'Hey – get out!' I said.

GSP chuckled.

'Oh, hello,' I laughed.

If you are a guy reading this, you know that when you are using a urinal next to another dude, you stare at the wall. So there's me and Georges St-Pierre stood shoulder to shoulder, our eyes locked dead ahead, taking a leak. We'd both obviously drunk a lot of water that day, because we were stood there for what seemed like a while.

'So,' Georges broke the silence, 'you've got a Range Rover?'

He'd obviously been watching my video blogs.

'Yeah,' I answered, 'but it's in the shop right now.'

'Oh those things mal-funct-ion all the time, man,' the former two-time UFC welterweight champion lamented. 'I had one. You gotta get rid of dat, man.'

I thanked him for the advice. We both zipped up and moved on to the sinks to wash our hands.

'Alright, buddy, let's get back into character.' I made an exaggerated 'mean face' to Georges and went back to my green room.

Twenty minutes after that, we were on set and live on air, and I was back to eviscerating him.

Despite creeping into my late thirties and despite my body constantly reminding me I was fighting on borrowed time, I was in the form of my life. I was riding a personal best streak of five consecutive wins in the UFC. I felt I had the beating of everyone in my division.

Jason had trained me for ten fights now and had unpicked all the psychological locks that had been holding back my full talent. The anger-induced swagger had been replaced by genuine confidence that, whoever I fought, whatever situation I found myself in, I had more than enough skill, experience and willpower to prevail.

The camp for the GSP fight went fantastically. I felt like I could drag more oxygen than ever into my lungs. I wore muscles tighter around my arms, shoulders and chest. My thighs were powerful and my punching power had increased again.

I've been told more than once that you're not really supposed to talk about what happens in sparring – or the BJJ equivalent 'tap and tell' – so you'll have to take my word for it that I was dropping UFC and Bellator fighters left and right. I felt like I had before the Anderson fight; more than a match for one of the all-time greats.

We were using a ton of training partners and the RVCA gym was packed. The sponsors wanted to take advantage of the visual and shoot footage for an upcoming campaign, so, eight days from the fight, we had a camera crew filming us.

Former *TUF 9* Team UK member Dean Amasinger was part of the GSP fight preparation too. Dean had retired from active competition in 2015 and was transitioning into coaching; he offered his services as a training partner and I was happy to have him around.

Unfortunately, in the last day of sparring he shot for a takedown and his full weight crashed through his shoulder into my ribs.

There was a searing, tearing sensation I'd never felt before and I knew immediately I was injured. I screamed – not in pain – but in frustration. The best camp of my life for the biggest fight of my life … and I'd been injured with a week to go.

An X-ray showed that it wasn't broken but the cartilage had been shorn off. It was extremely painful and would need a while to heal.

There was no way I was pulling out of the fight, though. This fight had been on and off for almost a year now, I'd turned down opportunities outside of the Octagon to ensure I was available to make this happen and – bottom line – I'd gone through too much for too long for this fight not to happen now.

One of my friends from California, a medical practitioner, suggested I take an injection of lidocaine just before the fight to reduce the pain and allow me full movement. I initially said no, but I triple-checked and lidocaine was not on the ten-page-long USADA list of banned substances.

'Okay, then, let's do that,' I said once I was satisfied.

But it wasn't so simple.

The best advice I could find was that while taking lidocaine before a fight was perfectly fine, if I wrote down I had injured ribs during the pre-fight medical at the weigh-in at New York, there was every chance the NYSAC would pull me from the event.

'Okay, I'll take the injection in my hotel room, before I leave for the arena,' I said.

Nope, that wouldn't work either.

'Lidocaine only lasts for a very short period,' I was told. 'We're talking twenty minutes to an hour. With your body working so hard in the fight, the effects will be gone sooner than that but, by then, the adrenaline released in the fight will take over and you won't need the lidocaine.'

'There's no way I can take a doctor into the dressing room with me,' I said. 'The Commission will obviously ask me what I'm taking and a whole can of worms will be opened just minutes before my fight. New York has already kicked off about licensing me about my eye … I think if I go to them with a rib injury on top of that they'll cancel the fight there and then.'

So, a crazy plan was formulated …

'Remember,' my medical friend said, 'if you get this wrong you'll puncture your lung.'

Worries about the rib injury were stacked on top of months of worrying about the NYSAC refusing to license me over my right eye.

Before applying, I underwent a one-hour operation to remove the plastic drain I'd worn on my eyeball for over four years. The drain had become preventative by that point and, although I'd had it in for my previous eight fights, I wanted to do all I could to ensure the Commission licensed me.

I'd initially provided them with, literally, an inch-thick file of scans, test results and a letter explaining it all from my eye doctor, who also noted that I have a 'heavy-set brow and recessed globes', which gave my eyes further protection. (Rebecca found this part absolutely hysterical. 'See? See!' she squealed. 'I always said you look like a caveman!')

That wasn't enough. The NYSAC had their own eye expert, they noted, and he disagreed with my doctor.

The people now in charge of the Commission were clearly – and understandably – extremely cautious out of concern of another multi-million-dollar lawsuit.

The NYSAC offered a way forward. If I signed a disclaimer stating that I would not bring any lawsuit against them in relation to my eyes, they would license me to compete at *UFC 217* on 4 November.

Madison Square Garden, located in 7th Avenue, Manhattan, is about as American as sports venues get. Although to a Brit, some of the history doesn't translate, to an American fight fan 'The Garden' conjures up a lineage that stretches all the way to Rocky Marciano in the 40s, Joe Louis in the 30s and even Jack Dempsey in the 20s.

Three UFC titles were on the line on that freezing November night and the limos and Uber XLs were pulling up three-deep alongside the iconic marquee on 7th Avenue.

The Garden is also known as the Mecca of basketball, with the NY Knicks calling MSG home since its current incarnation opened in 1968. And it was into the Knicks' recently refurbished locker room that I was directed when my team and I arrived at the fight venue a little after 9pm local time. The Knicks logo blazed up from the thick carpet, which itself was a cool blue contrast to the redwood and shining brass horseshoe of open 'lockers' that dominated the room.

The room was surprisingly small for the dressing room of a team of 6ft 7in basketballers. But there was more than enough room for myself, my team and Rose Namajunas and her crew. 'Thug Rose', an introverted 24-year-old outside the Octagon and a stone-cold executioner inside it, would be challenging Joanna Jedrzejczyk for the women's strawweight title on the card.

When the knock on the door came for Rose, I got ready to put my crazy plan into action. It was time.

Time to root the wrapped towel out of my bag and carry it to an empty stall in the bathroom; time to set my phone down on top of the toilet tank cover and, after hopefully getting three bars or more, calling my medical-expert friend on Facetime. And if that went well, it would be time to carefully unroll the towel and take out the two-inch syringe containing lidocaine and, with my digital medical assistant giving step-by-step instructions in real time, it would be time to inject myself in the ribcage in exactly the right spot to numb my injury but not puncture my left lung.

Eyeing my blue gym bag with the towel and syringe in it, I waited for my moment. But Commission members were in and out of the room. Then Big John McCarthy came in to give his instructions for the main event. A UFC camera crew wanted to know when they could film me warming up. A Reebok rep checked to see if all the kit was good. Then Rose came back – having won the title with a first-round KO.

This is lunacy! I thought. *My ribs will just have to hurt.* The stress of finding a window to go and take an online anatomy class, involving injecting myself in the toilets, was somewhat distracting me from preparing for my world title defence. If only I'd been as familiar with needles as Vitor Belfort.

I grabbed the blue gym bag and put it in the locker.

St-Pierre was two years younger than me and, as a result of his vigilant fighting style as much as his sabbatical from the sport, he had far fewer miles on the clock. While I am two inches taller than the Canadian, I never expected to have a size advantage in the Octagon; Georges is an incredible athlete with a deceptively large frame. His back, biceps and shoulders looked very large and his arms and legs were longer than mine too.

The 18,201 fans enjoyed booing me in the way they'd boo a pantomime villain or a pro-wrestling heel. They had a black hat to boo and a vanilla hat to cheer.

Both Georges and I understood what a victory against the other would cost. We bumped fists twice during referee Big John McCarthy's instructions.

Any thought of my rib injury melted away at the start of the fight. St-Pierre was circling constantly in the early going; clockwise and then counterclockwise and then back the other way, keeping the fight at jabbing distance. GSP had beaten some very good fighters for five rounds apiece purely with his jab. I lamented that my own jab was a relic of what it had been before the eye injury.

Georges threw a big left hook – the first of many – two minutes in. I didn't see the fist flying towards my right temple but I saw the way his feet, legs and trunk had moved and I sensed the punch. He hit nothing but air and I landed a one-two while he was still open.

A jab bit into my nose. I nodded to my opponent. That was a well-timed one. So was the right cross he stuck in my left ear. For a guy who'd not fought officially for four years GSP had started very sharply – which I expected – and was using striking rather than wrestling – which I had not anticipated.

He landed another solid jab. I clipped him with a right hook. With one minute to go he shot his first takedown. It was a single-leg near the cage that had me sitting on my arse, my back against the fence. Georges held on to my left leg and didn't move for several moments. I looked up at Big John and gestured for him to instruct my opponent to try to advance his position; when he did I posted off my right and regained my feet.

I was overthinking; my conscious mind was struggling to let my instincts take over and guide my actions in the fight.

We both fell short with a handful of punches each – then just as I was at the absolute apex of changing my weight to step to the left, Georges flew forward with a Superman jab. Because he'd timed it so exactly with the movement of my feet, the force of the blow knocked me backwards as I regained my balance. The timing of the punch couldn't have been more precise even with the use of an atomic clock. The crowd leapt to their feet cheering – then a spinning wheel kick bounced off the top of my head seconds before the round ended.

'I tell you what,' Rogan explained on commentary. 'GSP might have been lying – he might be even better. He might be better!'

No question, round one was a wash. Jason told me not to load up on my punches so much.

Round one was cut adrift in my mind. I started the fight from scratch in round two.

GSP came out kicking. He threw a side kick, a push kick, a leg kick. None landed but they were delivered with such crisp perfectionism the three judges would have been impressed nevertheless. He then threw a left hook, but this time did a better job of disguising it. I had to change the direction of the fight. I used the stutter-step left high kick that had worked so well on Henderson. St-Pierre skipped forward and pushed me back with a side kick to the body. He again threw a leaping left hook in an arc so wide there was no doubt now that he was looking to take advantage of my diminished eyesight on that side.

Rogan spotted it, too. 'Georges is really threatening with that left hook,' he informed the huge PPV audience. 'He's throwing it so wide it's insane. Michael's got to be careful about that.'

Georges has very few 'tells' in his game, but I had picked up when he was going to throw a leg kick. I was setting him up for one and, instead of moving to check it, I stepped and threw a right hand down the pipe. It detonated right on his jaw. Georges was hurt, big time. His features went blank and I knew he'd seen that white flash behind his eyes. I was taking over. Georges stayed closer to me, which brought my jab into the fight. At this range, where the need for depth perception was less pronounced, I could jab with him on even terms. I could see he was open for the right, and I landed another huge cross that rocked him to his heels.

With the fight moving away from him, Georges shot for the takedown. His level changes weren't particularly fast but he disguised his intentions very well. I scrambled and regained my balance, only for 'Rush' to pull at my shorts for illegal leverage so hard my left butt-cheek was exposed in the World's Most Famous Arena. It was the most aggressive pulling down of MMA shorts this side of Vitor Belfort's TRT clique.

'Don't hold on the shorts!' the ref told GSP, but the advantage had been taken. I was down, with GSP on top in half-guard. This was exactly where I didn't want to be. I clipped him with pushes to the ears, trying to distract him from working. I allowed my left arm to linger as I drew it back and forth towards his head – Georges took the bait. He whipped his left arm from round the back of my head and went for a keylock. As he moved, I shot my arm under him and created enough space for me to plant my feet and power up into a standing position.

Seconds after the stand-up battle resumed, I cracked him with a lead right hand. I could feel my groin protector moving around for some reason; it was a distraction I could have done without while matching wits with the most cerebral tactician in the game.

His jab was still effective but I was landing with increasing regularity now. I timed another low kick and landed a left hook.

I timed – and caught – another kick, sending Georges sprawling backwards to the fence. We exchanged jabs and I heard my corner shouting, 'He's feeling it, Mikey!' I landed the left kick to the head again, this time he barely got a hand up to block any of it. St-Pierre looked tired and I was chasing him now. I feinted with a jab and then a kick so I could land the right hand on his temple.

The horn ended a much better round for me. 'Your round!' Jason said. We'd both landed 17 shots, but I'd landed with the heavier artillery. I asked my corner to take a look at my cup. The challenger had pulled so hard on my shorts that he'd snapped the lacing which held my groin protector up. I always wore metal Muay Thai cups because they gave better protection, but now it wasn't tied in place the extra weight made the thing move around inside my shorts.

I expected the takedown to come at the start of the third round but, despite my best efforts, St-Pierre ended up in my full guard. Again, this was not where I wanted to be but I landed a solid right fist to his jaw from the bottom. Then an elbow strike cut St-Pierre's forehead wide open and another right opened the cut on his nose further. GSP tried to change position, posture up, and get his ground and pound working, but I realised I was giving far more than I got from the bottom. I was content with the rate of exchange; I would stay there slicing his face with elbows until St-Pierre gave me an opening to get up.

Georges threw everything he had into two elbows; one of them caught me above the hairline. He punched me in the body. Two more elbows from me tore at his eyebrows. He was bleeding all over me now. He pressed his face against my stomach, hiding his cuts from my elbows. For the third time in as many fights, my body and trunks were covered in blood. This time, though, it wasn't my own. While St-Pierre was so distracted by his bleeding I drew my soles to his hips and thrusted him off of me. The fight was back on the feet.

There was a cut on the bridge of his nose, too. He dabbed away at his eyes with his fingertips. Blood, I saw, was flowing into the challenger's eyes. I knew the feeling. I landed a big right hand. He landed one of his own. He landed an inside leg kick. I waited for another, it came, and I threw the right. GSP ducked under it and – BANG!

I was on the floor. It must have been a left hook. Didn't see it. He was in my guard. Much higher than before. Boom! A left elbow I didn't see. Boom! Another. Boom! Another. Another. Another. Another. A punch. Another punch. Elbow! My head was against the cage. I turned my body to the left. He was still hitting me. I turned right. I found a little space and tried to get up. He had my back. His hooks shot in. I couldn't turn. Rear naked choke. I fought his forearms. His squeeze was very tight. My brain was starving for oxygen. My thinking went fuzzy. I pulled at his arms but I couldn't escape. I wouldn't tap. I'd worked too hard for this title. Everything went fuzzy, then black …

…

…

…

… three men were kneeling over me. Their faces too close, their voices not close enough. One of them was John McCarthy. His big shoulders were blocking whatever was happening behind him. An instant later I knew what was happening behind me.

Georges St-Pierre was celebrating his win.

I'd lost.

The title was gone.

'Rear naked choke' is a misnomer. The technique doesn't work by obstructing the windpipe to stop you from breathing; it works by compressing the carotid arteries and jugular veins, limiting the blood flow to the brain and causing a temporary cerebral ischemia. In other words, you pass out.

It's not uncommon to wake up feeling confused, but I was fully aware of my surroundings even as I lay on the canvas. Georges walked over and helped me to my feet.

'It could have gone the other way, Michael,' the new UFC middleweight champion said.

On *The Joe Rogan Experience* six months later, GSP confirmed that he and his team had made good use of the worst-kept secret in the sport.

'The thing with Michael is he'd adjusted very well to this [eye issue], he adjusted so he kept me in his line of sight [with the good eye] all the time. So I had to wait for him to commit with the right hand, so he moved his line of sight to the left, before I could come over the top with the left hook. It was always when he missed the right hand he could be caught with that left hook.'

St-Pierre added: 'Bisping is a great example of hard work, perseverance and that anything is possible if you are courageous and don't give up. He is a tremendous fighter and great role model for the sport.'

Funny, that's exactly what I think of Georges St-Pierre. He is the man, someone you can point to as a role model in the sport; a champion who left the sport richer than he found it.

I hated losing my title. I'd given a decade of my life, months on end away from my family, my right eye and paid a butcher's bill of body parts to get that belt. I never wanted to lose that. But, it didn't cut me to the bone to have lost it to Georges, a clean fighter and one of the very best mixed martial artists of all time.

'How you doing, Dad?' Callum asked as he folded his long legs under the chair next to mine.

Rebecca had brought our two eldest kids into my dressing room (Lucas was still too young to come and was at home with his grandparents).

'Yeah, I'm okay,' I answered truthfully. 'I thought I had him in the second but, y'know, he's one of the best and he caught me. It's okay. You can't win them all.'

Ellie sat down on the other side of me. 'You definitely hurt him in round two,' she said, 'you were doing great.'

The conversation was upbeat. I'd shown my kids over the years that in any competition where there's a winner, there must be a loser. And while it's okay to be disappointed with a loss or setback, you don't get dejected.

'It's a sport,' I told the media at the post-fight press conference twenty minutes later. 'In sport, one side wins and one side loses. Tonight, Georges was the better man and he beat me fair and square. He caught me with a good shot, put me down and I remember trying to fight his hands in the choke but he was very strong. All those push-ups and protein shakes paid off for him, and good for him.

'What's next? I dunno. I feel like I can go again right now. I've no injuries at all. I feel great. I don't think this is the last you'll be seeing of me.'

CHAPTER TWENTY-ONE

ANYTHING'S POSSIBLE

The Friday after the fight in New York Ellie and Cal were back in school and I was driving myself, Rebecca and her parents to the Filling Station, my usual brunch location in Orange County. I'd missed the turkey chilli cheese omelettes.

The news from Las Vegas was the pay-per-view number for *UFC 217* was very good. Of course, I was gutted my reign as world champion was over but, years from November 2017, that disappointment would be long gone while the payout from the St-Pierre fight would still be earning interest.

The car radio was switched to Sirius XM and *The Luke Thomas Show* was on. Thomas is an MMA journalist, a big-bearded ex US serviceman with a passing resemblance to Bluto from *Popeye* fame. Luke had breaking news to report: 'Anderson Silva is out of UFC Shanghai on November twenty-fifth. Middleweight Kelvin Gastelum is left without an opponent for the headline fight of the UFC's first event in mainland China ...'

Turning the volume on the radio down a little, I turned to Rebecca in the front passenger seat.

'What do you think?' I asked. 'Should I take it?'

'What?' she said. 'You can't do that.'

I raised my eyebrows at her.

She shook her head, 'You're crazy …'

'Two paydays for one training camp,' I said.

My wife looked at me like I had two heads. 'Michael, you can't do that.'

I sure could. When we pulled up outside the Filling Station restaurant I fired off a quick text to Dana White.

Hear you need a main event for China. I know a guy.

Every fight since Anderson Silva had a sense of potentially being my finale but, ironically, when I flew to China I didn't feel in my heart that, win, lose or draw, this would be my last fight. When I boarded that plane to Shanghai, I was travelling those 14 hours to go there and win. This wasn't just a nice payday. It was a chance to do something a bit special and underline that I always battle back from adversity.

I'd no illusions about getting my title back. Even as champion I was taking it one fight at a time. GSP was supposed to defend the belt against Whittaker early in 2018 and Romero and Rockhold were already positioned as challengers after that. I was pragmatic.

'The first rule of MMA,' Forrest Griffin told me a long time before, 'is don't be forty.'

I would turn 39 in three months. The Gastelum fight would be my 39th as a professional mixed martial artist. Time had almost caught me. So while I was healthy enough to fight – I was going to fight.

Coming back and beating a genuine contender the same month I lost the title? That wouldn't be nothing and, touch wood, would set me up for a big farewell fight in the UK in 2018.

Bless my innocent heart. I'd assumed the dog and pony show I'd put on to get licensed in New York meant I'd quickly get approval to fight in China, where the UFC essentially serves as the regulator as well as promoter.

I'd assumed wrong. Even though I had literally one week to train for Kelvin, the UFC had me driving all over town doing another MRI, a heart stress test, blood work, you name it – along with, yes, another bloody eye exam.

As chance had it, my eye doctor had listened to *The Luke Thomas Show* too, while driving to his practice.

'I expected this call,' he said when he picked up the phone. 'I heard there's a UFC main event in need of a middleweight ...'

'That's right,' I said, 'I'm reaching for another vine.'

When I earned my first UFC contract by winning *The Ultimate Fighter* season three, Kelvin Gastelum still had four years of Cibola High School in Yuma, Arizona, in front of him. He was 22 years old when he followed in my footsteps and won *TUF 17* in 2015 and was 25 when we fought in front of 15,128 Chinese fans at the Shanghai Arena. A squat puncher with a sawn-off right cross and fastball left hook, Gastelum was a young man hurrying towards a title shot.

Making 185lb twice in 21 days was hell on earth. I remember looking at myself in the mirror and thinking, for the first time since before *UFC 100*, that I looked gaunt and underpowered. It's just not in my nature to make demands or ask for special stipulations in a fight, but I really wished I'd told the UFC I wanted this fight to be at 195lb.

While hitting the pads with Jason backstage, though, I told my trainer the fight wouldn't be going the distance. I felt good. I felt sharp.

That feeling fell away once I got to the Octagon. I felt like I was chasing myself across the Octagon in the opening minutes. I didn't feel fully present in the moment. In hindsight, I'd drained myself physically and emotionally for the GSP fight. Nevertheless, I began to settle down in the middle of the first round.

Then I was lying on my back looking at the lights.

I had no clue what had happened.

While nodding to the men asking me if I was okay, I pieced it together. I'd lost the fight by knockout.

When I got back to my feet I used self-deprecatory humour as a front to hide just how jumbled my thoughts were. Then I saw the finish play out in slow-motion on the giant screens around the arena. Just like GSP had, Gastelum had countered my cross by firing a left hook that my right eye didn't see coming.

Kelvin hit plenty hard, but there's no way that right + left combo would have knocked me out in the past. I'd have recovered, regrouped and got back into the fight. Instead – for the first time literally in my life – I'd lost two fights in a row.

Backstage everybody was saying nice things. No one else would have the balls to attempt what I'd just tried to do. I was a warrior. A legend.

Nothing anyone says makes you feel better in those lonely moments after a big loss, but you appreciate that people care enough to make the effort.

My dad and Little Mick had come out to see the fight – even on 14 days' notice they flew halfway around the world to support me. Jacko, who now lived in Australia, had flown to China to see me, too, and I'd had him work my corner along with Daz, Brady and Jason. They all joined me and my fight team in a post-fight drink. These people had literally followed me to the ends of the earth, and that kind of friendship is always worth a toast or two.

Sixty years after Shanghai's nightlife was driven underground by Mao's Communist Party, the most ridiculously plush nightclub in the city is perched 24 floors above street level. M1Nt has a vast dance floor, a lounge and restaurant with incredible panoramic views of the city. The centrepiece of the lounge is a giant floor-to-ceiling shark tank. The neon-lit water gave off a brilliant blue-white.

We sat down in deep leather chairs around a black marble table. The music from the dance floor on the other side of the bar was exactly loud enough. Drinks were on the way. Win or lose, I'd always gone out after a fight but, on that night, having six of the people who'd supported me the most with me, I was ready for a great night.

An hour in, I went over with Jacko to one of the 40-foot floor-to-ceiling windows that wrapped around the club. Glasses in hand, we took in the breathtaking and almost futuristic view of the biggest city on earth. A grey mist rising over the Yangtze River delta was blasted purples and lime-greens by lights from the Oriental Pearl Tower and Shimao International Plaza, two of the six or seven buildings that looked gigantic even from a distance. It was like something out of a movie.

A strobe light from the direction of dance floor yanked my attention back inside. We went back to our table. I sat down next to Jason this time and caught up to the conversation. There was another flash. I dropped out of the banter. The second blaze of white couldn't have come from the dance floor. A dreadful feeling crawled around my guts. I closed my right eye, leaving my good eye open. I breathed in and darted my left eyeball left and right.

Flash!

White light spiralled behind my vision.

I moved my good eye again.

Flash!

No …

Flash!

No, no, no.

Flash!

Fuck. Not this eye too.

As soon as I was off the plane at LAX airport I was on the phone to my eye doctor.

'My good eye,' I told him. 'My good eye is doing those flashes like the left did. I think the retina is detached in my good eye.'

My doctor did what he could to calm my nerves. He told me the flash I'd described didn't necessarily indicate a detached retina but, I don't mind admitting, I was terrified. I'd left the club in Shanghai soon after that first flash. Daz and Jason followed me back to the hotel to make sure I was okay. There were more flashes as I tried to sleep. It was identical to what had happened after the Belfort fight.

My doctor got me an appointment with another specialist within 24 hours of me calling him from LAX. I couldn't believe I was going through those tests again – and now for my left eye.

As ever, I used humour as a force field.

'So, do I pick my white stick up on the way out, doc?' I asked the optometrist jokingly.

The tall, middle-aged woman with the tied-back blonde hair was quiet for a second too long. 'I don't think we are there yet,' she said.

What!?! I was fucking joking.

I've fucked myself, I thought, *my pride, my ego have really fucked me this time.*

After what seemed like an eternity, my left eye was diagnosed as experiencing posterior vitreous detachment. There are millions of fine fibres attached to the surface of the retina, and as we age tens of thousands of those break off. It was natural enough, but it was happening to me earlier in life, and in my good eye. I was told that, because the process was already under way in my eye, there was an increased chance that the fibres would rip a hole in my retina.

'Or detach it entirely,' Rebecca repeated the optometrist's words. 'She said there's an increased chance that the fibres would tear a macular hole *and* there was an increased chance of the fibres pulling on the retina hard enough to detach it.'

We were at home. It was mid-January 2018 and we were talking about me fighting one more time. Well, I was talking about it. The UFC had confirmed a March 2018 event for the O$_2$ in London and I saw a chance to bow out of the sport exactly as I'd envisioned it. I was in discussions to fight on the card.

Rebecca – for the very first time – was flat-out telling me that I should retire. 'Your eye, Michael. Why? Why risk it? Nothing is worth your eyesight.'

I was listening to her. And to my manager, Audie, who was one of several people whose opinion I valued who wanted me to call it a day.

Only ... the moment I'd told new UFC matchmaker Mick Maynard that I wanted to fight in London, I'd fallen in love with the idea of performing one last time in front of the British fans, hearing 'Song 2' lift the roof off the O$_2$ one last time, of retiring on a win, of one final pay cheque as a UFC headliner.

Half the UFC roster wanted to fight me but Mick put together the fight I'd asked for: a rematch with Rashad Evans. I thought a rematch of my first ever loss, against somebody I now very much liked and respected, who was from my generation of UFC stars and who was also looking to call it a day soon ... I thought that would be a great final lap.

But, in the end, I couldn't reach an agreement with the UFC quickly enough to make the fight happen. I began edging towards making an announcement that I'd retired – but then another UK event, this time in May in Liverpool, was announced.

The Rashad fight could still happen. At 195lb, too. Another pay cheque, and that final goodbye to the UK fans. It was all right there for me. I kept going back and forth ... until the deadline to commit to competing in Liverpool came and went.

I was about 75/25 in favour of retiring at this point. I didn't want to announce it until I was 100 per cent sure; when I retired, it would be forever. I spoke with Jason Parillo again.

'Mike, no one's going to remember who your last fight was against,' he said. 'They'll remember you won the world title on short notice, that you were the champ, that you beat Anderson Silva and Dan Henderson and fought anybody they put in front of you.

'I get it, one more fight, one more payday. It's only once more, right? But if you lose your sight you would trade that last win in the UFC, give back that money – fuck, you'd spend every penny you've ever earned to be able to look at your kids again.'

Those words were still sinking in when I boarded a plane to New York. The *Believe You Me* podcast had really taken off and Luis J. Gomez and me had committed to doing two shows a month face to face rather than over a camera link. On the flight, I watched a movie I'd auditioned for, *Journeyman*, which was directed, written and starred Paddy Considine. It's a heart-wrenching story;

a champion fighter wins a world title but suffers an injury that devastates his family.

That was when I knew. For sure. I'd had enough. Enough money from the sport, enough titles, enough wins, enough ego. I'd beaten the best of the best; I'd won the world title. I'd kicked and clawed against every obstacle put in front of me for so long. Now it was time to stop.

The next day at the GaS Digital studio in New York City I began the 28 May 2018 episode of *Believe You Me* by announcing my retirement from mixed martial arts.

The reaction was humbling.

Within minutes of the episode's conclusion, I had tens of thousands of messages and comments on social media from MMA fans. I should retire more often, I decided. Dana called me and said I should be proud of everything I'd accomplished over the years and that he was looking forward to working with me as a broadcaster. The MMA media wrote some really touching retrospectives. A lot of fighters said some really generous things; I was particularly moved by what some of the younger British fighters said.

Still, people needed to be convinced this was final. Hunter Campbell from the UFC called a few days later, asking me if my retirement meant that I wanted out of the USADA drug-testing programme. As thorough as ever, Hunter made sure I was fully aware that withdrawing from the USADA programme would mean, should I change my mind, I'd need to be tested for six consecutive months before I could step into the Octagon and compete.

He reminded me that other fighters who'd quit the sport – including Urijah Faber and Ronda Rousey – continued in the testing pool 'just in case'.

'Hunter, that's exactly why I want you to pull me out of the USADA pool,' I said. 'I can't leave the door ajar. I'd see a big fight or a short-notice opportunity and I'd think to myself, "Hey, I'm in shape," and I'd be sending you and Dana a text. I can't – I won't – do that to my family. I need that six months cooling-off period between me and the Octagon. Take me out of the USADA pool, please. I really am done.'

When most people retire or leave a job they've had for 15 years, I imagine the first Monday morning feels a little weird. Not for me. I still train and I still go for runs almost every day. Between doing three podcasts a week and traversing North America several times a month doing broadcast work, I'm around the sport as much as ever.

Mixed martial arts is an amazing sport. I see a fight like Israel Adesanya vs Kelvin Gastelum or Dustin Poirier vs Max Holloway and I love the sport as much as I ever did, despite the pound of flesh it took from me. I read a good review of *Triple Threat* the other week where my 'surprisingly powerful performance' was noted along with the observation that 'years of UFC fighting has layered scar tissue over Bisping's boyish good looks'.

After retiring, the sight in my right eye continued to deteriorate and there's also nothing that can be done to repair the damage to my left knee. I was shooting a documentary in England in early 2019 and they wanted to film me running the same Clitheroe streets approaching the castle that I'd pounded thousands of times early in my career.

This time, though, the cold and the cobblestones pounded back.

But I'd do it all over again. In a heartbeat.

The final fight in the UK never happened – but I got to bid the British fans farewell anyway.

On 16 March 2019 I was working for American broadcaster ESPN, providing pre- and post-fight analysis alongside Karyn Bryant on the *UFC Fight Night* event at the O₂ Arena. It was odd being back at my old fortress wearing civilian clothes. The same Octagon where I'd beaten Anderson and Akiyama lay waiting with its doors open, but I wouldn't be walking up its stairs again.

'You wish you were backstage getting warmed up?' Karyn asked.

'Of course,' I said, 'I'll still feel that way if I attend an event here when I'm seventy.'

About halfway through the card one of the UFC production staffers asked me to go and take a front-row seat for a few minutes. They wanted to show me at Octagonside in between fights, so the fans in the arena and watching on British television could see I was in attendance.

It was a ruse. I heard commentator John Gooden make some sort of announcement but couldn't make out what. Then the arena went dark and the big screens played a really touching vignette recapping my career. Rebecca, my dad, my kids, former opponents and other champions were all featured. The UFC production team lead by Zach Candito did a beautiful job. I teared up.

Then came the kicker. At the end of the piece was the UFC HALL OF FAME logo and the words:

UFC Middleweight Champion
Winner of 20 UFC Fights
Pioneer of British MMA

I then got a standing ovation from 16,602 fans in the arena where I'd left parts of my heart and soul.

'Thank you,' I said to as many of them as I could make eye contact with. 'Thank you.'

About a week ago I took my coffee outside and sat on a deckchair and watched my three kids buzz in and out of the kitchen as they busily got ready for their day at school. Lucas was hunting a missing shoe with his never-ending energy; Ellie – so much like her mum and loving life in California – was grabbing breakfast and Callum, taller than me already and not far away from being stronger than his old man, too, was packing his wrestling gear.

Then Rebecca sat down next to me and put her head on my arm. We took a moment, sat in the warming sun and just watched our children start another day in their lives.

'You working on the book this morning?' she asked.

'Yeah, almost done,' I said. 'Trying to figure out how to end it.'

'Why not right here?' my wife said. 'This is what you fought for – providing a better life for our children. This is the proof you made it more than the gold belt in your office.'

I shook my head and pulled her close.

'How many more times do I have to say it, lady? *We! We* made it.'

AFTERWORD

What always terrified me was the thought of not being able to provide for my wife and children.

The odds were against me. I'm from a very ordinary background and, as you've read, I've made mistakes that made the path for me to succeed in life even narrower. But by taking a chance on a brand-new sport none of my friends had ever heard of, I beat those odds.

I won the championship of the world and I've parlayed that success into TV work, acting and several businesses. This isn't a humblebrag, this is proof that anybody reading this can be successful if they go for it.

Think back to the first chapter of this book. If you'd met me as I was aged 22, would you have predicted anything big for that guy? Of course not – but here I am.

We all have a skill, something we're good at. For me it was martial arts, but it could be computers or sewing or photography – who knows – and I'm encouraging my kids to figure out what that is for them.

In my experience, having travelled the world and met a lot of interesting and successful people, this skill is usually something we're good at already. Trust me, getting paid for doing something you once did purely for the love of it is one of life's greatest successes.

If you have confidence in yourself and are willing to make the sacrifices, it can be done. Believe you me.

Thank you for reading.

MICHAEL BISPING CAREER STATISTICS

Final MMA Career Record
30–9 (20 wins via KO/TKO)

Nickname: The Count
Born: 28 February 1979
Height: 6ft 1in
Reach (arm): 75½in
Reach (leg) 44½in
Fighting Stance: Converted orthodox (left-handed but fights as if right-handed)

Fight of the Night Awards (5)
Vs Elvis Sinosic, *UFC 70*, Manchester, England
Vs Denis Kang, *UFC 105*, Manchester, England
Vs Yoshihiro Akiyama, *UFC 120*, London, England
Vs Anderson Silva, *UFC Fight Night*, London, England
Vs Dan Henderson, *UFC 204*, Manchester, England

Performance of the Night Awards (2)
Vs Cung Le, *UFC Fight Night*, Macau, China
Vs Luke Rockhold, *UFC 199*, Los Angeles, USA

MMA Titles Won
Cage Rage light heavyweight championship
Cage Warriors light heavyweight championship
FX3 light heavyweight championship
The Ultimate Fighter 3 light heavyweight tournament winner
(Unofficial Strikeforce middleweight championship)
UFC middleweight championship

UFC Hall of Fame
Modern Era Wing, Class of 2019

UFC Records (correct at time of retirement)
- Most wins in UFC history (20)
- Most fights in UFC history (29)
- Most wins in UFC middleweight division (16)
- First winner of *The Ultimate Fighter* from outside USA
- Landed more significant strikes – 1,567 – than any fighter in UFC history

Other UFC Career Notes (correct at time of retirement)
- Spent 6 hours, 5 minutes and 33 seconds in the Octagon (more than any fighter other than Frankie Edgar)
- Completed 19 takedowns (eighth most in UFC history)
- Scored 6 knockdowns (third in UFC history)
- Headlined 14 UFC events
- Main-evented or co-main-evented 22 of 29 UFC appearances

- Headlined UFC events in a record 7 countries: England, Scotland, USA, Canada, Brazil, Australia and China
- Recovered from knockdowns to win fights 7 times (UFC record)
- First fighter to land over 100 strikes in 5 different fights
- Blocked/avoided 65.7 per cent of strikes from UFC opponents
- Landed 217 leg kicks, more than any other UFC middleweight
- Scored 5 knockdowns from clinch position, only Anderson Silva has scored more (7)
- Became champion in 26th UFC fight, latest into UFC career of any first-time champion
- Oldest first-time UFC champion (37 years, 3 months, 7 days)
- Scored fourth most knockouts in UFC history (10)
- Only *TUF* champion to go on to win and then successfully defend a UFC title
- First and only Briton to win a UFC world title
- Never, ever, lost a fight in the UK

ACKNOWLEDGEMENTS

The first person I 'met' remains the toughest person I know – my Mum. I got all the mental attributes that made a fighter and a champion from my mother – and I only got half of her toughness and ability to ignore life's setbacks.

My Dad has always been the greatest supporter of my martial arts career. He drove all over the UK and then flew all over the world to be in my corner. I sometimes wish I'd gotten a little more of his size – I'd have made a great UFC heavyweight champion – but what I did get from my dad, his sense of pride and discipline, made me the man I am today.

And completing the support system I've had since day one are my brothers and sisters, Stephen, Konrad, Adam, Maxine and Shireen. Thank you for your never-ending love and support.

To my old friends – the lads – from Clitheroe, thank you for the great times. You know who you are and exactly what I mean by great times!

I've always been extremely fortunate to have fantastically loyal and crazy/interesting mates and for those who aren't mentioned in the book, please understand that's purely due to me already going way over the word count. You know who you are I thank you from bottom of my heart.

I also didn't have space to detail just how important my time training with Allan Clarkin and everyone from the Black Knights

407

kickboxing gym in Burnley was in my life, but I gladly acknowledge it here.

Everyone in MMA owes Dana White and Lorenzo Ferritta a debt of gratitude but I want to give personal thanks for their belief and support over the years – and for always allowing me to be me. I also want to recognize the dozens of UFC staff who've gone above and beyond their job description over the years.

A career as long as the one I had in MMA is built on thousands upon thousands of hours of training and learning from hundreds of not only coaches but training partners. I owe thanks to everyone who swopped punches in the face with me in the name of self-improvement. I also want to recognise the support of my sponsors over the years and every gym that opened its doors to me, even if it was for one or two workouts while I was in town.

I owe more than my world championship to Jason Parrillo. He not only changed the trajectory of my MMA career, but helped me grow as a man as much as a fighter.

Another architect of my title reign is Brady Fink. He is always in my corner, in life as well as in MMA. Thank you, brother. I also want to acknowledge Daz Morris, a great striking coach and even better friend. Thanks also to Pat Tenore and the whole RVCA Sport family for allowing me to make the RVCA training centre the headquarters for the biggest successes of my career. Some of the best times of my life were spent at that gym with those people.

Everyone who steps into the Octagon, a ring or a BJJ mat is offering irrefutable proof of their courage. It takes guts to volunteer for a prize fight and I want to state I respected every opponent – from UFC legends to kids I grappled against in the 90s. It was an honour to complete with you.

It's a fact of human nature (or maybe just mine – ha!) that naysayers and haters can be every bit as motivating as supporters. So, I also owe a strange sort of thanks to some of my old school teachers, a few hundred internet trolls and some former 'team members'. Thank you for doubting me – you fuelled my desire to achieve more than you will ever know. Cheers! ;D

Thanks, of course, to the team at Penguin Random House UK for allowing me to tell my story and to my agent extraordinaire, Mike Staudt, for his unfailing support in general and for pitching this book in particular.

To my children Callum, Ellie and Lucas – your Dad is so proud of you. You were all the inspiration I ever needed. I love you more than I can put into words.

Finally, I'm going to try once more to get across just how indebted I am to my wife, Rebecca. Every success in this book is hers as much as mine. This book, the world title, the movies, TV work, podcast – none of it would ever have happened without you in my life, babe. You are my whole world. I love you.

– Michael Bisping

***

Thank you, Mike, for your trust, humour and friendship – not only while writing this book together but for the last 13 years.

Throughout this process, the archives of Sherdog.com, MMAJunkie.com, MMAFighting.com and several long-gone MMA websites were fantastic references. But Mike and I owe special thanks to my friends Tom Gerbasi, Elliot Worsell, Ariel Helwani and Rami Genauer. Their keen insight and input was invaluable.

I want to join Mike in thanking the team at Penguin Random House UK, especially Commissioning Editor Robyn Drury for her guidance and patience and copy editor Ian Allen, who not whack-a-moled typos but also made several suggestions that greatly improved the manuscript.

I also want to thank my Mum for her support and my Dad for sparking my interest in combat sports in the first place.

My wife, Jacquie, encourage me during the long nights and weekends writing this book required with the grace and empathy that I first fell in love with. Our son, Xander, also understood why Daddy had to (again) shut the door and do 'important work'.

But nothing's more important to me than you and your mum, Little Big Guy.

– Ant Evans

Picture Credits

Images 1, 2, 3, 7, 9, 12, 18, 19, 24, 29, 30 and 31 courtesy of Michael Bisping

Images 4, 5, 6, 8, 10, 11, 13, 14, 15, 16, 17, 20, 21, 22, 23, 25, 26, 27, 28 © Getty Images/Zuffa LLC